The Theatrical Gamut

Notes for a Post-Beckettian Stage

Edited by
Enoch Brater

Ann Arbor

THE UNIVERSITY OF MICHIGAN PRESS

A CIP catalogue record for this book is available from the British Library.

Library of Congress Cataloging-in-Publication Data

The theatrical gamut : notes for a post-Beckettian stage / edited by
Enoch Brater.
    p.   cm. — (Theater: theory/text/performance)
    Includes bibliographical references.
    ISBN 0-472-10583-3 (hardcover : acid-free paper)
    1. Theater. 2. Drama.   I. Brater, Enoch.   II. Series.
PN2037.T5   1995
792—dc20   95-2385
                                                    CIP

Grateful acknowledgment is made to the following journal for permission
to reprint previously copyrighted material: *Cahiers de la Comédie Française* for
"Training the French Actor: From Exercises to Experiment," by Bernard
Dort, Fall 1992.

THEATER: Theory/Text/Performance

Enoch Brater, Series Editor

For Ruby Cohn

Contents

Preface

ENOCH BRATER

The purpose of this "disguised" festschrift in honor of Ruby Cohn is to display the number of discourses that have come to maturity during the period of her long and impressive career. I use the word *disguised* here deliberately: for the intention of this collection is not merely to pay homage through an edition of sentimental tributes but rather to continue the rich critical dialogue about theater and drama that she has so often set in motion.

Cohn's work as a scholar tracks the many revolutions that have taken place in the development of a truly modern repertory and the critical community's response to them. Recognizing the primacy of Beckett in the continual reassessment of an ever-emerging dramatic vocabulary, hers was the first book to call our attention to the centrality of his playwriting to the dynamics of postwar western drama. *Samuel Beckett: The Comic Gamut* was not only the first book published on this playwright; it was by all accounts *the book*, along with the contemporaneous writings of Hugh Kenner, Edith Kern, Raymond Federman, and John Fletcher, that set the boundaries of Beckett criticism for an entire generation. *The Comic Gamut* was followed by two

more landmark studies: *Back to Beckett* and *Just Play: Beckett's Theater.*
Accompanying these books were a series of seminal essays in all the
major drama and theater periodicals on both sides of the Atlantic as
well as dozens of chapters in the major collections of essays devoted
to Beckett's work. Cohn has also edited and translated several volumes now rendered indispensable in all areas of Beckett studies: *Casebook on "Waiting for Godot," Disjecta: Miscellaneous Writings and a Dramatic Fragment by Samuel Beckett,* and Odette Aslan's *Roger Blin and
Twentieth-Century Playwrights,* a key study of the role of Beckett's principal French director in the rise of the Paris avant-garde.

As is reflected in the essays that follow, her work has by no means
been limited to Beckett (though as this book goes to press she is fast at
work on yet another "fresh go" on this twentieth-century master).
Hers is a household name among students of American drama where
her writing ranges widely through Miller, Williams, Shepard, Mamet,
Fornes, and Mabou Mines (my list is not complete). *Dialogue in American Drama* and *New American Dramatists, 1960–1990* have found their
place in the bibliography of every study in the field. So, too, is Cohn's
work justly celebrated for its encounter with contemporary London
theater; recently published is her encyclopedic *Retreats from Realism in
Recent English Drama,* a book that features her vast familiarity with
theater in Britain. Even more recently she has published *Anglo-
American Interplay in Recent Drama,* a title the scope and ambition of
which speaks for itself. French drama, too, is one of her many special-
ties, and here one need only cite, among other studies, *From "Desire"
to "Godot": Pocket Theater of Postwar Paris.* A student of comparative
literature, Cohn is also the author of *Modern Shakespeare Offshoots,* a
book that evaluates reconstructions and reinterpretations of Shakespeare in the hands of such contemporary figures as Edward Bond,
Dürrenmatt, Ionesco, Tom Stoppard, and Megan Terry.

But no survey of her publications can highlight on its own the way
she has been among the first to respond to new movements in European, British, and American drama. Opening our eyes to what was
happening, where it was happening, and *how* it was happening (and
how all of this continues to happen in the present tense), Cohn has
been a significant player in the development of postwar theater criti-

cism. Often a close reader, sometimes a theater historian, frequently a chronicler of unfolding production events, her critical writing has heralded the major innovations in a developing dramatic syntax and what she herself has called the integrity of each new "theatereality."

The essays in this volume, in themselves a panorama of other signicant voices in the field, continue the dialogue with dramatic writing that Ruby Cohn has helped to invigorate in her lively encounters with stage time and performance space. Collected here, then, is a critical gamut, the course few have run as efficiently as the American critic whose career this volume can only attempt to celebrate and esteem. This is, after all is said and done and recorded, merely one more *just* play, but one that hopes to place the work of Ruby Cohn, for the moment, on center stage.

But an actual journey back to Bali left me with very different thoughts. The only dance-dramas I was able to see were performed on a weekly schedule by troupes that included numerous schoolchildren of little skill and small powers of concentration. Single dancers and some of the leading drummers were the only artists who claimed attention. Everything was performed beneath crude lights before seated tourists who responded with camera flashes and the whirl of video recorders. I am told that if I had been present at an Odalan, or temple feast, I would have seen the ancient dance-dramas as they are being developed for performance in a new world. My timing was wrong for that, but I did find in Bali an experience that has challenged what I had previously thought about theater. Attending a cremation ceremony, in a village deep within the jungle, I reacted to this prearranged and staged event in a manner that has expanded my views of what an audience might contribute to theatrical performance.[2]

The cremation was held on a working day, a Friday, but five or six hundred people had taken time off from ordinary business to attend. I arrived a good hour before it was due to begin, but already the roadway outside the house of the deceased was crowded, as were the home and its courtyard, too. Further down the dirt lane, which had been leveled and tidied for the occasion, two gaudily decorated structures of bamboo, cloth, and tinsel stood waiting. One was a bier surmounted by a structure of many small stories, the other a large animal with a parasol poised beside it. Both towered above us all. The ceremony began with the body being brought out of the house and into the bier. Various offerings and gifts were brought with it—tokens of the deceased's life to accompany the passage of the soul out of the body—a photograph, a coconut filled with rice, a small eggshell lamp to represent the soul itself. Then bier and effigy were lifted onto many shoulders, and a procession gathered and made its way some half-mile through the jungle to an open space near the largest of the village temples. There the beast was placed under an awning, and then the corpse was moved from the bier and placed inside its stomach, which had been cut open to receive it. More offerings, including food and coins, were brought, and prayers were said. The deceased had been a policeman, and so ten of his colleagues in uniform formed up as a squad and made their own presentation. Everything was unhurried and soon it was clear that not everyone knew what to do or when. But at length all was ready for fire to be applied to the effigy and corpse. Flames rose into the sky and the last stage of the spirit's journey was completed.

What held my attention, more than any of the rituals or representations, was the crowd. First of all, it was not made up of the lonely grieving figures one finds at many funerals in the English-speaking world. Nor were these people actively participating unless a particular duty was briefly required of some of them, which was then completed and, as it were, forgotten. The crowd was a collection of small groups, which shifted in membership from time to time. Women and small children stood together, sometimes holding hands or with an arm around another's shoulders. Some of the young men walked in couples or stood linking their two little fingers together. A tight knot of them, wearing Harley Davidson T-shirts, were more restless, sometimes engaged in sharp bouts of talk or comment. Older people tended to keep somewhat apart. Everyone continued to have his or her own thoughts and his or her own concerns, which seemed as important to them as the ceremony or the deceased person's life and present fate. On this Friday morning, earning a living was forgotten for four or five hours while this gathering was present with the body and spirit of a deceased friend, family member, fellow villager, or police officer; and its members were also present with each other in whatever groupings suggested themselves. No one moment appeared to be more important than another and no place of vantage was privileged; there was no one way to face, no prescribed attitude or posture for prayer. No singing or chanting drew everyone into a single reaction; the music had ceased long before the flame was applied to the corpse. Various tourists, like myself, were also present, intermingling anywhere, and no attention was paid to them by anyone. Whatever we saw and whatever we did was part of one essential action; whatever we thought was our own business.

Attendance at this ceremony stays in my mind as the movements of the Balinese dancer-actors stayed in Artaud's. It has proved to be a more lasting memory than being present at any funeral, more than attendance at Native American ritual dances (where I have always been aware of my strangeness), more than encounters with English Mummers' plays, or seeing any official procession or public event, or watching a soccer match in England, Italy, or America. Was this because in Bali a nonexclusive, unprogrammed attentiveness was both singular to each watcher and also communal? In this remote village, the assembled company, many of whom must have traveled considerable distances, watched an artificial, lengthy, and significant happening as if it were an accustomed part of life. The event was favored by having a special day and time allotted to it, as decreed by the local temple priest, but not so that other concerns and relationships had to be put aside. None of the various components of the ceremony transfixed or transformed the crowd of spectators, but rather it seemed as if individuals offered attention to it from wherever they happened to be and whenever it suited them. It was encountered in an unforced but contagious mood—an alert, or possibly a wise, passivity.

Afterward I wondered whether I might have been part of a crowd of spectators that was more like an audience in an Elizabethan theater than any I had known before. We did not applaud and we knew the content of what we were watching—the journey of a spirit out of the body in which it had lived—but we had decided to give four or five hours to be in company on a working day to watch a representation of life and death. That much was Elizabethan. So, too, was the fact that the spectacle we watched had many and varying parts, as a whole lifetime was represented. Perhaps our freedom to invest any part of the show with our own concerns was also a characteristic of earlier theater.

Surviving evidence about Elizabethan theater audiences can be interpreted in many different ways, the more so in that scholars are writing about circumstances that have long since disappeared. It is possible to imagine that playgoing in Shakespeare's time was a submissive and sharply observant enterprise—much more like going to the theater in a conservatively repressive society in the present century. So Stephen Greenblatt writes:

The triumphant cunning of the theater is to make its spectators forget that they are participating in a practical activity, to invent a sphere that seems far removed from the manipulations of the every day. Shakespeare's theater is powerful and effective precisely to the extent that the audience believes it to be nonuseful and hence nonpractical.[3]

But nothing "precise" was involved with the power of the Balinese ceremony, although it did hold attention without fuss for hours on end. Nor had the triumph of this occasion anything to do with coercion or with forgetting daily concerns and individual relationships. It was a popular occasion. A meaningful content seemed to be taken for granted but that was not "far removed from the manipulations of the every day." The whole colorful and artificial show was practical: we could see how everything was contrived; it was assumed that all this had to be enacted; and everyone wanted to be part of it. All of this I found thought provoking and memorable, or, in Greenblatt's phrase, "powerful and effective."

How might Shakespeare have satisfied such a practical and independent audience? The earliest plays, with the exception of *The Comedy of Errors*, which is greatly indebted to the tighter forms of Roman comedy, have an ample and unhurried variety of incident, which would allow an audience to pick and choose, to give most attention to whatever caught their fancies and not to bother with episodes that did not. *The Two Gentlemen of Verona* is so written that its performance will give a great deal of pleasure without almost any of its scenes: Speed can be treated as redundant; Julia in talk with Lucetta in I.ii can make her drift clear enough in any twenty or so of the scene's 140 lines; Panthio talking with Antonio in I.iii.1–87 is expendable; and so on. Launce and his dog of II.iii is an amazing comic turn that no one would want to miss, but should that happen the play would be understood well enough without it; even if this were the place where someone first gave attention to the play, the rest would follow without much difficulty. The play's action proceeds with great variety, but all its scenes, many very short, start by clearly defining both what is afoot and much of the story so far.

Speed   Launce! by mine honesty, welcome to Padua . . .

(II.i.1)

Proteus To leave my Julia, shall I be forsworn;
         To love fair Silvia, shall I be forsworn; . . .

(II.vi.1–2)

Julia   Counsel, Lucetta; gentle girl, assist me; . . .
         How with my honour, I may undertake
         A journey to my loving Proteus.

(II.vii.1–7)

Duke   Sir Thurio, give us leave, I pray, awhile;
         We have some secrets to confer about. (*Exit* Thurio)
         Now tell me, Proteus, what's your will with me?

(III.i.1–3)

Duke   Sir Thurio, fear not but that she will love you
         Now Valentine is banish'd from her sight.

(III.ii.1–2)

Critics have often remarked on the variety of incident in Shakespeare's earlier plays but not so often on their instant credibility or the disposability of many of their scenes. The episode of Thurio's song, "Who is Silvia?" (III.ii.16–80), exemplifies all three characteristics.

A member of the audience could take his or her own way through *The Two Gentlemen* and still have an enjoyable entertainment to go along with more ordinary thoughts continuing at the same time. Fantasy and reality could mingle with mutual benefit. Perhaps this is why the most critical moment in the entire story is treated with utmost economy, or, to put a different face on it, with a completely inadequate explanation of what is going on in the minds of its principals. Perhaps the author and actors were well aware that, by the time of this last scene, the audience would still be sufficiently in charge of their own minds to put their own valuations on the shocking abruptness with which Proteus asks for pardon, Valentine gives him "All that was mine in Silvia," Julia faints, the ring is recognized, all is revealed, and everyone accepts the outcome, or at least no one protests. An independent audience will surely have here many opinions and will be set talking among themselves before the Outlaws enter with the Duke and Thurio. It is only now that condemnation is heard on stage as this hapless and disappointed lover is called "degenerate and base" (l. 136)—words that might well have been in the minds of the audience a few moments earlier. Pardon is extended to the Outlaws who had all been banished for murder, theft, or other crimes committed in the "fury of ungovern'd youth" (IV.i.44–52). But the audience's thoughts are sent almost at once in another direction: the Duke draws attention at the last moment to Julia's blushes as she stands speechless in boy's clothing (l. 165). This comedy needs robust playing and an audience with its own sense of right and wrong and of what is laughable.

In Shakespeare's early history plays the march of events and consequences of actions are given much more weight, but here also the audience can keep its own head. The sheer accumulation of scenes within the three Parts of *Henry VI* or in the long text of *Richard III* would make for bewilderment if all were given equal and adequate attention. In modern productions the plays are shaped and varied, illustrated, and given a precise point by careful rehearsal, strong lighting, scenic and sound devices, and fine tuning, means that were not available in Shakespeare's own day. In the less technically accomplished theaters of the nineteenth and earlier twentieth centuries, the *Henry VI*'s were not played at all and *Richard III* was heavily cut both within scenes and by the excision of whole episodes. However, if Shakespeare's early history plays were performed as representations that audience members were free to follow with their own various thoughts and interests, the curse of complexity and the burden of length would both be lifted; some scenes would hold attention and some would not, or only partly so. Actors could shine in the variety of their tasks, and the audience could perhaps enjoy a lively competition arising among them, all of which would add to the pleasure of the occasion and the efficacy of whatever was able to draw the whole crowd together.

It may be a mistake to think of an Elizabethan audience as being wholly caught up in a "nonuseful" and "nonpractical" world of a play, as if for a time living in a "sphere" far removed from ordinary life. A looser rein may have held them, as the Prologue to *Henry VIII* mockingly reminds us.

Those that can pity here
May, if they think it well, let fall a tear:
The subject will deserve it. Such as give
Their money out of hope they may believe
May here find truth too. Those that come to see
Only a show or two, and so agree
The play may pass, if they be still and willing,
I'll undertake may see away their shilling
Richly in two short hours . . .

(ll. 5–13)

The cunning of this theater lies in giving the audience its own head and so allowing its own thoughts to interact with the fantastic or "truthful" happenings of the play.

In *Richard II*, for instance, the pace of the dialogue is sometimes very slow as ceremonies are elaborated or arguments augmented. But the action is sometimes hurried so that Bolingbroke seems to start his return to England before there is time for him to begin his banishment. The dramaturgical principal seems to have been to create a number of stopping places in the story, which are then exposed and explored in varying ways. Some scenes can be dropped from an acting text with little loss of clarity and possibly with a gain in forward energy: in modern productions the Duchess of Gloucester does not always appear (I.ii) nor do the Earl of Salisbury and the Welsh Captain (II.iv); the Queen need not meet the Gardeners (III.iv); Aumerle, Bagot, and Fitzwater need not throw down their gages (IV.i); and the Duke of York need not call repeatedly for his boots and horse, or the Duchess of York kneel before the new king (V.ii and iii). The entire abdication of King Richard was omitted in the first three printings of the text, almost certainly in accord with stage practice at the time. The end of this history occurs in two separate scenes (one of Richard's death and the other of Bolingbroke's reception of the news) so that the audience is left to relate one to the other, to think well or ill of the murdered king, as he lies in his coffin, and also of the new king as he protests:

my soul is full of woe
That blood should sprinkle me to make me grow.

(V.vi.45–46)

As Shakespeare's career developed the structure of his plays became less amenable to excision and the focus that is brought upon a few principal characters was more strongly sustained. This much is clear in a comparison of, say, *A Midsummer Night's Dream* with *Twelfth Night*, which followed not many years after, or of *Richard III* and *Henry V* with *Macbeth*. It is as if the dramatist has become far more in charge and wants to lead his audience, by a kind of force, closer into the heart of some mystery. But Shakespeare's development in these matters was not all one way, as if he knew that his audience remained ready to take matters into their own heads when that was what he wanted them to do. So *King Lear* has a more ample structure, allowing two stories to interweave and drawing a wide range of incidents and characters in their wake. Between the Quarto and Folio texts of *Lear* we see various adjustments taking place, as episodes are added, dropped, or adjusted; perhaps a change in audience attentiveness suggested a change in the arrangement of the playing script so that the earlier Quarto version may remain the closer representation of what Shakespeare wished his play to be.

But, whatever compulsion Shakespeare began to exercise on the audience, several of his old plays continued to be performed, allowing the audience to exercise its earlier freedom. In *Pericles*, and perhaps in parts of *The Winter's Tale*, this former independence seems to be positively provoked. Perhaps when Shakespeare was at his most commanding he knew he could rely on a spirited counterpull from the wayward minds of his audience, which remained intent on its own manipulations and able to bring a sturdy sense of common reality to the engagement.

In *The Advancement of Learning*, of 1605, Francis Bacon upheld the power of theater "to improve mankind in virtue."

> The action of the theater . . . was carefully watched by the ancients . . . and indeed many wise men and great philosophers have thought it to the mind as the bow to the fiddle.

A fiddle might have only one string, but Bacon was probably thinking of several, for he goes on to write of a theater audience as of a company of persons whose contact with each other is part of their enjoyment:

certain it is, though a great secret in nature, that the minds of men in company are more open to affections and impressions than when alone.[4]

In Shakespeare's dialogue a constant awakening of the audience's individual thoughts and experiences can be observed. When Richard II is being most fanciful, and his predicament seemingly most unlike that of his audience in the theater, Shakespeare made him touch the simplest of its feelings.

> I live with bread like you, feel want,
> Taste grief, need friends.
>
> (III.ii.175–76)

This appeal to what could be called the "manipulations of the every day" is made confidently at almost every juncture in the most gripping and highly wrought of the later plays. As *Othello* drives toward its conclusion, the dramatic focus narrowing with great intensity, the direct and very ordinary appeal recurs, especially in Desdemona's words but also in the impassioned utterances of Othello. Sometimes this is accomplished by means of simple words: "My wife! my wife! what wife? I have no wife!" (V.ii.100). Sometimes actuality is present in a passing but strongly placed image.

> Methinks it should be now a huge eclipse
> Of sun and moon, and that th' affrighted globe
> Did *yawn* at alteration.
>
> (V.ii.102–4)

Ordinary words and affective, everyday imagery often go together.

> Where should Othello go?
> Now how dost thou look now? O ill-starred wench
> Pale as thy smock!
>
> (V.ii.274–76)

In *Macbeth*, an appeal to common experience is perhaps the most arresting of all, drawing not only daily events and perceptions into its account of a metaphysical, political, and moral dilemma but also the actual attendance of the audience at the current performance.

> To-morrow, and to-morrow, and to-morrow,
> Creeps in this petty pace from day to day
> To the last syllable of recorded time,
> And all our yesterdays have lighted fools
> The way to dusty death. Out, out, brief candle!
> Life's but a walking shadow, a poor player,
> That struts and frets his hour upon the stage,
> And then is heard no more; it is a tale
> Told by an idiot, full of sound and fury,
> Signifying nothing.
>
> (V.v.19–28)

An active, independent crowd could contribute a great immediacy and close involvement to the conclusion of Shakespeare's most terrible tragedy. To what effect? In some sense, they were being encouraged to make the play their own.

In one passage, for which Artaud drew as much on hearsay as on his own experience, *The Theater and Its Double* claims that Balinese dance-dramas, for all their extreme artificiality, were based in the experience of their audiences back on the remote island where they were meant to be performed. Not only did these performances give a "sovereign idea of the theater," but the spectacle was "popular, it seems, and secular . . . like the common bread of artistic sensations among those people."[5] He had sensed that an audience could enter, on its own terms, into highly artificial, fantastic, and imaginative creations. Even shorn of the original context of performance, Artaud recognized this potentiality in the Balinese dance-dramas; as an artist working for a similar vitality, he could act as an audience of one in freedom:

> after an instant the magic identification is made: WE KNOW IT IS WE WHO ARE SPEAKING.[6]

Perhaps only an isolated twentieth-century literary intellectual could think otherwise of Shakespeare's plays in performance in his own time and place.

Shakespeare's plays are attuned to an independent audience. Some of the evidence surviving from his day shows how thoroughly spectators took the drama to themselves. Thomas Heywood's account of "our domestic histories" in his *Apology for Actors* (1612) is often quoted.

> What English blood seeing the person of any bold English man presented and doth not hug his fame, and honey at his valor, pursuing him in his enterprise with his best wishes? (Sig. B4)

The active verbs used of the audience are remarkable: *hugging* and *honeying*, as if responding sexually (compare "honeying and making love Over the nasty sty" in *Hamlet*, III.iv.93–94); and *pursuing*, as if mounting the stage in imagination. Contemplating the forthcoming theatricals, Duke Theseus in *A Midsummer Night's Dream* explains how much he is willing to give as an audience: when some anxious performers "dumbly have broke off,"

> Out of this silence yet I pick'd a welcome;
> And in the modesty of fearful duty
> I read as much as from the rattling tongue
> Of saucy and audacious eloquence.

Thinking of the actors about to entertain him and his guests, he looks forward to an active participation.

> Our sport shall be to take what they mistake;
> And what poor duty cannot do, noble respect
> Takes it in might, not merit.
>
> (V.i.89–105)

In the event, each member of the audience on stage in this play is revealed to the audience in the theater by his or her engagement in *Pyramus and Thisbe*.

Mistress Quickly in *Henry IV, Part I*; Polonius, Hamlet, Ophelia, Gertrude, and Claudius in *Hamlet*; and the superior young courtiers in

Love's Labor's Lost are all, like Puck in the *Dream*, more than passive "auditors" in what is performed for their pleasures.[7]

An active and independent audience can be unruly if a free response is encouraged, and there is evidence for this in the theaters of Shakespeare's day. Restraint was needed, in an unaggressive but persistent way, beyond the enticement of a varied or gripping dramatic fare. At the cremation ceremony on Bali nothing was out of hand. The occasion was serious, of course, but that was impressed on every watcher by the two bright and ingenious constructions that dominated the entire scene even among the tallest of the jungle trees: they spoke at all times of life and death, and of the journey of a soul.

In the theater of Shakespeare's day, dramatists may be seen to rely on similarly dominating visual devices to hold attention over long periods and to impress an audience by more permanent means than ever-changing words and human actions. This is clearest in Marlowe's plays: the cage for Bajazeth, the chariot drawn by kings for Tamburlaine, and the embalmed body of Zenocrate all exercise a spell in *Tamburlaine* whenever they are on stage, and they can hold in the memory after the performance is done. Faustus's books and the presence of two contrasting angels likewise speak beyond a dramatic instant. In Jonson's *Volpone*, the hero's gold, and in his *Alchemist* the implements of alchemy, are also pervasively powerful visual images.

Shakespeare managed permanent visual images less obviously. They are mostly noticeable in the histories where throne, crown, and heraldic impresa maintain signs of power and opposition while being necessary elements of the story. In *King John*, the crown is at first given solemn significance; then, when it is tendered to and fro between John and Pandolph, the Papal Legate, at the start of Act V, scene i, the possession of it as mere sign is open to ridicule. In the abdication scene of *Richard II*, after the king takes off his crown, the two rivals for power stand on either side, holding it. In *Henry IV, Part I*, the king is presented in three successive scenes (I.i, I.iii, and III.ii) in which he is sitting on a throne or chair of state and giving audience; these contrast with the presentation of his restless son and the necessarily devious rebels. Only when ready for battle is Henry seen without the trappings of established power; then he is clad in armor and surrounded by soldiers.

Shakespeare does sometimes use more extraordinary visual signs to provide an anchor, as it were, for the audience's reactions, but these are usually connected intimately with individual characters. Prospero's cloak and staff, representing his power over nature, are dominant in *The Tempest*; especially meaningful when they are laid aside or exchanged for other clothes, they help establish a special kind of reality proper to the entire play. In *King Lear* the visual trappings of power are potent at first, but a divestment occurs so that, augmented by the nakedness of Poor Tom, the king's unkingly appearance, together with his white hairs and enfeebled body, have huge and long-lasting impact. Whatever the audience thinks of what Lear does and what is done to him, the sight of a struggling and wearied infirmity affects any watcher deeply: pain, endurance, senility, or madness in such a person draw attention, and his resumption of anger or command are seen only in relation to such realities.

Such visual statements obviously contribute to the plays from first to last. Others come into prominence during the course of the action. So, once an audience has seen Bottom's ass's head, Malvolio's cross-gartering, Rosalind's disguise, and those of other heroines who "turn to men" (*Merchant of Venice*, III.iv.78), they cast lasting influences over the plays as well as revealing individual character.

Hamlet's mourning clothes make an off-center impact as soon as he appears silently among the court dressed for a regal celebration, but later his figure will merge with others as they enter in mourning for Ophelia's funeral. The blackness of Aaron and Othello, and more briefly and awkwardly of Morroco in the *Merchant*, is used to startling and dangerous effect. The early "Peacham drawing" representing a scene of *Titus Andronicus* in performance shows how unmistakable at all times this sign must have been.

Probably Shakespeare's boldest and most open use of a dominant visual sign is Shylock's "Jewish gaberdine" (*Merchant*, I.iii.113) and other marks of his ethnic difference. For Act V, they are not present on stage anymore, but now it is absence that becomes noticeable. Although the act begins with talk of the harmonizing music of the spheres (see V.i.60–65), Jessica is present and identified at the beginning and end of the scene as Shylock's daughter (see ll. 15 and 291–93). She says not a word after Portia and the others return to the stage, although she is twice addressed unmistakably, but her association with her father is emphasized on each occasion she is addressed so that Shylock, too, can be in the minds of the audience. The end of his story is not seen or heard, but, during the wrangles, jokes, and "happiness" of the last phases of the other stories, the sight of Jessica can be sufficient to make the audience imagine what has happened and is happening to him. The characters on stage seem to agree that the conclusion of the comedy is

> like the mending of highways
> In summer, where the ways are fair enough.
>
> (V.i.263–64)

But in the mind's eye some members of the audience may sense otherwise.

The critic's task can be to explore a dynamic between actors and audience as a play comes to life between them both. It is not merely to decode a hieroglyph or provide meanings for a series of signs written on paper but rather to sense what can happen, with the instigation of the text, both on stage and in the mind of the audience. Of these two elements, the latter is the more difficult yet the more crucial to understanding. When the audience is independent, so that its members continue to inhabit their own world as well as that of the play, it is their thoughts that must "deck" the actors' presentation of kings—as the Prologue to *Henry V* reminds its hearers—and that of all other dramatis personae. A play for such an audience is an agent for arousal, memory, argument, resentment, and delight, all experienced with a sense of discovery and intimacy, and sometimes with sensations of hugging, honeying, and pursuing. Uncertainty is part of the pleasure as in all games. Repudiation can follow suddenly after identification; other reactions can grow continuously, only occasionally held back. Timing is a large part of the skill needed to handle any audience, but the more independent its response the more this must be so. Phrasing and suggestion can be all-important, as they are for a stand-up comic with no feed and no settled script in support. Above all the play can supply the "common bread" of the imagination of its audience.

Shakespeare's plays are amazingly open for anyone's enjoyment: the pleasures of reading them are endless, and they have won applause from many different audiences. But in the twentieth century more complicated and directed ways of response have been developed by solitary scholar-critics and by some teachers of classes and seminars. Theater producers simplify the plays and keep audiences enthralled and seated in the dark. In some ways those who know Shakespeare are today at the greatest disadvantage as theater audiences. The plays come to lively, meaningful, and sometimes startling life on stage, but in this process audiences have lost an ancient freedom. So it was an almost total surprise to find myself on Bali among a crowd of spectators the various members of which were both attentive and independent. As a member of an audience, I had rediscovered the sense of self-possession.

That strange ceremony aroused unexpected thoughts and sensations in me, which were intimately connected with my own life, whereas in our theaters in the West I am often asked to submit to what is placed before me. Companies in strong financial positions vie with each other and for notoriety by bringing to the staging of Shakespeare's plays the audience-controlling power developed for twentieth-century megamusicals. Sensational visual effects of set, costumes, and especially stage lighting, the force and controlling rhythms of sound and music, and, when money and time can be stretched so far, the careful drilling of lines of actors, are all brought into action. Even small-scale companies strive to follow the same route toward making Shakespeare's plays their own and impressing audiences with a brand-name product. The experience given is a polar opposite to that of watching a cremation ceremony in Bali. It seems as if theater producers cannot trust their audiences or can only see one way of staging Shakespeare.

In present-day theaters, however, an audience is not always expected to submit to the staging of a script. In more recent plays, at least
from *Waiting for Godot* to the latest piece of scripted performance art,
dramatists and their directors have continually prodded audiences into
more active responses. Sometimes they seem more concerned with
new ways of provoking a reaction than they are with a search for
stronger dialogue or more significant action. Even a play that repro-
duces ordinary life on stage with some conviction can unsettle an audience's view: so, for *The Nest* (1975), Franz Xaver Kroetz insisted that a
truck driver empty eight barrels of poison, one after another, into a lake
without speaking a word—that is, until the audience becomes sufficiently bored to notice small changes for themselves or to lose the play
entirely. Plays surprise audiences by moving backward or forward in
time with little or no warning: for example, Harold Pinter's *Betrayal*
(1978) and Richard Nelson's *Sensibility and Sense* (1989). Samuel Beckett
unsettled audiences by a succession of new demands, so that they had
to make some sense of a play lasting only thirty-five seconds (*Breath*,
1966), or of one lasting twenty minutes, which is then repeated word
for word but not necessarily in the same order (*Play*, 1964), or of one
opening and closing with unintelligible speech from behind a stage
curtain and between that a "play" in which one woman's mouth was all
that could be seen with absolute clarity (*Not I*, 1973). Today the members of an audience may be puzzled, surprised, or wearied, or they may
have to struggle to keep intent on the play before them, and by these
means they may come away with perceptions that are more than usually of their own making. These are not communal and independent
audiences, as in Bali, but at least the dramatists have restored a personal freedom of thought and responsibility.

For some new plays anything goes in an effort to awaken an audience. Its members may be free to walk around and talk, take refresh-
ment, or consult various exhibitions, monitors, or alternative dramas.
Sometimes an audience is asked to decide which way the actors
should develop the story or to become part of the dramatic event.
Actors may speak directly to the audience, either as themselves or in
character. Messages are hung over the stage to explain what is hap-

pening or to deliver information that no one on stage is able to speak. Thirty years ago, in a preface to his *Workhouse Donkey* (1964), John Arden looked for even more audience freedom.

> I would have been happy had it been possible for *The Workhouse Donkey* to have lasted, say, six or seven or thirteen hours (excluding intervals), and for the audience to come and go throughout the performance. . . . A theatre presenting such an entertainment would, of course . . . take on some of the characteristics of a fairground or amusement park . . .[8]

Together with Joan Littlewood and others, he was speaking in favor of a theater that he could call "vital." Intermittently the search goes on with more or less conviction, but this seldom affects the staging of Shakespeare.

It is not necessary to go back to Bali to find some elements of the audience for which Shakespeare's plays seem to have been written. Reviews and previews in the press are always speaking of a more active role for audiences and it may be that a change in the staging of Shakespeare is about to happen in our English-speaking theaters. Two random examples of these straws in the wind may be taken from the London *Times* within one week of 1993. The first is a review of *Emanuelle Enchanted* published on June 10.

> By refusing to spoon-feed the audience or pacify them with visual prettiness, *Emanuelle Enchanted* stimulates spectators into helping themselves. It makes them search for their own connections and meanings amongst the cryptic fragments. . . . One can be bored or flummoxed, but that is part of Forced Entertainment's agenda. . . . this is courageously radical, intelligent, provocative work.

The second quotes a Brazilian author-director speaking about his new show, *A Guerra Santa*, on June 16.

> When you are in a Baroque church, the architecture doesn't make you look towards any specific focal point; you have to take in everything at once. And that's what I am trying to do in this show; there are always many things happening. And as a viewer, you have to choose what to observe.

These two of very many voices suggest that those who make plays from nothing are moving some little way back to Bali. Perhaps they may encourage producers of Shakespeare in the English-speaking world to move in the same direction. The first really large step would be to keep the audience in the same light as the performers—or to keep them, for the most part, on their feet.

NOTES

1. Antonin Artaud, *The Theater and Its Double*, trans. Mary C. Richards (New York: Grove Press, 1958), 57, 59, 66.
2. This essay does not offer a responsible account of Balinese cremation rituals and, still less, an assessment of Balinese "culture." Its sole concern is to show how a visit to one ceremony awakened, in one spectator, a lively response to well-known evidence about the theater practice of Elizabethans and suggested ways of reading and staging their plays that are, at present, not widely employed.
3. Stephen Greenblatt, *Shakespearean Negotiations: The Circulation of Social Energy in Renaissance England* (Berkeley: University of California Press, 1988), 18.
4. Francis Bacon, *The Advancement of Learning*, II.xiii. This passage is quoted in appendix 2 of Andrew Gurr's *Playgoing in Shakespeare's London* (Cambridge: Cambridge University Press, 1987), which prints a useful list of over two hundred contemporary references to playgoing, from 1563 onward. Of those dating from 1625 and earlier, the following add to the picture of a communal and independent audience stirred by their own thoughts as well as those derived from the performance of a play: numbers 15, 18, 19, 21, 23, 32, 33, 38, 40, 43, 46, 51, 56, 69, 74, 78, 79, 88, 93, 99, 101, 102, 117, 118, and 120.
5. Artaud, *The Theater and Its Double*, 59.
6. Ibid., 67.
7. See *A Midsummer Night's Dream*, III.i.68–70. See also I, *Henry IV*, II.iv.379–85; *Hamlet*, II.ii.492–98 and III.ii.131–284; and *Love's Labor's Lost*, V.ii.543, 703. Christopher Sly's reactions in *The Taming of the Shrew* are more uncertain evidence, since Sly scarcely knows where he is or what is happening to him. But it is relevant, in the context of this inquiry, to notice that Sly's self-interest, as the play is performed for his benefit, outweighs very obviously any matter belonging to the dramatic fiction.
8. John Arden, *The Workhouse Donkey* (London: Methuen, 1964), 8.

Training the French Actor: From Exercise to Experiment

BERNARD DORT

BEFORE STANISLAVSKI

Stanislavski is the Galileo of acting. He turned actor training topsy-turvy, substituting one center for another. Before Stanislavski the center was the character, or, more precisely, the role, and that role was set once and for all by tradition. The actor had to repeat what his illustrious predecessor did, who in turn had copied his predecessor. To be sure, the actor might introduce a few corrections or improvements, but he had to do so without disturbing the basic conception. And these slight modifications might be corrected or improved upon by his successors. Essentially, then, the art of the actor was one of reproduction, and his goal was an ensemble of the roles of his profession, which he was to interpret on the basis of established models. Learning to act was therefore transitive: one studied a certain role, one copied a certain model. In Diderot's terminology, the art of the actor was interpretive not conceptual.

FROM INTERPRETATION TO CREATION

Stanislavski accomplished what was only suggested by Diderot, who is something like the Copernicus of this revolution of Galileo. With the former, the actor changes function and perhaps his/her very nature. Against an art of representation that is pure and simple imitation, Stanislavski opposes an art of creation. And it is the actor, not the role, who is at the center of his system. Learning to act becomes intransitive. You have to be an actor before undertaking a particular role, and that requires a long apprenticeship in depth. Finally, it means creating a new kind of human being, the actor, a man or woman capable of playing, or rather incarnating, all roles. And something more.

This leads to a double and contradictory result. The technique required by the actor broadens and diversifies; it is no longer based on a few specific disciplines like diction and bearing; rather, it assembles many different kinds of processes, which presuppose continuous training. At the same time, the very concept of technique is subverted; the actor not only has to perform but also to invent and create. His/her art subdues technique; it relies on technique but goes further; it is indebted to technique but is free of it in the theater. Beyond technique or in opposition to it, the actor's study develops.

SUBVERSION OF PROFESSION AND CHARACTER

The milestones cannot be dated with precision. The Napoleonic prescription of specific *emploi* is out of date. Although the terms of *emploi* were used at the Comédie Française until the 1950s, it was already old-fashioned, and yet it was the basis of actors' training and of the organization of the company. The idea of genre is even more obsolete. The birth of *drame* dissolved the separation between tragedy and comedy while introducing so many intermediate forms that each play was virtually its own genre. Today we speak of a text rather than a play. Even the notion of character was reexamined. Thus, the actor is within or beyond the character, or whatever replaces it; he/she plays behavior but does not construct a homogenous whole; he/she views and comments from the outside, examining an object that is unstable and multiple rather than an analogue of him/herself who is defined once and for all. In addition, the actor's workplace may vary; it is no longer the stage alone, but also the small or large screen, where the image replaces actual presence.

In short, the actor must be prepared to lend him/herself to everything. Is it not possible "to make theater out of anything," in the words of Vitez (the recently deceased head of the Comédie Française)?

The training of such an actor no longer relies on a well-regulated and rather stable profession. It has to anticipate a praxis that is protean and variable.

At the beginning of the century Antoine declared disapprovingly: "To present the individual whom they represent, actors have only two instruments, the voice and the face. The rest of their body has no share in the action." The actors have to be reminded that "movement is the most intense expression of the actor" and "the whole physical body is part of the character." The body is no longer raw material; it has to be exercised, trained, as in sports. In his program for the Studio in 1914, Meyerhold emphasized "the human body in space, gesture as impulse, summoned by the body alone." In opposition to western academic tradition, which is based on declamation and minimal gesture, Meyerhold refers to popular traditions and to Asian theater: "the study of the processes of *Commedia dell'arte* or of Japanese theater," which he judges "preferable to anything." Later, he even wished the actor to remake his/her body, to rebuild it. Artaud, a week before his death, was dreaming of

> a theater that, at each performance, would *corporeally* give something to the one playing as well as to the one who comes to see the playing, and for that matter one doesn't play, one acts. The theater is in reality *the genesis* of creation.

This revaluation—or ostentation—of the body requires a new ethics. When Copeau founded the school of the Vieux Colombier, he addressed himself not to specialists but

> to the whole man, causing him to be aware of all his expressive faculties, sending the actor to the school of poetry and the poet to the school of the stage. For the intensive training undergone by the actor in view of the immediate needs of production; for the rough and summary lessons in technical realities given to the author, I wanted to substitute a wide professional culture, a free dramatic life shared by men of the theater.

THE ACTOR, A COMPLETE ARTIST

On the one hand, the instrument, this body that must bend to every possible kind of expression; on the other hand, the consciousness of the artist, his/her responsibility. Actors' training today takes both goals into consideration, even making their difficult convergence its prime objective. Such training assumes new forms, new methods, which are many, different, and changing. Nevertheless, they share one characteristic: they extend far beyond traditional interpretation. They aim at being rather than doing. (Copeau quotes "the simple and profound words of Goethe: *before doing, one must be.* For one does only what one is.")

Let us speak of two broad categories: exercises and studios. Exercises precede production. They aim at the acquisition of certain techniques, which, in isolation, do not cover the whole area of activity of the actor. They are specifically theatrical or they overlap other physical or psychological disciplines. Since Stanislavski, improvisation occupies a privileged position, but that improvisation is less a preparation for the interpretation of a given role than a way for the actor to perfect his/her instrument, his/her very self. Studio work involves a different process; it is no longer a question of perfecting an instrument but of testing it, and in so doing committing the actor to his/her responsibility. In contrast to exercises, the studio is global, collective, and turned toward representation. The student participates as an actor with full privileges. The group functions like a theater company.

Collaboration of other theater professions is required (from scenography to stage management, including light and sound). And the final product is a performance, which is entirely different from a production. The rule of the studio is not efficacy but experimentation. At each step of the process the techniques are probed; one individual confronts another, one hypothesis confronts another. The only certainty is the experiment. And the final performance should retain this spirit of the temporary and uncertain so as not to become a production and thus betray itself.

This experimental practice, common today, also begins with Stanislavski. The first studio was probably the Studio Theater that he founded in fall 1905, assigning Meyerhold to head it. As is well known, the experiment failed and resulted in a break between Stanislavski and Meyerhold, which lasted thirty years. It turned on the nature of the final performance: a director's production or research conducted by actors. The very name Studio Theater already carried this ambivalence; Meyerhold wanted *theater* whereas Stanislavski expected a *studio* (a place for study) to revivify the Art Theater. Since then the theater of the twentieth century has been marked by such studios or laboratories. And in actors' training, the exercises may stress techniques, but the studio is a crucible of learning.

SCENE STUDY

Where, then, should we situate the dominant practice in actors' training in France—scene study—which remains the touchstone of most theater schools? At the very least, its status is ambiguous. In training based on the profession or the role, scene study is central. If the scene is well-chosen—that is, if it is a key scene of the play—it allows the student to pierce to the essence of a character or a role as if it were a contraction of the whole text. Everything must be said and shown in a minimum of time and even of space. The scene depends upon an instantaneous identification, and it postulates an immediate fusion of being and doing. Which is to demand a great deal. Dramaturgically speaking, it is perhaps absurd. (I confess that I often remain skeptical, and even hostile, when I see young actors work hard at playing the meeting of Rodrigue and Chimène—III–4—or the scene in which Hermione convinces Orestes to kill Pyrrhus—IV–3—or one of the two conversations between Elmire and Tartuffe. Not only are these scenes virtually senseless when they are played out of context—it is true that the interpreters are supposed to know this context; they are supposed to have read and thought about the play, but this is not, alas, always the case—but how can students succeed instantaneously when experienced actors need the duration of the performance— unless the students imitate their elders?) Actually, the French habit of scene contests belongs to pre-Stanislavskian training, based on a model. It harkens back to "the art of representing" not to an apprenticeship of the actor as a responsible creator.

Nevertheless, the practice continues. It is the very basis of the "course in interpretation" that still forms the spine of the French national conservatory. And Antoine Vitez was far from renouncing it, although he was an innovative teacher who was nurtured on the great masters of the twentieth century—Stanislavski, Meyerhold, and Brecht. But, while conserving the practice, Vitez transformed it. He introduced a kind of relativity into it. With him scene study became an experimental exercise. By constant variation and even distortion, Vitez "denormalized" the scene. It became the locus of a statement— about the essence of a role or a situation. It was transformed into an experimental space. Thus, far from remaining an anachronistic practice, the scene could now be a meeting point of exercise and studio, the occasion for interplay between styles and sense, between techniques of representation and exigencies of incarnation, between continuity and discontinuity—in short, between all possibilities for the actor. By its very gratuity, scene study called for an act of consciousness, not of success or failure but of choice, of actorly responsibility in a semantic exercise. Hence, in contrast to the boredom of the scene contest, there arose a feeling of invention and liberty so that one can dream of a theater free of shackles. But it must be liberated from competition and prizes. Scene study is valuable only in and for the training school. It should be neither a way into the school, nor should it conclude the schooling. It is exclusively a laboratory.

INTERPRETATION AGAIN

In contrast to traditional actors' training, the modern school wishes to teach the actor to free him/herself from imitation without striving for originality at all costs. It is not easy. The actor has to find or invent a voice, a body, a culture, and he/she can do this only by discarding everything that was formerly considered natural or ideal. Grotowski characterized his *way* as "negative—not a collection of methods, but an elimination of blocks." The very word *to interpret*, shamed by Stanislavski, now has a new sense borrowed from literature; it no longer means to translate what was already in the text but to imagine, to uncover the virtualities of this text, to embark it on a path of changes so that it will not remain dead wood.

Vitez said: "The actor is an artist who is conscious of the tricks he proposes." The training school is the laboratory of that consciousness. There techniques are converted to learning. On leaving school, the student is not an actor; at best he/she is ready to become an actor. The rest takes a lifetime.

Translated by Ruby Cohn

Molly's "Happy Nights" and Winnie's "Happy Days"

ANTONIA RODRÍGUEZ-GAGO

If one were to choose the most contrasting female characters in twentieth-century literature written in English, one would probably select Joyce's Molly Bloom in *Ulysses* and Beckett's Winnie in *Happy Days*. Molly is a fictional character traditionally interpreted as a sensual, and sexual, life force, a fertile Mother Earth symbol, while Winnie is a dramatic character most often considered as a metaphor for the barrenness, futility, and boredom of life, a figure whose physical and mental deterioration negates all possibility of improvement. Winnie contrasts clearly with Molly, a fictional protagonist who embodies the principle of affirmation, or, in Joyce's words, "der Fleisch der stets bejaht" (the flesh that always affirms).[1] If one tries to consider these two distinct but equally intriguing female protagonists in a new light, one is surprised not only by their obviously contrasting characters but especially by the striking similarities in the nature and content of their virtuoso "solo" performances.

I cannot help but think that when, in 1960, Beckett started writing a monologue entitled "X female Solo," a kind of female companion to Krapp, he couldn't resist using some aspects and features of what is perhaps the most famous female monologue of this century—which he knew so well—and, with his inimitable sense of humor, used them for his own purposes in the creation of Winnie, a female character that in many aspects seems a parody of Molly Bloom, perhaps an "inverted parody" as the initials of their names seem to suggest (*W* being an inverted *M*). It is also significant that Willie, when he first appeared as a companion to Winnie, was called simply "B," Bloom's initial. I am not arguing that Beckett's intention, when he wrote *Happy Days*, was to create a parody of Joyce's famous couple; but I am quite convinced that some aspects of character, situation, recurring themes, motives and obsessions, which Winnie shares with Molly, are not there by mere chance. I would like to illustrate this point, presenting some of the obvious resemblances and also some of the remarkable contrasts between Molly's "happy nights" and Winnie's "happy days."

The structure of Molly's interior monologue and of Winnie's "dialogue of one" is basically musical, with a central theme and recurring variations. Another common trait is the sheer *oral* quality of both their speeches, so that readers and spectators become listeners and confidants of Molly's and Winnie's innermost thoughts and trivial chatter.

Although Molly's interior monologue was written to be read, not theatrically performed, her colloquial tone and the natural flow of her language deludes us into believing that she is a "voice" who talks, sharing with us her obsessions, doubts, confusions, and reveries. Speaking only to herself, Molly becomes, paradoxically, a great dramatic performer who has her audience spellbound with the power and energy of her language—and obviously with the provocative subject matter of her interior monologue. Through her words we enter Molly's conscience and accompany her in an "internal journey," moving back and forth in time, from her present situation in 7 Eccles Street, Dublin, to past memories of her girlhood in Gibraltar.

Winnie is also a great performer who manages to hold her audience's attention not only by the power of her speech but above all by her unique dramatic situation. She is trapped in the earth, literally buried by it, yet she seems totally undaunted by her desperate condition, performing a series of everyday actions with the utmost naturalness. Like Molly, Winnie is a great talker who tries to come to terms with her present situation by talking about it. Though Winnie's fragmented and often incoherent speech, punctuated by pauses and silences, has nothing to do with Molly's powerful and incessant stream of words, both speeches are appropriately suited to presenting not only their different life experiences, recalled or "invented," but to convey an accurate image of their individual personalities. If language denotes being, Molly's and Winnie's "solos" are therefore acts of self-translation that reveal two fascinating female characters.

Let us now consider Molly and Winnie as if they were both stage characters (Molly has been successfully taken to the stage and film) and compare their physical situation as well as their living spaces. Molly is "paralyzed" in her bed next to a silent and sleeping husband, and Winnie is "stuck up to her diddies in the bleeding ground"[2] next to an almost invisible, mostly silent, and half-sleeping husband. There is an evident resemblance in these situations, but there is also a clear difference. Molly's "recital" is given during the night, or at least late in the evening, because she cannot sleep. She is a "night-talker": her powerful solo performance is a kind of lullaby that sends her to sleep for "another happy night." Winnie, on the other hand, is a "day-talker"; her "recital" takes place under a "blazing light," but her words bring her also to the end of "another happy day." It is not difficult to see, then, the ironic correspondence in their situations and to notice Beckett's deliberate distortion in his creation of Winnie. It is a mark of Beckett's great ingenuity to transform the fertile Mother/Earth/Molly (the "voracious sexual animal," in Robert Adams's words),[3] into the sterile Mother/Earth/Winnie, literally planted in a barren and scorched earth.

If we consider their living spaces, the contrasts seem to be even greater, but again one can discover parodic elements enlivening each situation. Molly is comfortably located in her living space, her bed. In one of her many significant exclamations she says, "O I like my bed."[4] Winnie occasionally complains about her physical confinement, though not very often; she is an incorrigible optimist who "will not admit that she was born merely to die."⁵ She complains mainly about the heat, the "blaze of hellish light" (p. 11), the infernal oven in which she has been placed. She even contemplates a future in which she might "burst into flames" or perhaps be, little by little, "charred to a black cinder" (p. 29), the heat being the principal source of her physical torture. Like Winnie, Molly complains about the heat: "this blanket is too heavy on me" (p. 896). But unlike Winnie she can alleviate her situation by removing the blanket: "that's better." Because of the heat, Molly "could not read a line" (p. 897) when she was a girl in Gibraltar. The heat is for both a symptom of physical discomfort, an image of their problematic present situation and of the confined, stifling existence they are fated to share.

As I mention above, Molly's and Winnie's "solos," with their mixture of discourses, evolve around a central theme: *the need for another.* Sentimental affairs, present and past, real or fictitious, are variations around this central theme. Both Molly and Winnie start their recitals thinking about their husbands. In the case of Molly, the spring that opens the Pandora's box that is Molly's mind is Bloom's unusual request to have breakfast in bed: "Yes because he never did a thing like that before as to ask to get his breakfast in bed with a couple of eggs since the *City Arms* hotel . . ." (p. 971). Bloom's request in the past has an easy explanation for Molly: he wanted to make himself interesting to that "old faggot Mrs. Riordan." But his request now is much more intriguing. The first sentence, of the eight that make up her soliloquy, is devoted to Molly's questions and reflections about the possible causes of her husband's strange behavior. He wishes, perhaps, to awaken her interest in himself or, suspecting her relationship with Boylan, he wants perhaps to exercise his marital authority. Molly's multiple reflections end with the reassuring conviction that she can get Bloom back if she likes. The significant thing here is that it is Bloom's request that opens the stream of Molly's thoughts.

Winnie is forced to start her solo by the piercing sound of a bell, not by any request from her husband, but the first thing she does after her prayers and morning toilette is to attract her husband's attention.

Another heavenly day . . . For Jesus Christ sake Amen . . . World without end Amen . . . Begin, Winnie . . . Begin your day, Winnie . . . Hoo-oo! . . . Hoo-oo! . . . Poor Willie . . . poor dear Willie- . . . -sleep for ever- . . . marvellous gift- . . . -nothing to touch it- . . . -in my opinion- (pp. 10–11)

Winnie is going to give us a good show of "her life and opinions" as she retraces the routines and rituals of another of her many "happy days."

Molly's and Winnie's openings couldn't be more diverse. And yet one sees resemblances deliberately distorted, which reveal, perhaps, Beckett's parodic game. Bloom demands Molly's attention, and this starts her monologue. At the opening of *Happy Days* we have the opposite situation: Willie is in this instance the object of Winnie's continuous request for attention. She needs a spectator for her performance, and, although Willie's few monosyllabic answers amount to a parody of dialogue, Winnie's incessant chatter becomes a "dialogue of one" (Katharine Worth's expression) because it is addressed to that other, her husband. But Willie is not merely the recipient of Winnie's continuous request for attention; playing a similar role to Bloom, he is also responsible for his wife's reflections, observations, meditations, and allusions. Their husbands' mere presence enables Molly and Winnie to go on—to go on "talking," that is. Winnie is, moreover, very much aware of this.

Ah yes, if only I could bear to be alone, I mean prattle away with not a soul to hear. . . . Not that I flatter myself you hear much, no Willie, God forbid. . . . Days perhaps when you hear nothing. . . . But days too when you answer. . . . That is what enables me to go on, go on talking that is. . . . (p. 18)

"Marriage farce," as Ruby Cohn has noticed,[6] plays an important role in *Happy Days*, and it also plays a relevant role in *Ulysses*. Sleeping next to his wife, Leopold Bloom is, in Joyce's words, "body Poldy"—just a sleeping body next to Molly who is certainly given "the last word."[7]

Willie in *Happy Days* is silent or sleeping during the greater part of the performance; directing the play, Beckett compared him to "a turtle very much from the earth."[8] The physicality of these two male characters is quite evident, and there are other resemblances as well. They both possess pornographic cards and enjoy sexual jokes. Willie's prolonged contemplation of his pornographic card seems a parodic echo of Bloom's close observation of Gerty MacDowell in "Nausica." But the greatest joke of them all, on Beckett's part, is substituting Willie, the "great crawler," for Bloom, the "great wanderer." There is another correspondence: both Willie and Bloom are sources of "intellectual" information for their wives. Two dialogues will illustrate this point. The first, between Bloom and Molly, occurs in the fourth chapter of *Ulysses*, when Molly questions him about the meaning of a word: "-Metempsychosis, he said, frowning. It's Greek: from the Greek. That means the transmigration of souls" (p. 77). Molly wants the explanation in plain words and it takes a few more pages to complete it. The most relevant piece of information that Willie helps Winnie elucidate is the meaning of the word *hog*.

> *Winnie:* What *is* a hog, Willie, please! . . .
> *Willie:* Castrated male swine . . . Reared for slaughter.

Winnie, quite happy with this explanation, exclaims, "Oh this *is* a happy day" (p. 36). Equating the words *metempsychosis* and *hog* as goals for intellectual inquiry, Beckett seems to be mocking not only his predecessor but also the relative importance of all human knowledge.

In the fourth sentence of her soliloquy, Molly expresses the boredom and monotony of her present life, having dismissed her lover Boylan from her thoughts as a "savage brute" at the end of the previous sentence. To escape from her present boredom she takes an imaginary journey into the past, recalling her first love when she was a young girl in Gibraltar. This is her evocation.

> Mulveys was the first . . . he was the first man kissed me under the Moorish wall my sweetheart when a boy it never entered my head what kissing meant till he put his tongue in my mouth . . . what was his name

Jack Joey Harry Mulvey was it yes I think . . . moustache had he . . . (pp. 901–3)

Let us now consider Winnie's recollection of a similar scene from her past. Like Molly, Winnie has a bad memory for names, but she also enjoys evoking sentimental memories.

> My first kiss! . . . A Mr. Johnson, or Johnston, or perhaps I should say Johnstone. Very bushy moustache very tawny . . . Almost ginger! . . . Within a toolshed, though whose I cannot conceive. We had no toolshed and he most certainly had no toolshed.
>
> (p. 15)

Beckett kept most of the explicit sexual connotations from earlier versions of the play, and he later omitted two lines in this scene that may be significant if we compare them to Molly's recollections.[9] In the first typescript of the play, Beckett offers us more information about Mr. Johnson.

> A Mr. Johnston, or Johnson, very bushy moustache, (very brown), I suppose that is what vanquished my scruples. Old enough to be my father in those days and indeed it later transpired my grandfather. He was eager I recall to put his tongue in my mouth.

Molly's Mulvey is young, while Winnie's Johnson is old, though age is not mentioned in the last version of *Happy Days*. Both lovers share a moustache, and kiss their women similarly. *J* is the initial they both share. Mulvey's Christian name was perhaps Jack or Joe—or even Harry—we cannot trust Molly's memory. Significantly, Winnie's lover's surname was Johnson or Johnston—or perhaps even Johnstone. The "setting" of the two affairs is, however, quite different. Molly meets her man in the open air: "under the Moorish wall." Winnie's and Johnson's affair is more private; it occurs "within a toolshed," hidden from the public view perhaps because of the difference in the lovers' ages. Both evocations make use of a genuinely poetic language that alternates "from sex to sensibility,"[10] for Molly and Winnie like to depict themselves as romantic heroines. Although

Molly, according to Suzette Henke, tries to represent herself in her reveries as the kind of "sensuous heroine of the pornographic novels she's read,"[11] I agree with Charles Peake when he says that Molly is more "a romantic than a sensual heroine."[12]

Let us briefly consider Molly's and Winnie's "classics." In the second act of *Happy Days* Winnie, trying unsuccessfully to remember a piece of poetry, exclaims:

> one loses one's classics . . . Oh not all . . . A part . . . A part remains . . .
> That is what I find so wonderful, a part remains, of one's classics, to help
> one through the day. (p. 43)

Winnie's fragmentary way of "misquoting" makes it impossible for the audience, in most cases, to identify the originals. She doesn't name a single author, or title, though she frequently quotes "wonderful lines," "unforgetable lines," or "exquisite lines." Unlike Winnie, Molly gives the reference, though often inaccurate or incomplete, of the books she has read or is reading. These include a mixture of pornographic books such as *Ruby: the Pride of the Ring*, in which she finds the intriguing word *metempsychosis*, and the latest book Bloom has brought her to read, *Sweets of Sin*, written "by a gentleman of fashion some other Mr de Kock I suppose" (p. 908). Molly also mentions more serious readings such as Byron's poems and a novel of the nineteenth-century Spanish novelist Juan Valera (probably *Pepita Jiménez*, though the title is not mentioned; Mrs. Rubio lent it to her, but she never tried to read it). She remembers having read a book with a "Molly" in it, but she dislikes books with her name in them: "like that one he gave me about the one from Flanders a whore always shoplifting anything she could" (p. 896). The novel is obviously *Moll Flanders*, but again she has forgotten its title.

Molly's reading is, then, quite unconventional, and she rarely chooses her own books. Winnie, by contrast, seems to have had a much better and more traditional education, if one considers the fragments of poetry that she quotes, or rather misquotes. Fragmented lines from Shakespeare, Milton, Yeats, and other poets are among her many literary allusions. Reading seems once to have been for both Molly and Winnie a way to fill their days. Words from past readings are now just a precious possession that they use to pass the time.

As I have said above, both Molly and Winnie have a defective memory, and the way they misquote illustrates this point. In addition, Molly has problems with spelling; and both her monologue and Winnie's speech are ungrammatical from a conventional point of view. I would like to give two significant examples of misquotation and also of misspelling. We listen to Winnie first.

> What is that wonderful line? . . . Oh fleeting joys . . . Oh something lasting woe. (p. 13)

The line she quotes is from *Paradise Lost*, Book X: "O fleeting joys of Paradise, dear bought with such lasting woes." Winnie's memory is weak and fragmented, like her body, but the words she remembers apply ironically to her present situation. Molly's misquotation, from Robert Southey's "The Cataract of Lodore," similarly relates significantly to her situation: "O how the waters come down at Lahore" (p. 915). The correct line is "How does the water, / Come down at Lodore." Molly substitutes the letters *a* and *h* for *o* and *d* in the word *Lodore*, which becomes *Lahore*. *Lo* becomes *la*, the Spanish definite article; *dore* becomes *hore*, phonetically *whore*. This change perhaps shows Molly's guilty conscience after committing adultery; she thinks she is a whore, as Patrick Colm Hogan suggests in his Lacanian reading of her monologue.[13] Her menstrual flow is ironically compared with the "waters of Lodore."

The only philosopher mentioned by name by both Molly and Winnie is Aristotle. As Richard Ellmann points out, "Molly's only acquaintance with Aristotle is the apocryphal and semi-pornographic" *Aristotle's Masterpiece;* she "malaprops" his name into "some old Aristocrat or whatever his name is."[14] She mistakes the name Aristotle for the noun *aristocrat*, a sure sign of her deficient education. Winnie's "acquaintance" with Aristotle is mentioned almost at the end of the play when she is considering different kinds of sadness.

Sadness after intimate sexual intercourse one is familiar with of course . . .
You would concur with Aristotle there, Willie, I fancy. (p. 42)

In these allusions to the Greek philosopher, both Molly and Winnie
"flesh philosophy," as the "wisdom of the body penetrates the wisdom of the mind."[15]

The significant point here is that both Winnie and Molly have their
"classics" to turn to when all else fails. They are "great talkers" who
make up their lives with the only means at their disposal, language,
taking us from time present to time past, and also visualizing time
future. Like Buñuel, they seem to believe that dreams and reveries are
essential in our lives, that "time doesn't alter anything. One lives
inside oneself. Journeys don't exist."[16] Only internal journeys matter.
For Molly and Winnie, as for "the dead voices" of *Godot*, living is not
enough; they have to talk about it. In a certain sense, their talking is
their living. Through recollections of their past they try to come to
terms with the presentness of their situations. Molly's and Winnie's
powerful "solos," orchestrated musically around a central theme with
recurring variations, are essentially acts of such self-translation into
words.

I would like to finish this essay with a brief reflection on Molly's and
Winnie's different use of language. Molly's ungrammatical but continuous flow of words contrasts sharply with Winnie's self-questioning
and fragmented speech. Molly's is a paradigm of Rimbaud's language
of "soul that speaks to the soul," a language that seems to contain
everything, "smells, sounds, colours."[17] Her natural, colloquial, and
very often incoherent speech is perfectly timed to present her complex
and often paradoxical personality: sensitive and intelligent at times,
vulgar, illogical, and incoherent at others. At the end of her solo, Molly
seems to come to terms with her own situation, and, carried away by
the power of her own language, she ends her monologue with the
definitive affirmation, "I will yes."

Winnie's fragmented language also reflects a complicated personality; sometimes she is aware of her terrible predicament, but most
often she is blind to it. She is "an interrupted being" (Beckett's

phrase) who cannot concentrate on anything, who jumps constantly from one subject to another, unable to finish anything. Her fragmented language is an image of her fragmented mind. Winnie suffers from "pernicious optimism," which prevents her from seeing her condition as it is; and this is, perhaps, the reason why she, like Molly, ends up by "saying yes to this atrocious affair of life, like the 'oui' in *Ulysses*."[18]

Molly's and Winnie's ways of using language are paradigmatic of the different use of language in the hands of their respective authors. Beckett believed that language always failed to express "being," perhaps because this being was hidden behind a barrier of words; he tried to break this wall of language to get at the something or nothing hidden behind it. Joyce thought, on the contrary, that all was possible with language, that he could do everything with words. "The more Joyce knew the more he could," Beckett said. "He is tending toward omniscience and omnipotence as an artist. I am working with impotence and ignorance."[19] Joyce's attitude toward language was one of integration, Beckett's one of disintegration. Molly and Winnie, "revolving it all" in their minds and contrasting their past and present experiences in their powerful dramatic solo performances, exemplify and embody the Joycean attitude of creation through integration, and the Beckettian attitude of creation through disintegration.

The surface of Molly's speech, not broken by any punctuation, is a smooth, powerful, and integrative flow, though the reader has to break this flow continuously and reread in order to get at the meaning of the words. The spectator of *Happy Days* is aware from the start, Winnie's body being half-hidden, that all experience is fragmentary. Winnie's speech, continually broken by actions, pauses, and silences, is paradigmatic of Beckett's construction through fragmentation and disintegration. Using such opposite methods, and having contrasting conceptions about the value and power of language, Joyce and Beckett have created Molly's "happy nights" and Winnie's "happy days." Two fascinating and convincing female protagonists recount and retell their own problematic experiences; each is emblematic, moreover, of the creative process at work in the imagination of two great stylists of the modernist tradition.

NOTES

1. Richard Ellmann, *Selected Letters of James Joyce* (London: Faber and Faber, 1975), 285.
2. Samuel Beckett, *Happy Days* (London: Faber and Faber, 1970), 32. All quotations in this essay are from this edition.
3. Robert Adams, "Common Sense and Beyond," as quoted in Suzette A. Henke, *James Joyce and the Politics of Desire* (London: Routledge, 1990), 248.
4. James Joyce, *Ulysses* (London: The Bodly Head, 1966), 918. All quotations are from this edition.
5. Ruby Cohn, *Back to Beckett* (Princeton: Princeton University Press, 1973), 192–93.
6. Ruby Cohn, *Just Play: Beckett's Theater* (Princeton: Princeton University Press, 1980), 13.
7. Ellmann, *Selected Letters of James Joyce*, 274.
8. James Knowlson, Samuel Beckett, *"Happy Days": A Bilingual Edition* (London: Faber and Faber, 1978), 104.
9. S. E. Gontarski, *Beckett's "Happy Days": A Manuscript Study* (Columbus: Ohio State University Libraries, 1977), 41.
10. Enoch Brater uses this expression, referring to Winnie's language, in *Beyond Minimalism: Beckett's Late Style in the Theater* (New York: Oxford University Press, 1987), 16.
11. See Henke, *James Joyce*, 127.
12. Charles Peake, *James Joyce the Citizen and the Artist* (London: Edward Arnold, 1977), 302.
13. Patrick Colm Hogan, "Molly Bloom's Lacanian Firtree: Law, Ambiguity, and the Limits of Paradise," *James Joyce Quarterly* 29, 1 (Fall 1991): 110.
14. Richard Ellmann, *Ulysses on the Liffey* (London: Faber and Faber, 1974), 163.
15. Ibid.
16. Luis Buñuel, *Mi Ultimo Suspiro* (Barcelona: Plaza and Janés, 1982), 98.
17. Rimbaud's letter to Paul Demeny, 1871. See *Rimbaud*, ed. Oliver Bernard (Harmondsworth: Macmillan, 1962), 13.
18. Quoted by Martha Fehsenfeld in Linda Ben-Zvi, ed., *Women in Beckett: Performance and Critical Perspectives* (Urbana: University of Illinois Press, 1990), 57.
19. Israel Shenker, "An Interview with Beckett," in *Samuel Beckett: The Critical Heritage*, ed. Lawrence Graver and Raymond Federman (London: Routledge and Kegan Paul, 1979), 148.

Beckett's German Context

MARTIN ESSLIN

Beckett not only wrote some of his most important works in impeccable, inspired, and highly inventive French, having studied Romance
languages at Trinity, but he was also brilliantly proficient in both
Italian and Spanish and knew Portuguese well. What is less well
known, and even less well documented, is his extensive knowledge
of German and his wide erudition in German literature. The letter that
he wrote in German in 1937 to Axel Kaun (published by Ruby Cohn in
her collection of Beckett's miscellaneous writings, *Disjecta*) reveals the
sophistication of his German style. But even in his earliest work of
fiction, *Dream of Fair to Middling Women*, written at the age of twenty-
six, in 1932, Beckett displayed a playful facility in inserting German
expressions into his text.

Already, by chapter two, Belacqua, the hero of the novel, finds
himself in Vienna in pursuit of his beloved, the Smeraldina-Rima,
who has gone there to study the piano. Having "stepped hastily out
of the train at the Westbahnhof," Belacqua soon goes to find the
lady who, in fact, has ended up at a more ambitious establishment,
"studying music and eurythmics in the very vanguardful Schule

Dunkelbrau, ten miles out of town, on the fringe of the wild old, grand old park of Mödelberg."¹ This school is fairly easily identifiable as the establishment of two well-known eurythmic dancers, the sisters Wiesenthal, at Laxenburg, near the little town of Mödling, a few miles south of Vienna. Students there were, so Belacqua learns, taught "Harmonie, Anatomie, Psychologie, Improvisation, with a powerful ictus on the last syllable in each case."² Belacqua's jealousy is aroused by the interest taken in his beloved by "Herr Arschlochweh, Swiss and melancholy and highbrow and the Improvisationslehrer."³ *Arschlochweh*, literally translatable as "arse-hole-woe," is clearly a playful version of "a pain in the ass."

The whole of the Vienna episode in the novel, which also gives proof of Beckett's considerable familiarity with the topography of the Austrian capital, and later the passage set in Germany, are liberally peppered with German expressions, usually functioning as comic examples of multisyllabic, ponderous Teutonic clumsiness and lack of refinement. Yet, in the long letter Beckett wrote in German five years later to his friend, the writer and translator Axel Kaun, he explains his use of the language—Kaun, after all, as a translater of English novels, would have easily understood a letter written in English—with the fact that "it is actually getting more and more difficult, and indeed, senseless, to me, to write an official English."⁴ This, seven years before he decided to write his major works in French . . .

The letter to Axel Kaun starts with Beckett's answer to Kaun's suggestion, when he was asked to propose possible German texts Beckett might translate, that he should have a try with the poems of Joachim Ringelnatz (pseudonym for Hans Bötticher, 1883–1934), a cabarettist, nonsense-verse writer and humorist. In fact, Beckett starts his letter with an allusion to one of the Ringelnatz's poems; he had been on the point of replying to Kaun's letter when, like Ringelnatz's male postage stamp, he had to go on a journey. The poem in question, "Der Briefmark," runs as follows.

Ein männlicher Briefmark erlebte
Was Schönes bevor er klebte.

Er war von einer Prinzessin beleckt.
Da war die Liebe in ihm erweckt.
Er wollte sie wiederküssen,
Da hat er verreisen müssen.
So liebte er sie vergebens.
Das ist die Tragik des Lebens . . .[5]

In English, in a literal translation, "The Male Postage Stamp" reads:

A male postage stamp experienced
Something beautiful before he stuck.
He was licked by a princess.
That aroused love in his breast.
He wanted to kiss her back.
But he had to travel on.
So he loved her in vain.
That is life's tragedy . . .

This rather witty poem in its slight impropriety could not reconcile Beckett to its author, whom he dubbed a "rhyme-coolie," and who "as a poet seems to have been of Goethe's opinion that he would rather write NOTHING, than not write."[6] Here Goethe makes an appearance as an author with whom Beckett is familiar. There is another, far more subtle, allusion to Goethe in the same letter, however, when Beckett talks about his disgust with the terrible, arbitrary materiality of the word-surface in contemporary literature, his longing for his language of silence, which, like the pauses in Beethoven's seventh symphony, would offer glimpses into hitherto unplumbed depths. "Ich weiss," he goes on,

es gibt Leute, empfindsame und intelligente Leute, für die es an Still-schweigen gar nicht fehlt. Ich kann nicht umhin anzunehmen, dass sie schwerhörig sind. Denn im Walde der Symbole, die keine sind, schweigen die Vöglein der Deutung, die keine ist, nie.

I know there are people, sensitive and intelligent people, for whom there is no lack of silence. I cannot but assume that they must be hard of hearing. For in the forest of symbols, that aren't any, the little birds of interpretation, that isn't any, are never silent.

This sentence is exceptionally rich in allusions, quite apart from the fact that its structure, possible only in German, is untranslatable, insofar as the syllable *nie* (never) drops with a subtle and surprising fall at the end. The forest of symbols comes from Baudelaire's poem "Coincidences,"[7] while the little birds that are silent point to Goethe's famous short lyric, "Wanderers Nachtlied" (Wanderer's Night Song), which ends with the lines:

> Die Vöglein schweigen im Walde
> Warte nur, balde
> Ruhest du auch.

> The little birds are silent in the forest
> Wait a while, soon
> You too will find rest.

Another famous lyric by Goethe is subtly alluded to in Beckett's story *First Love*. The narrator of that story has met a prostitute, Lulu or Anna, and thinks he has fallen in love with her, very much against his better judgment.

> I longed to be gone, to know if it was over. I asked her to sing me a song. I thought at first she was going to refuse, I mean simply not sing, but no, after a moment she began to sing and sang for some time, all the time the same song it seemed to me, without change of attitude. I did not know the song, I had never heard it before and shall never hear it again. It had something to do with lemon trees, or orange trees, I forget, that is all I remember, and for me that is no mean feat, to remember it had something to do with lemon trees, or orange trees, I forget, for of all the other songs I have ever heard in my life, and I have heard plenty, it being apparently impossible, physically impossible short of being deaf, to get through this world, even my way, without hearing singing, I have retained nothing, not a word, not a note, or so few words, so few notes, that what that nothing, this sentence has gone on long enough.[8]

The song, it is beyond doubt, is Goethe's famous "Mignons Lied" from *Wilhelm Meisters Lehrjahre* (Wilhelm Meister's Apprentice Years) in which that thirteen- or fourteen-year-old waif sings of her longing to go to Italy. The first verse reads:

> Kennst du das Land, wo die Zitronen blühn,
> Im dunklen Laub die Gold-Orangen glühn,
> Ein sanfter Wind vom blauen Himmel weht,
> Die Myrte still und hoch der Lorbeer steht,
> Kennst du es wohl?
> Dahin, dahin
> Möcht ich mit dir, o mein Geliebter, ziehn![9]

> Do you know the land where the lemon trees bloom,
> Gold oranges gleam in the dark foliage,
> A soft wind blows from a blue sky,
> Where still the myrtle, high the laurel stands,
> Do you know it well?
> There, there
> I want to go with you, oh my beloved!

The narrator of the story insists that he did not know or recognize the song, as he is incapable of retaining a word, even a note—which is strange because he seems a highly learned man, having heard of love "at home, in school, in brothel and at church, and read romances, in prose and verse, under the guidance of my tutor, in six or seven languages, both dead and living."[10]

There are some parallels between Mignon and Lulu/Anna. Mignon has been rescued from mistreatment by the head of a troupe of tight-rope walkers by Wilhelm Meister, simply by buying her from her tormentor. And she dies of unrequited love for her benefactor, while the narrator of *First Love* abandons Lulu/Anna when she bears him a child.

Another lovelorn female figure from German literature to whom Beckett alludes more than once is Effi Briest, the unhappy heroine of Theodor Fontane's novel of the same name; in *Krapp's Last Tape* the solitary old man sums up his last year.

Scalded the eyes out of me reading *Effie* again, a page a day, with tears again. Effie . . . (*Pause*) Could have been happy with her, up there on the Baltic, and the pines and the dunes . . .[11]

Fontane (1819–98) is the great master of the German nineteenth-century realistic novel. *Effi Briest* (1895) tells the story of a girl still in her teens married to a much older, stiff bureaucratic careerist. She is pursued by and falls in love with a dashing cavalry officer and they spend some idyllic times on the shores of the Baltic near Rostock. Long after the affair has ended, and Effi's husband has been promoted to Berlin, he finds by chance a bundle of love letters from that long past episode. Effi loses her child, is banished from her home, and dies of grief. Krapp clearly connects Effi's idyll with his own love affair somewhere on the shores of the Baltic. Beckett greatly admired Fontane's straightforward, unadorned way of telling this sad story.

That Beckett's knowledge of German literature extended further than just some recognized highbrow classics emerges from his perhaps most significant borrowing from German popular, oral literature—the song that Vladimir sings at the opening of Act II of *Waiting for Godot.*

A dog came in the kitchen
And stole a crust of bread.
Then cook up with a ladle
And beat him till he was dead.

Then all the dogs came running
And dug the dog a tomb
And wrote upon the tombstone
For the eyes of dogs to come:

A dog came in the kitchen . . . etc.

This ditty is sung by children all over the German-speaking world. I remember being greatly amused by it when I was about eleven years old. The version that appears in the German translation of the play,[12] certainly based on the translator Elmar Tophoven's memory, differs slightly from the one that I sang—the cook in Tophoven's version beats the dog to a pulp (*zu Brei*); in mine he beat him "in twain" (*entzwei*), etc.—a sure sign that this is a text transmitted orally from generation to generation. It probably originated as a students' song sometime in the eighteenth century.

The significance of the song, which may not clearly emerge at first hearing in the play, where Vladimir stops and interrupts himself while singing it, lies in the fact that it is an image of endlessness, even eternity. Strictly speaking, one has to go on singing it forever. It folds back on itself; the second verse restarts, in the inscription on the tombstone, the whole story from the beginning, and so on, ad infinitum. It is thus a powerful image echoing the main thesis of the play—life as endless repetition of meaninglessness.

The intertexuality of Beckett's work is of the subtlest kind: he is simply so deeply imbued with the fruits of his reading—some of which may have become quite subconscious—that references to literary models or points from which a thought might have been bounced off may lie deeply buried. One such—and I may be wrong about it—seems to me to be contained in one of Beckett's least known dramatic pieces, *Fragment de Théâtre II*.[13] This shows a figure (C) standing in front of "a high double window open on bright night sky. Moon invisible." After awhile two other figures (A and B) enter and seat themselves at a table on which lies a briefcase crammed with documents. A and B are bureaucratic pedants. They are reviewing the reasons for and against C's committing suicide by jumping from the window, raising episodes for and against that proposition from his past, and discussing his invariably hopeless prospects. Toward the end a bird is heard singing. Out of the darkness of one of the corners the two investigators produce a cage. One of the birds in it is dead; the other sings. The investigation is over: "A goes to the window, strikes a match, holds it high and inspects C's face." He is intrigued by what he has seen, strikes another match and inspects C's face again. He exclaims: "Well, I'll be" (in the French original: "Ça, par exemple!"). The play ends with the stage direction: "A takes out his handkerchief and raises it timidly towards C's face."[14] Clearly C has started to cry; a tear is rolling down his cheek.

It seems to me that this short play, like so many of Beckett's dramatic pieces from *Endgame* to *Catastrophe*, is a monodrama, happening inside an individual's mind—an individual is in this case contemplating suicide. At the very beginning of his career as a writer, in *Dream of Fair to Middling Women*, Beckett had spoken, in describing what went on in Belacqua's mind, of

> the fuss that went on about the monologue and dialogue and polylogue and catalogue, all exclusively interieur. And the Gedankenflucht! The pons asinorum was a Gedankenflucht. In the umbra and the tunnel no exchanges, no flight and flow, no Bachkrankheit, but thought moving alive in the darkened mind gone wombtomb.[15]

If this short playlet is thus an example of "polylogue interieur," we are witnessing an individual making up his mind whether to end his life or not and at the end shedding a tear and remaining alive. The allusion here seems to be a sly and ironic one to the scene in Goethe's *Faust* in which the hero, about to drink the poisoned cup to end his misery, hears the Easter hymn from the church next to his study, sheds a tear, and resolves to remain alive in spite of all.

> O tönet fort, ihr süssen Himmelslieder!
> Die Träne quillt, die Erde hat mich wieder!

> Oh sound on, you sweet songs of heaven!
> The tear pours forth, the earth has me again.

Here, in true parodistic diminution of the model that is being cited, the person involved is no Faust, though clearly a minor poet or intellectual, and the song he hears is not an Easter hymn affirming Christ's resurrection but that of a caged bird whose mate has died. And the tear, though obviously present as it is being wiped off his face, is never actually mentioned. The reference to Goethe and *Faust* may be recondite, but seeing a performance of the play it struck me with immense force, the famous and oft-cited line compellingly rose in my mind: the tear pours forth, the earth has me again.

Here, then, are just some of the references and allusions to German literature in Beckett's work. As Beckett's knowledge of German was so good, and as he collaborated very closely with his German translator, the late Elmar Tophoven, the German texts of his works often shed interesting light on Beckett's intentions and meanings. To give but one example, the title *Lessness* (as a translation of the original *Sans*) appears in the German version as *Lösigkeit*. Now, while *lessness* might be seen as a newly formed noun in English, the German *-lösigkeit* cannot be a noun but can only exist as a suffix denoting absence. Hence the English *lessness* is in fact *-lessness*, as in *endlessness, hopelessness, joylessness*, and so on. Beckett's work is surely, as he asserted, no more than "fundamental sounds," but these noises proceed from a mind that closely resembles the narrator of *First Love*, well versed in six or seven languages, "both dead and living."

NOTES

1. Samuel Beckett, *Dream of Fair to Middling Women* (Dublin: Black Cat Press, 1992), 12–13.
2. Ibid., 13–14.
3. Ibid., 14.
4. "Es wird mir tatsächlich immer schwieriger, ja sinnloser, ein offizielles Englisch zu schreiben." See Samuel Beckett, *Disjecta*, ed. Ruby Cohn (London: John Calder, 1983), 52.
5. From Joachim Ringelnatz, *Gedichte* (Berlin: Rowohlt, 1935), 41.
6. "Als Dichter aber scheint er Goethes Meinung gewesen zu sein: Lieber NICHTS zu schreiben als nicht zu schreiben." See Beckett, *Disjecta*, 52.
7.

La Nature est un temple ou des vivants piliers
Laissent parfois sortir de confuses paroles;
L'homme y passe à travers des forêts de symboles
Qui l'observent avec des regards familiers.

(Charles Baudelaire, *Oeuvres Complètes* [Paris: Bibliothèque de la Pleiade, Gallimard, 1962], 11.)
8. Samuel Beckett, *First Love* (London: Calder and Boyars, 1973), 38–39.
9. Goethe, *Wilhem Meisters Lehrjahre*, book III, ch. 1. (Zurich: Artemis, 1948), 155.
10. Beckett, *First Love*, 31.

11. Samuel Beckett, *Krapp's Last Tape*, in *Krapp's Last Tape and Other Pieces* (New York: Grove Press, 1960), 25.

12.

Ein Hund kam in die Küche
Und stahl dem Koch ein Ei.
Da nahm der Koch den Löffel
Und schlug den Hund zu Brei.

Da kamen die anderen Hunde
Und gruben ihm ein Grab.
Und setzten ihm ein'n Grabstein
Worauf geschrieben stand:

Ein Hund kam in die Küche, etc.

13. Samuel Beckett, *Fragment de Théâtre II*, in *Pas suivi de quatre esquisses* (Paris: Editions de Minuit, 1978). English version: *Rough for Theatre II*, in *Collected Shorter Plays of Samuel Beckett* (London: Faber and Faber, 1984), 75–89.

14. See page 89 of the English version, and page 61 of the French version. *Fragment de Théâtre II* (*Theatre II*): "Ça, par exemple (A sort son mouchoir et l'approche timidement au visage de C)"; "Well, I'll be . . . (A takes out his handkerchief and raises it timidly towards C's face)."

15. Beckett, *Dream of Fair to Middling Women*, 45.

Memory Inscribed in the Body: *Krapp's Last Tape* and the Noh Play *Izutsu*

YASUNARI TAKAHASHI

If someone who knows Samuel Beckett's *Krapp's Last Tape* happens to be watching the performance of the second part (he or she may have walked out by then) of the noh play *Izutsu* (meaning 'well-curb') written by Zeami (1364–1443),[1] there will come a moment when he or she may be galvanized by a discovery of something unexpected, a stage picture that may spark a memory. The heroine, a young lady, having danced a long and slow dance, stops by the well-curb (the sole prop on an empty stage), bends slightly forward, looks into the well, and freezes. This posture will be felt to be strangely Krappian, reminiscent (or rather prescient) of the old man with his head bent close to the tape recorder. I know I am speaking for myself; surely, to be honest, in order for the shock of recognition to be complete (or even to occur), one would need to understand what is being said by her. Suffice it, at this juncture, to point to a sheer visual echo that may possibly be descried between the two stage images. I shall go on to demonstrate that what the young lady is gracefully *looking* into is memories of her past, just as Krapp, an irascible old man, is *listening* to memories of his past.

Like *Krapp*, *Izutsu* is a drama of memory, and it is probably in the nature of this genre of drama that time is structured like Chinese boxes. *Krapp* is certainly a supreme example, but *Izutsu* is no less remarkable in its dramaturgy.

The play opens with a traveling priest arriving at the ruins of a temple dedicated to the ninth-century poet Narihira, a man of legendary fame for both his poetic talent and his gallantry. An attractive woman enters and starts offering the water, which she draws from the well, to the grass-covered mound (actually no realistic gesture is made; all she does is chant words that versify the autumnal loneliness of the landscape and the mutability of human life). The priest asks wonderingly if she is related to the poet. She answers that she lives in the neighborhood but denies that she has any relationship—how can she, she says, considering that Narihira was *already* a legendary figure a long time ago?[2] (Note the pluperfect here, the first hint of Chinese boxes.)

She seems, however, to be extremely familiar with the poet's life. At the request of the priest, she begins to relate biographical episodes, beginning with the fact that he lived here with his wife. Her narrative recedes further in time to the childhood shared by Narihira and his future wife when they played together by this same well, then it proceeds forward a little to their adolescence when they met here again after a long separation and discovered love for each other. She describes how he first confessed his long-held emotion in the form of a love poem:

> Playing by the well-curb,
> I used to measure my height against it;
> Much taller have I grown
> Since last I saw you . . .

to which she replied also poetically:

> The short hair that I parted
> When we compared our heights here

Now flows loose down my back.
For whom but you should it be tied up?[3]

The pun, which defies translation, playing on *izutsu* ('well-curb') and *tsuzu* ('nineteen', their age), emphasizes the effect of time folded upon itself.

It is perhaps small wonder that the priest is seized by suspicion or awe as to who this seemingly omniscient woman can be; he urgently asks her name. She "blushingly" replies that she is none other than that wife of Narihira's she has been telling him about, whereupon she vanishes.[4] Why, it may be asked, does she blush? There is no doubt that, because of her modesty, she is *ashamed* of the insistency of her desire (definitely not wholly Platonic), which will not let her soul rest in peace but impels her to haunt, even as a ghost, the place of her erstwhile love. And we are probably allowed to surmise that she has been doing this coercive haunting for the past few hundred years (!). Despite that idyllic young love and the poetic betrothal, her married life does not seem to have been an entirely happy one (according to her narrative, Narihira is known to have once flirted with another woman). She says she came to be known in the world as "the woman who waits" because of her famous poem on the patient agony of waiting, and her passion of love was far from quenched when she, surviving her husband, lived to be an old woman. And it has now transpired that she has been yearning for him even in the other world.

Left alone, the priest somehow feels that if he drowses now, "Time may revolve in dream, / Bringing back the past into the present." Therefore, waiting for a dream-vision to appear, he falls asleep on an (invisible) "mossy stone" (the end of the first part).[5]

As if in answer to the priest's shamanic power, the second part begins with the reentrance of the same ghostly heroine—but with a difference. There is a strange case of transvestism here, for she is wearing a male cape on top of her female robe (which she wore in the first part) and a male hat on her head (her mask, that of a young woman, is unchanged). It is a curious androgynous figure. The puzzled audience (in the person of the priest) soon learns that the cape and the hat are Narihira's belongings. She explains her behavior herself.

Many a year has passed
Since our memorable moments by the well-curb;
Many a year since bereft of my husband;
I now feel on my body this cape he left me,
And as it touches me, to my blushful amazement,
I am possessed by him, and I dance.

Obviously the reminiscences she divulged earlier to the priest must have activated a surge of emotion in her. Driven by an irrepressible impulse, she donned the dearly kept mementos of her husband, and the moment they touched her she was possessed by him. There is an interesting syntactical ambiguity here: the sentence translated above as "I am possessed" could also be interpreted as "I have possessed him." The ambiguity seems profoundly apt. As phenomenologists of the body have shown,[6] to touch is necessarily to be touched and vice versa. If so, to don a man's cape would mean both embracing him and being embraced by him, and it would then be impossible to distinguish between the active and the passive modes of *possession:* she has possessed him just as much as she has been possessed by him. They have possessed each other. Or she has become him, and he her.

She could have cried, "I am Narihira!" However, Zeami not being Emily Brontë, his heroine "blushes"—again. In order to appreciate the rich ambiguity of the word, we should realize that tonight something unique has happened to her (which we as the audience are privileged to witness). She did what she had never done before: she put on her loved one's clothes. This may certainly be a "shameful" thing to do, but there is no denying that she is happily amazed by what has ensued: a mutual possession. Union with her husband has at long last been achieved, so that she, who "blushed" because of modesty earlier, now does so in spite of it. She is glad, to the point of suffusion, of her body being literally overlapped with her husband's.

We are now watching the heroine's dance. The dance, of central importance, is several things at once: a dance of possession and transformation (partly agonizing as in many primitive dances), a kind of physical exercise to rub the nascent sensation of union with her husband into her body, and an expression of the joy of union. Resuming her speech after the dance, she approaches the well-curb, stops by it, and bends forward slightly to look into the well—that characteristic posture to which I drew special attention. We know, though we do not see, what she sees in the water mirror at the bottom: the androgynous image. The possession she has been feeling on her body is here turned into an objective recognition, an awareness that the metamorphosis is both fiction and reality. That does not, however, prevent her from being fascinated by the image, as is clear from the words recited alternately by the chorus and the heroine.

Chorus: The image down there,
Wearing my dearest's hat and cape:
It is no woman, but a man,
The living image of Narihira.
Heroine: How dear the face I see!
Chorus: How dear the face, though it be mine!

We are not told what is left for her to do: if her union has been achieved once and for all, then it will be logical to assume that, released from the agony of waiting and yearning, she will never return to haunt this site. But the author apparently prefers to leave it vague. The chorus, after comparing "the ghostly figure of the dead husband" to "the scent of a withered flower," sings of "the matin bell bringing in the first light of dawn" and of "the wind blowing among the pine trees," and the play ends with words that may sound like an inverted version of Prospero's speech on life and dream.

The dream is broken, one wakes up,
The dream is broken, day dawns.

It is not only the priest who wakes up but the audience as well. It realizes that the whole second part has been a vision dreamed by the priest (hence the usual term applied to this type of noh, *mugen-noh,* i.e., dream-noh). This consciousness on the part of the audience may be said to constitute the outermost layer of the multiple theatrical experience, thus completing the dizzying palimpsest structure that is the play *Izutsu*.

Krapp's Last Tape, another theatrical attempt at the hero's autobiography, is a tour de force as a construct of Chinese boxes. Krapp stores his tapes in boxes with serial numbers applied to them, and inside each tape is encapsulated a fixed span of time in his life, that is, a memory of a year summarized on each birthday. Each tape contains a reference to an older tape, which Krapp must listen to as "a help before embarking on a new." So the audience of the play is faced with several levels of time: the real time on the stage (Krapp on his sixty-ninth birthday, the present), the year that has just gone by (the present perfect, or the near past), the birthday thirty years ago (Krapp on his thirty-ninth birthday, the more remote past), the year ending on that day, the year "at least ten or twelve years" before that year (Krapp on his twenty-ninth or twenty-seventh birthday, definitely the pluperfect), and the time of "youth," which that Krapp "sneers at" (the still more distant pluperfect).

"The dark backward and abysm of time" may extend indefinitely backward, because, though it is true that Krapp must have started this recording habit on a certain birthday, the audience can by no means be sure that Krapp did not talk about his still earlier days on some of the tapes that have not chanced to surface in the play. Might he not have indeed referred to what he remembered about his first birthday, or even about a famously Beckettian birth trauma or prenatal existence, for that matter?

What induced Krapp to think in the first place of the rather bizarre project of annual tape-recording, or what has sustained his compulsive habit over such a long period, is never explained in the play. Be that as it may, Krapp's meticulously observed habit strikes us as almost a reductio ad absurdum of two fundamental tenets of modern man, *homo cartesianus*. The first concerns the theory of knowledge: everything must and can be subjected to measurement, division, analysis, classification; to know an object is to stand apart from it and observe it; to know is to control and manipulate; to know is essentially to possess and govern. In short, the thesis initiated in the seventeenth century that knowledge is power has since become an unshakable assumption. And time is no exception to the rule, though it should be mentioned in fairness that Descartes himself remained uncommitted about the nature of time.

The second tenet, curiously combined with the first, is that the only thing that is indivisible is man himself: the act of thinking is in itself an irrefutable proof of the identity of an individual (a thing that cannot be divided). Krapp's practice is indeed a whole-hearted dedication to the twin modern ideas of self and knowledge: he demonstrates with devastating faithfulness the belief that one can triumphantly confirm the continuity of one's self by dividing, recording, and reproducing at will one's past, which constitutes one's self.

What the play presents, in fact, is the last stage in his life leading to the moment when Krapp's practice and the underlying belief begin to fall to pieces. Ironically, despite all his savage discontent with life, he does not at first give up the practice; he seems to take it for granted that he will do the recording yet again this year. Nearer the end, he still says to himself, "Go on with this drivel in the morning," revealing how deeply ingrained the habit has become. Then he goes on to mutter, "Or leave it at that. (*Pause.*) Leave it at that." It is only after this that the crisis manifests itself. "Wrenching off" the tape he has been recording, he resets the other tape, and the play ends with Krapp staring before him as the tape runs on in silence. The audience realizes that this is his last tape, though a vexing ambiguity remains as to whether *this* refers to the wrenched-off one (the last he recorded) or the other one (the last he listened to).

Differences in the nature of time and memory as theatrically embodied by *Izutsu* and *Krapp* may be too obvious to be labored over. The similarities in the theme of memory and the multiple time-structure only set off the vast gap that separates the two plays. For instance, to confirm the compulsive urge to remember shared by both protagonists does anything but blur a salient contrast, that is, the one between the tenacity of memory in *Izutsu* and the quasi-amnesia in *Krapp*: the woman cannot forget while the old man cannot remember. She has her memory physically attached to the well-curb; she, as a ghost, is almost a genius loci; all she needs to regain the time past seems to be some cue such as the visit of a priest. He confines himself in his solitary den; he needs to have his memory stirred by a ledger containing a classified index of the past years, which he consults with difficulty owing to his weak sight. But even entries of crucial events, like "Memorable Equinox," fail to ring a bell, let alone the word *viduity*, which sends him off to a dictionary.

Krapp's failure of memory looms all the more grotesque because of the tape recorder, a modern apparatus designed to ensure memory. If he responds to what the tape narrates, he does so not with a flash of recognition but with a slowness suggestive of a veil obstructing immediacy. This discrepancy between the voice and Krapp, which often functions to create an excruciatingly seriocomic effect, reminds us by contrast of *Izutsu*, where the rememberer and the remembered, subject and object of memory, are identical, the only discrepancy being in the relation between the woman and the priest.[7]

The impotent fascination with memory that both binds and distances Krapp is nowhere more touching than when he listens to the central episode on the "punt," arguably one of the most hauntingly lyrical scenes in the whole Beckett canon. It is a scene of "farewell to love," and, notwithstanding the arrogant tone that permeates the voice of the middle-aged Krapp, the sentiment communicated rings true. The moment of eye contact ("I bent over her to get [her eyes] in the shadow and they opened. (*Pause. Low.*) Let me in."), rare in Beckett, and which may be cynically sneered at as cheaply melodramatic, is of particular interest in that the picture of the younger Krapp bending over the girl for the last time seems to repeat, albeit obliquely, the posture of the old Krapp bending over the last tape. This is followed by what may or may not be taken as a symbolic description of sexual intercourse: "We drifted in among the flags and stuck. The way they went down, sighing, before the stem!" Then comes the ending: "I lay down across her with my face in her breasts and my hand on her. We lay without moving. But under us all moved, and moved us, gently, up and down, and from side to side."

Whether one feels the ending to be climactic or anticlimactic, it would be fair to take it that Krapp and the girl have achieved union of a sort, complete with the sense of attunement to the rhythm of the surrounding element. The union is fleeting and deceptive (for they are separating); it is a far cry from Iago's two-backed monster, or Donne's ecstasy of two "interanimated souls," or Heathcliff and Cathy's passionate identification. But it does claim a place in the republic of love in literature and drama where the picture of Krapp on top of the girl floating on the water may echo, however distantly, the image of that ghostly androgyne of *Izutsu* (also floating on the water).

But what is more important than the image seen is the person seeing, or, more precisely, the way the relation between the two is theatrically represented. It is here that one comes face to face with that prototypical stage icon shared by the two protagonists: the woman bending over the well-curb and the man bending over the tape recorder, both concentrating on memories of time past. The difference is that the woman in Zeami sees her union with Narihira while the old man in Beckett only hears and impotently tries to remember and visualize the embrace depicted by the voice. Hearing, at least in this case, is obviously in less direct touch with reality than seeing.

The androgynous image reflected in the water mirror surprises the woman, rivets her attention, then sublimates her long-frustrated desire to the point of her "blushing," and finally (probably) releases her from the bondage to time. The old man, too, is surprised in a way by the narrated vision (for he did not recognize the entry "Farewell to Love" in the ledger), and his fascination is evident in the fact that he plays the passage again. But that fact has further dramatic purposes to serve: it shows ironically the inadequacy of Krapp's memory, which is in need of repetition, and it also accentuates the ultimate fact that memory is sadly impotent to redeem the present.

It may be further noted that the audience of *Izutsu* experiences somewhat similar indirectness in being unable to see the image at the bottom of the well: it resembles Krapp in that it can only try to see the image in its mind's eye. Both plays have this in common: the center, the ultimate vision, is consciously left invisible by the dramatists. But what radiates from that vacant center in each case could not differ more. Zeami's exquisitely graceful female ghost allows us a sort of non-Aristotelian catharsis as she disappears at the end. Beckett's furiously unsatisfied old man is never released from the bond of memory and time, nor does he seem ever to stop threatening us with the blank stare that is the last we see of him as the curtain falls.

Drama is often said to have its origin in the memorial ritual for the dead, and anyway memory has always been a great subject of drama. In the history of world drama, *Izutsu* and *Krapp's Last Tape* seem to represent two extremist approaches to the subject. The former I hold to be the purest example of what I would propose to term *memory-as-theater*, while the latter seems to mark the ne plus ultra of *drama-about-memory*.

When summarized in discursive prose, *Izutsu* stands in danger of looking as if it were a performance illustrating a series of stories according to a diachronic principle of cause and effect. Actually, what we witness on the stage is the multifold, fluid, and synchronic way that time is folded upon itself, the palimpsest of memory itself. To twist Beckett's dictum on *Finnegans Wake*, the play is not *about* memory, it *is* that memory. Conflict or dialogue with "the other," which is almost synonymous with drama in a usually understood sense, is not of absolute necessity to make this *memory-as-theater* possible (the priest is a minimal necessity, a mere excuse, or a cue). It is a special kind of monodrama, dedicated to embodying, not analyzing, the epiphanic moment of memory. We have seen how the heroine's memory is compulsively physicalized, being as it is closely related to the place (the site of her love), to the object (the well-curb), and most powerfully to the man's clothing, which, embodying his body, literally seizes her body and confounds the law of identity. To quote the unforgettable locus classicus from Zeami's late play, *Kinuta*, "memory is inscribed in the body, though time is flown and nothing remains."[8]
The privileged site where this strange palimpsest writing actually takes place is, of course, the body of the actor. A successful performance of *Izutsu* would be one in which the privilege of the narrative was subverted (if not obliterated) by the privilege of the actor's body, the articulated story being absorbed by the hieroglyph delineated on the stage by the body in motion. Ultimately, memory and desire could

be sublimated, and the ghost redeemed, only by the body of the Yeatsian dancer.[9]

Oedipus Rex may help to illustrate the point. Unquestionably the greatest masterpiece of drama-about-memory in the western or any history, it cannot be called a specimen of memory-as-theater. It is impeccable as a dramatized narrative *about* a man's lost memory, *about* the time past reemerging into, and eventually overwhelming, the time present. But Oedipus himself has no memory to worry about (except that forgettable killing of an old man at the crossways), so he cannot begin to try to remember. Crime is something outside him that he can order others to seek out. To tell the truth, there is a profound irony built into the story: memory is literally inscribed in his body, that is, his swollen foot, and also in his name, which, besides referring to his foot, is a viciously resonant pun meaning "I know." But since he does not know it, memory remains outside him. The drama consists in the admirable tension, the perfect balance, between the absence of his memory and the existence of his crime.

The tragic heroism with which Oedipus accepts the discovery of the past in the denouement never fails to produce the Aristotelian catharsis in the audience, but it is as it were the end product of a masterful drama-about-memory; it does not (and need not, of course) make the play a memory-as-theater. Oedipus does achieve a splendid physicality when, on knowing the truth, he gouges out his own eyes, but that again is not of quite the same sort as what we saw in *Izutsu*. Privileged supremacy, in the whole economy of theater experience, is tipped toward the narrative whose interest does not differ essentially from that of a detective story.

To come back finally to *Krapp's Last Tape*, I have always felt that there is something apocalyptic about it. The play, in this perspective, comes to look like an angel come to announce the death of drama-about-memory, a mainstream tradition in western drama proudly enriched by masterpieces from *Oedipus*, to Shakespeare's romance plays, to Ibsen's *Ghosts*, and so on. Beckett has stripped memory of all mysteries that may have accrued to it in the course of history. He denies Memory the status of Truth, the daughter of Time, who is bound to be revealed and restored by her father, as suggested in the well-known Renaissance emblem. On the contrary, time and memory have fallen to mechanical repeatability while truth has lost its aura of infallibility. Unlike Oedipus, Krapp has all his memories on file, tape-recorded and indexed. And, unlike any hero in the genre, Krapp is in no danger of being surprised by some stranger in possession of a secret truth from the past (besides, he lives a completely solitary life).

The only chance of the protagonist meeting "the other," of that indispensable dramatic conflict being brought about, must therefore reside in Krapp's encounter with his past self *as if it were for the first time.* That is, he must be deprived of his memory in order for the play to be possible. Hence the paradox: Krapp must be, in terms of memory, both omnipotent (armed with a tape recorder) and impotent (an amnesiac). And the paradox is completed by the irony that there cannot be any encounter or conflict: no dialogue is possible between Krapp and his past self. In other words, memory here has none of the power that was (and still is, of course) assumed to propel the dramatic action. It is powerless to spin a narrative that ought to be sufficiently consecutive and interesting to be unraveled and enacted by players. Assumptions that sustain the accepted dramaturgy of drama-about-memory have thus been undermined. *Krapp's Last Tape* has apparently proved that the only drama that could possibly be envisaged in this situation would be a drama about the impossibility of drama-about-memory—such as *Krapp's Last Tape.*

What about the body? Here, again, Krapp is nothing if not self-contradictory. He is both cerebral and physical, each to an extraordinary degree. We have seen how grotesquely Cartesian his mind is; we have here only to think of another name dear to Beckett, that is, Proust. If Proust can be regarded as one of the major writers who have attempted to break through the limitations of modern rationalism, exploring especially the elusive region of time and memory, it looks as if Krapp is gloating over the solution of the Proustian problem. Proust would have joyously appropriated Zeami's phrase about memory inscribed in the body, for he thought of memory as something intimately entwined with physical sensations (often seemingly trivial ones), totally out of the control of conscious will; and it is only through such *mémoires involontaires* that *le temps perdu* can be rediscovered, freeing us from time's bondage. Krapp's idea that one has time and memory literally at one's fingertips, that a mere touch of fingers on a tape recorder is enough to evoke memory of whatever time in the past he chooses, is inhumanly cerebral, nothing less than a cruel parody of the Proustian ideal.

It might be theoretically possible to argue that the disintegration of Krapp's Cartesian method at the end of the play implied the reintegration of Proustian memory, but it is tempting to think that, by exposing the vanity of human intellect in the person of Krapp, Beckett has dealt an unsparing quietus to the whole western thought and drama about the problematics of time/memory/body, including Descartes and Proust, Sophocles and Ibsen.

On the other hand, it is true that there is something fiercely physical about Krapp. The very decrepitude of his body—weak eyesight and hearing, hoary hair and red nose (in Beckett's original version), big shoes and shuffling gate—gives him a peculiar presence on the stage. Added to the actual actions, like eating bananas, carrying the ledger, etc., there are references to "unattainable laxation," the feel of the black ball, sex with Fanny, a year as "the sour curd and the iron stool," etc., which are impressive precisely because of scarcity and brevity. One could perhaps even venture to call Krapp one of the most unforgettable characters in modern theater in respect of sheer physical presence. And that highlights all the more the fact that this body is incapable of having any memory inscribed in it any longer; he admits that there is "nothing to say, not a squeak" about the past year. One wonders how much the actor playing Krapp must envy the noh actor and his (comparatively) privileged body.

Krapp is a play that bears testimony to a twofold impossibility: that neither drama-about-memory nor memory-as-theater is any longer possible. The only possibility left to modern or postmodern experience seems to be to go on facing this impossibility, this void, just as Krapp goes on staring before him at the end. This stark vision of nothingness, by denuding itself of all the extraneous trappings that throttle the traditional drama-about-memory, brings *Krapp* (and Beckett's other plays) closer to *Izutsu* than to any western play, even though *Izutsu*, as stark and austere in form as *Krapp*, is a theater-as-memory blessed with a vision of fulfillment.

One wonders if extremes meet, as the proverb goes. But if Krapp's blank eyes may be interpreted, by a stretch of imagination, as a ghastly simulacrum of Oedipus's tragic eye sockets, who knows whether the audience looking deep with its mind's eye into the Japanese well-curb may not find, to its surprise, an old westerner's face staring back? Or, conversely, the "spool" on the modern machine may be found to contain in it a time tunnel leading to the bottom of a medieval well.[10]

NOTES

1. The translation from *Izutsu* in this paper is my own. For a complete translation, see Japanese Classics Translation Committee of the Japan Society for the Promotion of Science, *The Noh Drama: Ten Plays from the Japanese* (Tokyo: Charles E. Tuttle, 1955).

2. Narihira (825–80) is commonly regarded as the hero of the *Stories of Ise*, a collection of short stories of great popularity, written probably in the tenth to eleventh centuries, so that the real Narihira indeed lived "a long time ago" if the play is set in the time of Zeami's writing (i.e., ca. 1400), which is likely, though not specified.

3. A girl in those days tied her hair up when married.

4. The chorus sings that "she hides herself behind the well-curb," but actually she exists through the curtain at the end of the *hashigakari* (the bridgelike corridor connecting the main stage and the exit) from which she entered.

5. As an "interlude" between the first and second parts, there is a dialogue between the priest and "the villager," who gives a fairly straightforward and prosaic account of Narihira and his wife.

6. I am indebted in this connection to Megumu Sakabe, *Furerukoto no Tetsugaku* [Philosophy of touching] (Tokyo: Iwanami Shoten, 1983), in which the author discusses, among other thinkers, Bergson and Minkowski.

7. Or one could reshuffle the pattern, equating Krapp with the priest and the taped voice with the woman, in which case *Krapp* becomes a variation of *mugen-noh*, with Krapp (*waki* 'secondary player' the priest in *Izutsu*) witnessing the apparition of the voice-as-ghost (*shite* 'protagonist'). For a detailed discussion of this point, see the present writer's articles, "Theatre of the Mind: Beckett and Noh," *Encounter* 58, 4 (April 1982); and "The

Ghost Trio: Beckett, Yeats, and Noh," *Cambridge Review* 107, 2295 (December 1986), reprinted in Yoshihiko Ikegami, ed., *The Empire of Signs: Semiotic Essays on Japanese Culture* (Amsterdam: John Benjamins, 1991).

8. My translation. For a complete translation, see Ezra Pound and Ernest Fenollosa, *The Classic Noh Theatre of Japan* (New York: New Directions, 1959).

9. Or by "the body without organs" dreamt of by Artaud and others. See Gilles Deleuze and Felix Guattari, *L'Anti-Oedipe* (Paris: Les Editions de Minuit, 1975).

10. For curiosity's sake: an *izutsu* is a square framework with a round hole inside it, while a tape recorder is a square box with two round spools on it. The logotype of the Samuel Beckett Society of America has a shape a little like an *izutsu*.

Delogocentering Silence: Beckett's Ultimate Unwording

CARLA LOCATELLI

"If this was said
that's why it was said."

—Buddha's *The Four Pillars of Knowledge*

"dream of a silence, a dream of silence"

—Samuel Beckett, *The Unnamable*

"For when his own light went out
he was not left in the dark."

—Beckett, *Stirrings Still*

The main focus of this essay regards Beckett's lifelong relation to the problematics of silence, a topic that has already been discussed by Beckett critics in the past but not very recently.[1] Furthermore, I believe that the legitimacy of the present investigation rests on new evidence: the fact that the very notion of silence necessarily keeps changing in western culture because we have no way of really speaking silence nor of indicating that whenever silence is spoken (about), it needs de-finition, that is, a de-limitation from within discourse. In

Beckett's words: "Silence, yes, but what silence! For it is all very fine to keep silence, but one has also to consider the kind of silence one keeps."[2]

Based on their cultural presuppositions, critics have produced several readings of the Beckettian silence throughout the years, but their interpretations seem to have been less daring than Beckett's actual conception of silence, which has been dynamic, open-ended, polymorphic, and certainly not restricted to the aspect(s) of silence highlighted by fashionable hermeneutical presuppositions. We have witnessed the succession of existentialist interpretations of silence, either spiritualistic or atheist, followed by Heideggerian "poetics" of silence. In more recent times, we have seen the flourishing of structuralist notions of silence, which implied it as the very locus of linguistic authenticity or, at best, as the primary weapon for linguistic demystification.

In the long run, all of these critical positions seem culturally more conservative than Beckett's daring experiments with dynamic *iconographies* and *performances* of silence. In fact, if we look back at how silence is inscribed and/or presupposed by the Beckettian corpus, we can easily perceive a lucid and systematic exploration of various and successive cultural notions of silence, which point to ever-renewed avant-garde connotations and implications, some of which are still waiting for critical valorization today.

Obviously, the danger of ideological hyperdeterminations of silence is a serious threat, not only because any reference to silence is necessarily verbal, and thus empirically breaks silence, but also because some pragmatics of silence often work as interpretants of silence in discourse, leaving "no lack of void," as Vladimir points out in *Waiting for Godot*. Thus, silence is understood in our culture mostly as part of verbal interaction, often construed (but constricted) by intentional listening.

We could say that either unchallenged referential logocentrism, or a sort of "situational semantics," always in-form silence, rather than denote it as unspeakable. Culturally, we understand silence from within a linguistic perspective, but, in real experience, we "hear/understand it" otherwise. How can discourse express the difference between "no sound" and "silence"? Can a verbal text speak the difference between "no language" and "silence"? Not very often in our culture, since the very polymorphism of silence-representation has only expanded the linguistic paradigm referring to silence, depending on varying ideological presuppositions, or has alluded to a greater variety of pragmatic situations, often implying listening as the construction of some still *verbal* coherence. Beckett, on the contrary, tried to express real silence, beyond "the usual silence, spent listening, spent waiting, *waiting for the voice* . . ."[3]

In very recent times, some critics have started thinking (about) silence beyond materialistic vs. metaphysical dichotomies, and we are just beginning to perceive the limits of a theory of silence resting solely on semantico-pragmatic coordinates of predication.[4] Beckett anticipated this awareness by telling us that the unutterable must be uttered in order to remain precisely unutterable and thus let silence *speak through* it: "I shall have to speak of things of which *I cannot speak*, [. . .] And at the same time I am obliged to speak. *I shall never be silent never.*"[5] Silence is something of which we cannot speak, but speak we must, so that we should also have no illusion as to our ever being able to be silent.

Beckett's relentless work of unwording has called to our attention the obvious fact that we cannot speak silence, so that "there is no lack of silence,"[6] but that "somewhere in this churn of words at last, I would still have to reconstitute the right lesson"[7] beyond language, voice, murmurs, and "long black pauses." His work kept pointing to silence, beyond its diverse semantico-paradigmatic meanings, and beyond its varying significance in our culture. The unnegotiable integrity that Beckett implies in his positing of silence is one of the original features of his conception in our contemporary culture.

As a matter of fact, Beckett confronted the problem as no other thinker in our century had done before because he dramatized language, thus making silence audible beyond linguistic description. Innovatively, he valorized aural stimuli, working with rhythm and repetition, as much as the iconic stimuli, which are obviously the predominant form of *evidentia* provided by our culture. Furthermore, his persistent and acute gaze on stillness gave silence the form of a spatial objective-correlative, and thus a new visibility, capable of pushing philosophical investigation beyond the traditional practice of implicit logocentrism in the description of silence.

The time has come for us to note and wonder why Beckett never asked the metaphysical question "what is silence?" even though he asked "what is the word[?]"[8] I believe that the very absence of this question highlights a particularly interesting resistance to silence definition, a resistance that ultimately discloses the actual impossibility of definition and interrogation in those metaphysical terms.

Even the most intense longing for silence never led Beckett to define it. As a matter of fact, a whole novel, *The Unnamable*, can be seen as silence posing, rather than silence defining, and not without a profound self-irony concerning "my speech-parched voice" and the presumably meritorious task of continuing to speak.

> I am doing my best, and failing again, yet again. I don't mind failing, it's a pleasure, but I want to go silent. [. . .] Strange notion in any case, and eminently open to suspicion, that of a task to be performed, before one can be at rest. *Strange task*, which consists in *speaking of oneself. Strange hope,* turned towards *silence and peace.*[9]

The apparently evasive Buddhist tautology quoted in the epigraph ("If this was said, that's why it was said") calls to our attention the radical possibility of the presence *or* absence of language, regardless of representational meaning, or, as Beckett put it, "without ulterior object."[10] This subtractive thought should also help us conceive of silence without ulterior meaning, that is, without psychological, mystical, or philosophical connotations, and without logocentric hyperdetermination.

In this light we can see how the alternative saying/not saying does not necessarily translate into the logocentric dichotomy language/silence, and why the very translation of non-language into silence is subject to the strongest resistance and critique in Beckett. Not only has he raised the issue of linguistic representation, to which I will return later, but he has also shown us how unwarranted is our culturally accepted projection of the linguistic system onto silence because it reduces it either to a linguistic metonymy (pauses, interruptions, or suspensions of the semantic chain) or implies it as linguistic *Grund*.[11] As a matter of fact, retrospectively it is easy to see how often he has warned us about the naïveté of our thinking habits, which de facto inscribe silence into language. When silence is conceived as starting from a linguistic perspective and remains stubbornly held within the hegemony of the linguistic domain, it becomes a mere linguistic object, surreptitiously needy of interpretation. As a matter of fact, by so doing we foreclose the possibility of conceiving silence as we experience it: simultaneously heard-understood, thus functioning very differently from language, in which hearing and understanding are separable.[12]

The fine imperceptibility of the cultural analogy that makes the meaning of "absence of language" work as an equivalent of silence is precisely what demands further investigation. Beckett's poem "nei-ther"[13] warns us about such an unwarranted analogy, calling to mind similar significant differences: "from impenetrable self to impenetra-ble unself"; "heedless" and "unheeded"; "unheard footfalls only sound" (a sound created by listening) and "no sound."

Most of the problems of contemporary hermeneutics are under-scored in this poem: the intentionality of thought ("intent on the one gleam or the other"); the ineliminability of (self)representation ("from impenetrable self to impenetrable unself"); the unverifiability of being ("to and fro in shadow from inner to outershadow [. . .] unspeakable home"), and the difference between hearing and understanding ("un-heard footfalls only sound").

If we can manage not to think of silence as always determined by the totalizing alternative language/silence, we could disentangle its conception from the negative associations that hyperdetermine it in discourse, and we may even start delogocentering silence. After all, silence has been conceived as absence, negativity, or *manqué* because language has always remained implied in its definitions, in its descrip-tions, and in its conceptualization. And yet, if silence is heard, it is because it is heard, not because it is *said*.

The investigation of Beckett's non-attempts to define silence, as well as the analysis of his semantic and performative reference to it, has revealed to me the lethal effect of our logocentric predication of silence in relation to the actual possibility of articulating it more adequately in discourse. Silence cannot be expressed linguistically because it is other-than-language (rather than non-language), and we should not forget that real silence is not a conceptual meaning but a complex and procedural experience of meaning.

Beckett's narratives and poems offer an evolving critique of the concept of silence, and his narrative silences valorize different semantic valences, while drama also activates different semio-systems, particularly those addressing and affecting the body (i.e., sound, rhythm, light). In his prose works repetition and unwording make of physical perception the prerequisite for conceptualization, while a correlative systematic de-symbolization of semiosis occurs in drama. Both these semiotic procedures alert us to a process of meaning formation that is not necessarily dependent on verbal-symbolic language. In other words, Beckett frames and encodes his representation of silence using systems of signs that are primarily material (fundamental sounds, rhythm, and light) rather than constituted by arbitrary signifiers. In the long run, this semiotic practice empowers his investigation of silence to move beyond logocentrism because language is relativized by its proximity to other semio-systems.

In this light, it is easy to understand why Beckett never tried to describe silence; rather, he believed that "to restore silence is the role of objects,"[14] not a task that words, qua language, can ever accomplish. The materiality of his signifiers has then enacted the echoes of a semantic allusion to an integral silence, an indivisible system of articulation of the human experience comparable to language, light, and sound. Beckett has shown us that silence cannot be predicated by language without becoming ipso facto a linguistic object; in order to avoid making it too dependent on language we could apply to it a quote from Emily Dickinson: "Invisible, as Music— / But positive, as Sound— / It beckons, and it baffles— / . . ."[15]

EPISTEMIC COORDINATES AND CULTURAL FRAMES OF SILENCE

One of the aims of this paper is to indicate that silence should not be conceived once and for all, that is, outside an anthropologically determined episteme, lest we subscribe to the transcendental sublimity conferred to it by the mystic or idealist tradition whose influence can still be seen in Heidegger, one of the last, but certainly not the least, of the metaphysical rhetoricians of our century. Therefore, I suggest we introduce and develop the notion of *cultural figures of silence*, particularly in order to fight against the foreclosure of the silence issue entailed by some contemporary investigations. We still merely oppose silence to language, and invariably inscribe the former into the latter. Yet, this binary opposition (language/silence) represses the important difference between silence in communication and silence as a semiotic system. Furthermore, it implies a strong metaphysical conception of language, which is susceptible of being charged further with a "presence/absence" axiology, connoting language as the positive and silence as its negative.

The repression of the fact that such a dichotomy logocenters silence, also because it presupposes an "always already there" of language, is not without consequences. For one thing, it reifies the panlinguistic domain at the expense of the unsayable by making the unnamable coextensive with silence. For another, it represses investigation of the event-quality of (non)writing. Finally, it produces a saturation of the sayable on the part of the said, which forecloses the question of speaking itself.

The silence issue is thus actually foreclosed, not only because a methodologic tropology implies referential impossibility, but because it cannot imply the radical alternative of saying/not-saying as a real possibility.[16] While modernist silence has been conceived as an expressive possibility, more or less fulfilled (just like romantic silence), postmodern silence has de facto become a critical impossibility because of the implicit panlogocentrism of dominant tropological critiques of the literary sign.[17]

However, Beckett has freed silence from the conceptual and epistemic limitations engendered by both traditional and current linguistic representations whose logocentrism has remained culturally unchallenged throughout the centuries. He has shown us how gratuitous our projections of language onto silence are, as well as the arbitrariness of our territorialization of silence within the linguistic system. Furthermore, he has called to our attention the fact that linguistic representations condemn silence to being an object (and thus always surreptitiously in need of qualification) rather than a function or an instrument of the human hermeneutics of experience.[18]

In Beckett, sound modulation such as the lessening of sound just when a certain sound is repeated (for example, the repeated chime, "a little fainter" and "even a little fainter still," in *Footfalls*) indicates the crucial difference between "being short of" and "being without."[19] We are short of silence, but not quite without it, just because we cannot name it or cannot verify its presence.

Among others, Tom Bishop has acknowledged the fact that "Silence is one of the key markers in Beckett's work [. . .] really at the very base of Beckett's writing. . . ." He has carefully elucidated the "paradox of necessity and impossibility" (i.e., "the need to say, coupled with the impossibility of saying"), which qualifies the strategic silence of Beckett's production, especially in the fifties and sixties. Yet it is interesting to note that when he discusses Beckett's ontology of silence (rather than silence as a strategy in communication) he has a hard time elucidating what seems to be an inevitable and paradoxical contradiction.

/*Silence*/ is something very tangible for Beckett, a presence if one dare say; *of course an absence, but a "presence"* nevertheless because one is so aware of the fact that Beckett's work is organized around the time of silence.[20]

I think that it was in order to explore this seeming contradiction, which is to say in order to elucidate "a presence [. . .] organized around the time of silence," that Beckett himself evolved the traditional ontological dichotomy of presence/absence—silence/language—into the dynamic correlations of each one of the terms, typical of his late works. There is a silence of language (of which Beckett seems particularly aware in the first *Trilogy* and in *Texts for Nothing*) and a language of silence, which *makes* a lot of difference even if it does not *say* it. Beckett himself remarks that ". . . silence to *tell* the truth does not appear to have been very conspicuous up to now . . ."[21]

On the way to a signification of silence as a semiotic system comparable to language, we find in Beckett many reminders of the presence of silence in communication. For example, Henry in *Embers* (1959) denounces the fallacy of our habitual association of silence with absence and of language with presence: "My father, back from the dead, to be with me. / ". . ." / Can he hear me? *Pause.* Yes, he must hear me. *Pause.* To answer me? *Pause.* No, he doesn't answer me. *Pause.* Just be with me. *Pause.*"[22] Similarly, Mrs. Rooney in *All That Fall* (1963) warns us: "Do not imagine, because I am silent, that I am not present, and alive, to all that is going on."[23]

In the dialectics of silence and language, what seems an absence is a presence, susceptible of being made visible only by reciprocal contextualization rather than by denotation. Silence can be implied as a relational element, that is, as semantic absence, in the presence of language, but language needs the global in-difference of a systemic silence in order to activate its semantic discretions. The reciprocal implications, but also the parallel existence of the two systems, becomes clear in the late Beckett when the strategic silence of pauses (a semantic silence) and the silence of language (due to linguistic failure) are played against the background of a "real silence" resisting linguistic representation(s).

In this respect, the epistemic distinction between "the usual silence" and "real silence" made in *The Unnamable* anticipates the strategies of Beckett's attempt to "restore" silence, indicating very clearly the problematics of silence representation:

> the usual silence, spent listening, spent waiting, waiting for the voice [. . .] it will be the silence, the one that does not last, spent listening, *spent waiting, for it to be broken*, for the voice to break it, perhaps there is no other, I don't know.

However, "that's not the real silence, [. . .] what can be said of real silence, I don't know."[24]

Beckett implied and explored the idea of "usual silence" in all of his works but made of "real silence" the previously unexplored *enjeu* of his mature works. Here the representation of representation takes the place of a previous critique of mimesis and narration. The early Beckettian connotation of silence as antilinguistic ontology (in the thirties) evolved into a later, complex idea of silence as onto-semiotic necessity (in the seventies and eighties). This complex idea was realized after "the horrifying discovery that when they [words] are not speaking they continue to speak; when they stop they go on; are never silent, for in them silence ceaselessly speaks."[25] Silence *is* in any utterance: this was the innovative and crucial cognitive perspective of the First Trilogy where silence no longer blocked discourse but rather worked in it, ready to show the unavoidable "ill said" of representational language.

Beckett's latest works, in particular, move beyond a critique of representation and imply an unprecedented notion of silence, as simultaneously strategic and categorical, both paradigmatic and systemic. As a matter of fact, ever since *The Unnamable*,

> what we have before us is not a book because it is more than a book. It is a direct *confrontation with the process* from which all books derive—with the original *point at which the work is inevitably lost*, that always destroys the work.[26]

In our direct confrontation with Beckett's works, we shall now see how his semantic dislocations, "devious deictics,"[27] and unusual performatives manage to restore silence, making it "semblable à une résolution de Mozart, [est] parfaitement *intelligible* et parfaitement *inexplicable*."[28]

It is my intention to provide a diachronic spectrum of examples from Beckett's works, attesting to the originality and evolution of his semiotic strategies because they imply original ways of positing silence, at different historical moments. Specifically, I plan to elucidate how the disruption of discursive coherence in the earlier works became a critique of representation in the middle works and finally how discursive deconstruction gave way to a powerful systemic contextualization of the reciprocal implicatures and the analogies between silence and language in the late plays and prose works.

EVOLVING SEMIOTIC STRATEGIES THAT SPEAK SILENCE

I believe that Beckett's complex idea of silence formed progressively and could move away from the ideological presuppositions of a hermeneutics of suspicion thanks to his actual work on semiotic strategies devised to "state silences more competently."[29] This critical project is already present in Beckett's first novel, *Dream of Fair to Middling Women* (1932), in which he "harbors his own esthetic cogitations" and Belacqua, the protagonist, "espouses [an] incoherent art"[30] whose ideal qualification seems perfect for a modern valorization of silence, both on the part of the reader and of the writer. "The experience of my reader shall be between the phrases, *in the silence,* communicated by the intervals, not the terms of the statement [. . .] his experience shall be the menace, the miracle, the memory, of *an unspeakable trajectory,*" says Belacqua, immediately adding: "*I shall state silences* more competently than ever a better man spangled the butterflies of vertigo."[31] In spite of the extended (and in this case probably excessive) playfulness of Beckett's literary allusions (especially to Samuel Johnson), we can find here a very serious declaration of a poetics in which truth is at stake while narrative mimesis is challenged. Silence has to be more competently stated, and "the terms of the statement" have to reveal, ultimately, "an *unspeakable* trajectory," so that the reader's ideal experience is that of silence "between the phrases."

As they explain the means and teleology of this new writing program, Beckett-Belacqua highlight the necessity of threatening traditional textual coherence through the fragmentariness and dissonance introduced by recurrent pauses: "I think now [. . .] of the dehiscing, the dynamic décousu of a Rembrant, *the implication lurking behind the pictorial pretext* threatening to invade pigment and oscuro."[32] The choice of a botanical metaphor such as "the dehiscing" implies the image of a rupture at maturity and of fertility signalled by the breaking of the outer form of the fruit.[33] Through this metamorphosis (which in narration implies the rupture of narrative coherence) "the implication lurking behind" comes to the surface, and the representational pre-text becomes the context of an unveiling. In other words, once representational discourse is deprived of its expressive and referential power, it can allude to the implication lurking behind it, which, for Beckett, meant that the text could make silence visible.

Silence is the locus of "an unspeakable trajectory" made accessible through the work of a:

disfaction, a désuni, an Ungebund, a flottement, a tremblement, a tremor, a tremolo, a disaggregating, a disintegrating, an efflorescence, a breaking down and multiplication of tissue, the corrosive ground-swell of Art.[34]

We should notice that the variety of languages (English, French, and German) that articulate this semantic paradigm of aesthetic fragmentation calls to our attention the translinguistic scope of Beckett's reference to silence, which can be alluded to by focusing on language but not on any one language.[35]

When Beckett worked within the linguistic system and against literary hypercodifications, he connoted silence as a potential locus of authenticity, as the agent of the truth that language makes inaccessible. His letter to Axel Kaun (1937) expresses clear ontological preoccupations and relates them to a positive idea of silence.

> As we cannot eliminate language all at once, we should at least leave nothing undone that might contribute to its falling into disrepute. *To bore one hole after another* in it, until *what lurks behind it*—be it something or nothing—*begins to seep through;* I cannot imagine a higher goal for a writer today.[36]

Truth was at stake for Beckett as it was for the existentialists. As a matter of fact, "In the frenzy of utterance the concern with truth"[37] remains constant throughout the Beckettian production as much as the reciprocal implication of language and silence is explored and relentlessly tested.

In so doing, Beckett recommended playing within the systemic frame of language, making its means and ends collide: "In this dissonance between the means and their use it will perhaps become possible to feel a whisper of that final music or that silence that underlies all."[38] Once the structure of representation (the means) and the semantics and pragmatics of the system (their use) could be played against each other, the reciprocity of the implication of language and silence would be clarified, and a new access to truth would be open.

Fragmentation and redundance were to become Beckett's habitual semiotic practices, particularly in drama. Ruby Cohn has pointed out that:

In the printed text of *En attendant Godot* the most frequent repetitions are two scenic directions: *Silence* and *Pause*. . . . They act like theatrical punctuation, a pause often marking hesitation or qualification, whereas silence is a brush with despair before making a fresh start.[39]

The semantics of dramatic pauses, "marking hesitation or qualification" in relation to dramatic action, highlight the possibility of a distinction between silence and a pause, or silence and suspension, a distinction that Beckett will progressively exploit while working toward the creation of unfamiliar semantic effects in his critique of language. In fact, Beckett's drama *performs* pauses to such an extent that the coherence of dramatic action is often threatened. At the same time, his prose invokes the use of pauses as desirable antidotes to logocentric totalizing.[40]

While insisting that silence "underlies All,"[41] Beckett showed us that qua silence it is not discernible in "discrete units," and that it is this very irreducibility that makes silence *sound* threatening ("silence is a brush with despair"). "Yet only then can you detect, beyond the fatuous clamour, the silence of which the universe is made."[42] Probably we are so willing to translate silence into pauses because we *can* determine their meaning, and thus feel that we are in control, that we can make sense of phenomena and of the world. However, this semantic control produces the impression of "no lack of void,"[43] simply because someone, not necessarily a personal subject, is always speaking, and even speaking the silence that speaks in words.[44] Indeed, there are many people "for whom there is no lack of silence," but, Beckett comments, "I cannot but assume that they are hard of hearing."[45]

After the formulation of the Beckettian theory of the obligation to express with nothing to express, silence becomes a resistance, that is, not only a pause, or a conceptual opposite, but the temporal endurance of the absence of language. Its dialectics with language signifies the radical risk of communication and the disquieting gratuitousness of our "making sense." Thus, the Beckettian obligation to express takes on a different meaning: the paradoxical meaning of an optional necessity. Humans need to speak in order to pass the time, and they cannot avoid speaking (i.e., thinking linguistically) even if the passing of time is not necessarily a linguistic condition. Gogo states it very clearly: "In the meantime let's try and converse calmly, since we're incapable of keeping silent [. . .] We always find something, eh Didi, to give us the impression we exist?"[46] The shocking epiphany of *Godot* involves the fact that we feel "no lack of void" (or no lack of silence) because we simply cannot bear facing the world after the loss of "the impression we exist." However, Beckett comments rather humorously on our incessant naming: "Deplorable mania, when something *happens*, to inquire *what*. [. . .] There are *sounds* here, from time to time, *let that suffice*."[47]

If "something happens," it is linguistically framed, so that even when silence happens it is linguistically and psychologically framed and becomes a pause (absence of sound) or its meaning, charged with the semantic value produced by the verbal chain encompassing it. Real silence, on the contrary, the one that has the power of "making a fresh start," does not allow discretion nor inscription into the linguistic system. This explains why it is very hard to hear/understand it. Not even the creation of better pauses, of larger holes, and of more massive subtractions in the texture of language can warrant the hearing of silence.

> I speak *softer*, every year a little softer. Perhaps. Slower too, every year a little *slower*. [. . .] If so the *pauses would be longer*, between the words, the sentences, the syllables, [. . .] And *I should hear, at every little pause, if it's the silence I say* when I say that only the words break it. *But nothing of the kind*, that's not how it is, it's for ever the same murmur, flowing unbroken, like a single endless word . . .[48]

The multiplication of pauses and their length is no guarantee of a better articulation of silence so long as listening is predetermined by logocentric or semantic presuppositions.

The Beckettian invitation to let sounds suffice alerts us not only to the difference between speech and sound but also to the subtle difference between silence and absence of sound. The latter distinction is particularly helpful in differentiating silence from language because it deconstructs the logocentrism of listening. One of Beckett's poems expresses with great skill the absence of silence, dissolved by a listening that mistakes "no sound" for silence itself: "steps sole sound / long sole sound / until unbidden stay / then no sound / on all that strand / long no sound / until unbidden go."[49] The predication of "steps" as "sole sound" shows the perceptive experience of listening as intentionally framed, as the result of an interpretation that in-forms perception and thus forbids "keeping silence" even when for "long [there is] no sound." In the poem, while we visualize steps (having already, to begin with, interpreted sound, and translated it into the image of steps), we are made aware of the fact that we rely on their psychic trace while conceptualizing the perception of an alternating "sound/absence of sound." In fact "no sound" and even "long no sound" imply reference to an absent sound-meaning (absence of steps) rather than a reference to real silence. The expression "long no sound" indicates the impossibility of hearing silence so long as we expect to hear something. Thus, the image that apparently comes closest to silence in fact highlights its absence because of the logocentrism of our listening. Not until the end of the poem do we stop listening, and we are ready to hear silence: we no longer expect to hear steps and the (non)sound of steps. When the word *steps* literally goes, at the end of the poem, we hear silence, because sound, both as materiality and as meaning, really fails. The image of steps (interpreted sound) no longer interprets the absence of sound (interpreted silence); they go, finally, "unbidden," that is, unrecognized. In the silence following the end of the poem we realize the totalizing power of the predication that opened it ("steps sole sound"), hyperdetermining our understanding of "no sound," and barring our access to the audibility of real silence. In *The Unnamable* the same risk of a logocentered listening is expressed but in descriptive rather than performative terms: "*I listened. One might as well speak* and be done with."[50]

Another quotation from one of Beckett's poems comes to mind in relation to his critique of our cultural perception of silence: "je ne m'entende plus / me taire."[51] Beckett highlights the risk of not being capable of listening to silence because we cannot suspend the understanding of what we hear or the understanding of ourselves hearing. Good listening, on the other hand, the one Beckett refers to as something lost ("je ne m'entende plus"), would permit the distinction between "being silent in silence" and "keeping silence," disentangling the cultural confusion between silence as ontology and silence as linguistic supplement (what we understand of our experience of silence). As a matter of fact, the lexical choice of *s'entendre* indicates the simultaneity of hearing/understanding oneself, and "je m'entends me taire" would mean "I hear/understand silence in me being silent." However, in this very perception the logic of interpretation displaces, invades, and rules the understanding of silence: "Not one person in a hundred knows how *to be silent and listen*, no, not even to conceive what such a thing means."[52] The absolute impossibility of speaking a silence simultaneously heard-understood could be resisted, though certainly not overcome, by trying to establish a delogocentering perspective in using language. *The Unnamable* puts it rather bluntly: "First dirty, then make clean"; as a matter of fact, he tries to deconstruct the conceptual and representational functions of language: "No, I must not try to *think*, simply *utter*. Method or no method I shall have to banish them in the end, the beings, things, shapes, sounds and light with which *my haste to speak has encumbered this place.*"[53]

On the way to his theorized literature of the unword, Beckett thought that the valorization of actual utterance could be a good means of alluding to silence (though again in absentia of silence, of course). For example, the Opener in *Cascando* (1963) enacts the representation of the enunciation as follows: "They say, He opens nothing, he has nothing to open, it's in his head. [. . .] I don't protest any more, I don't say any more, / There is nothing in my head. / I don't answer any more. / *I open and close.*"[54] The real confrontation of silence and language as onto-semiotic systems can be expressed only by moving beyond refutation and even assertion ("I don't protest"; "I don't say"). Only a real "*nothing* in my head" can underscore the radical alternative of opening and closing, that is, of speaking/being in silence, beyond linguistic interpretation ("I don't *say* any more") and dialogical understanding ("I don't *answer*").

Silence and language do not function in the late Beckett as the opposites of a metaphysical dichotomy; rather they achieve visibility as independent semio-systems but through reciprocal contextualization. Even when Beckett seemed to subscribe to the metaphysical implications of the hermeneutics of suspicion (whereby truth was in need of revelation through some form of demystification), he did not really oppose silence and language: "The forms are many in which the unchanging seeks relief from its formlessness."[55] Language provides the forms of silence's formlessness, as much as "the forms are many," because something is always silent in them.[56] Through a progressive shift of focus in his works, from literature as linguistic hypercodification (in the thirties and forties) to language itself (in the fifties and sixties), the somewhat metaphysical silence of the early Beckettian production (which implied silence as the horizon of language) was gradually transformed into the "imperfect silence" of the First Trilogy, a silence so imperfect because always broken by "a voice that speaks, knowing that it lies, indifferent to what it says."[57]

Progressively both language and silence were conceived in weaker metaphysical form, that is, not only beyond the dichotomy that traditionally opposes them but also beyond the frame of mind that always inscribes silence into language as a component of the same semiosystem. In the long run, silence and silences were highlighted as different realities, and only silences remained necessarily bound to language as pauses (sound) and as meaning (sense). In other words, after having contributed to the critique of language articulated by his contemporary hermeneutics of suspicion, Beckett came to connote silence as a semiotic system capable of articulation through contextualization and thus comparable to the linguistic system but not circumscribed by it.

One of the means through which Beckett represented silence was the creation of "systemic tropes" within a text, that is, the creation of visual or oral figures imitating the dynamics of silence/language contextual implication. Spatial icons (the most significant of which is the light/dark alternation and variation), the spatialization of language on the page, or the combination of visual and rhythmic variations have the power to asseverate the icons of silence produced by discourse. The correlation of movement and sound, and the metaphoric spatialization of sound, allows Beckett to highlight the "global" nature of silence and to indicate that it is comparable to entire visual, phono-semantic, rhythmic, or sound systems rather than to specific units within each of these systems. In other words, through his systemic metaphors, simultaneously relying on more than one semiotic system, Beckett called to our attention the difference between language, speech, and sound, indicating that, qua systems, each one of them could be conceived as analogous to silence.

In the process of silence representation, Beckett also mixed genres that traditionally would have been mutually exclusive, and his subsequent combination of different semiotic systems (sound, rhythm, light), or of denotative and performative language in the same text, can be seen as the logical development of those earlier procedures working to deconstruct the solid texture of articulated discourse.[58] In complex "acts of language" (in the seventies and eighties), Beckett alluded to silence through the coexistence of different semiotic codes, simultaneously articulating contradictory, or incomplete, semantic units. Especially in drama, he translated silence into metaphors of movement (after having used the key metaphor of voices in the First Trilogy),[59] so as to indicate not just a dynamic silence but the dynamics of silence resisting (its) linguistic representation. In both the late drama and the late prose works, silence was articulated by successive contextualization so that it could be perceived not as the blueprint of language but as its reversible context.

In order to re-produce the perceptive experience of silence and express its auditory visibility, Beckett developed a very productive open con-textualization of utterances-texts; he challenged linguistic pantextualism by showing the mobilization of texts into contexts (context which then functioned as texts for a later context). The Beckettian dynamics of text contextualization, a true experimental form of open semiosis, has provided an unusual way of approaching silence beyond what appeared to be the traditional standard procedures for its manifestation: apophatic and apotropic modes of discourse.[60]

The representation of representation, which is typical of the late Beckettian production, implies an unprecedented notion of silence, simultaneously strategic and "categorical," both paradigmatic and systemic. In this respect, *Rockaby* (1981), *Ohio Impromptu* (1981), *Catastrophe* (1982), and *What Where* (1983) are emblematic plays[61] that express

a double representation of silence: as a *system* compatible and coextensive with language and as *meaning*, specifically determined by the
pauses in the discrete segmentation of the language spoken.
The "Nothing is left to tell" that closes *Ohio Impromptu* (1981),
a doubly contextualized play representing reading and narration,
comes after the four-times repeated "Little is left to tell," marking the
silence of "the night when having closed the book and dawn at hand
he did not disappear but sat *on without a word.*"[62] The absence of words
("Nothing is left to tell") marks here a series of successively contextualized silences: (1) the absence of the "sad tale"; (2) the absence of
reading/listening (to the sad tale); and, finally, (3) the end of the
dramatic action (representing, at that final point, the absence of
reading/listening). Nothing can be *said* of real silence, but the powerful semiosis through which the saying is contextualized into reading,
and then reading is contextualized in relation to a represented listening, until the Listener and the audience are left with nothing to listen
to, makes us ready to *hear* silence. The successive, relentless contextualization carried out throughout the play, which originates precisely
by representing the already there of language in the dialogic interaction of Listener and Reader, takes us progressively away from pre-
presentation and finally delogocenters our forms of listening, transforming listening into an uninterpreted hearing. After playing the
dialectics of the implication of text and context, made visible also by
the iconography of a Listener and a Reader "as alike in appearance as
possible," we are ready to hear the silence of being silent, beyond the
silences of a story and of storytelling. Indeed, we reach the threshold
that opens onto silence: "*Nothing* is left to tell."[63]

NOTES

1. See Georges Bataille, "Le silence de Molloy" in *Critique* 58 (May 1951),
translated as "Molloy's Silence" in *Modern Critical Interpretations: Samuel
Beckett's "Molloy," "Malone Dies," "The Unnamable,"* ed. Harold Bloom
(New York: Chelsea House, 1988); Hélène Baldwin, *Samuel Beckett's Real
Silence* (University Park: Pennsylvania State University Press, 1981); Tom
Bishop, "The Temptation of Silence," in *As No Other Dare Fail,* ed. John

Calder (London: John Calder, 1986), 24–29; and John Fletcher, "Bailing Out the Silence," in *Samuel Beckett's "Waiting for Godot,"* ed. Harold Bloom (New York: Chelsea House, 1987), 11–22.

2. Samuel Beckett, *The Unnamable*, in *Molloy, Malone Dies, The Unnamable: Three Novels by Samuel Beckett* (New York: Grove Press, 1958), 309. Hereafter reference to the works of the trilogy is to this edition, indicating only novel title and page number.

3. *The Unnamable*, 413 (italics mine).

4. See Michel Foucault, *Archeologie du savoir* (Paris: Gallimard, 1969); Jacques Derrida, *Speech and Phenomena*, ed. and trans. D. B. Allison (Evanston, Ill.: Northwestern University Press, 1973); Bernard P. Dauenhauer, *Silence: The Phenomenon and its Ontological Significance* (Bloomington: Indiana University Press, 1980); Jürgen Habermas, *The Theory of Communicative Action*, trans. T. McCarthy (Boston: Beacon Press, 1984); and Pier Aldo Rovatti, *L'esercizio del silenzio* (Milan: Cortina, 1992). For a semiotic approach, see Gian Paolo Caprettini, "Per una tipologia del silenzio" in *Le forme del silenzio e della parola*, ed. M. Baldini and S. Zucal (Brescia: Morcelliana, 1990).

5. *The Unnamable*, 291 (italics mine).

6. Samuel Beckett, "German Letter of 1937," in *Disjecta: Miscellaneous Writings and a Dramatic Fragment*, ed. Ruby Cohn (New York: Grove Press, 1984), 172. Hereafter cited as *Disjecta*.

7. *The Unnamable*, 311.

8. Samuel Beckett, "what is the word," in *As the Story Was Told* (London: John Calder, 1990), 131. It is also worth noticing the instability conferred to such a metaphysical question by Beckett's original French version as "comment dire." On this point see Enoch Brater, *The Drama in the Text: Beckett's Late Fiction* (New York: Oxford University Press, 1994), 164–73.

9. *The Unnamable*, 310–11 (italics mine).

10. Ibid., 310.

11. One of the earliest and most lucid warnings against logocentric conceptions of silence, which remained unchallenged by contemporary "hermeneutics of suspicion," is to be found in Michel Foucault's work. See *The Archaeology of Knowledge*, trans. A. M. Sheridan Smith (London: Tavistock, 1972); and "Theatrum Philosophicum" and "Language to Infinity," in *Language, Counter-memory, Practice*, ed. D. F. Bouchard (Ithaca: Cornell University Press, 1977), 165–96, 56–60. For an extended discussion of the issue, see also Carla Locatelli, "Unwording Beyond Negation, Erasures and *Reticentia*: Beckett's Committed Silence," in *Engagement and Indifference: Beckett and the Political*, ed. Henry Sussman, forthcoming.

12. For an outline of recent philosophical debates on the difference between interpretation and understanding, and a discussion on the truth of herme-

neutics, see Gianni Vattimo and Maurizio Ferraris, "Introduzione," in *Filosofia '91* (Rome-Bari: Laterza, 1992); Karl Otto Apel, "Idee regolative o evento del senso? Tentativo di definire il logos dell'ermeneutica," in *Ermeneutica e filosofia pratica* (Venice: Marsilio, 1990), 17–40; Karl Otto Apel, "Fallibilismus, Konsenstheorie der Wahrheit und Letztbegründung," in *Philosophie und Begründung* (Frankfurt: Suhrkamp, 1987); Hans Georg Gadamer, *Wahrheit und Methode* (Tübingen: Mohr, 1960); and Jürgen Habermas, *Theorie des kommunikativen Handelns* (Frankfurt: Suhrkamp, 1983). For the sake of the present discussion of Beckett's work, I find Gadamer's defense of the logic of question and answer particularly interesting. In his view, understanding is dialogical, and dialectics is the logical structure of dialogue. Beckett's work seems a coherent testimony of a hermeneutics so dialogical that the very terms of the interrogation are not given once and for all but are relentlessly negotiated. I have developed a discussion on Beckettian hermeneutics in my *Unwording the World: Beckett's Prose Works After the Nobel Prize* (Philadelphia: University of Pennsylvania Press, 1990).

13. "neither," in Samuel Beckett, *As the Story Was Told* 108–9.

14. *Molloy*, 13.

15. The poem does not refer to silence but to "A Species [that] stands beyond—." See Emily Dickinson, "Poem 501," in *The Complete Poems of Emily Dickinson*, ed. Thomas H. Johnson (Boston: Little Brown, 1960), 243.

16. Some feminist theorists have indicated the importance of the actuality of the enunciation in a discussion of women's silence and the quest for an appropriated voice. See, in particular, Patrizia Violi, *L'infinito singolare: Considerazioni sulla differenza sessuale nel linguaggio* (Verona: Essedue Edizioni, 1986).

17. For an extended discussion of the relation of tropology and silence, see Locatelli, "Unwording Beyond Negation," 18. For a contextual definition of the hermeneutics of experience in relation to the hermeneutics of suspicion, see Locatelli, *Unwording the World*.

19. "There is more than a difference of degree between being short, short of the world, short of self, and being without these esteemed commodities. The one is a predicament, the other not" (Samuel Beckett, "Bram van Velde," in *Disjecta*, 143).

20. Tom Bishop, "The Temptation of Silence," in *As No Other Dare Fail*, 26, 25, 24 (italics mine).

21. *The Unnamable*, 388–89 (italics mine).

22. Samuel Beckett, *Embers*, in *Collected Shorter Plays* (New York: Grove Press, 1984), 93.

23. Samuel Beckett, *All That Fall*, in *Collected Shorter Plays*, 25.

24. *The Unnamable*, 413–14, 408 (italics mine).

25. Maurice Blanchot, "Where Now? Who Now?" in *Samuel Beckett's "Molloy," "Malone Dies," "The Unnamable,"* 23.
26. Ibid., 26 (italics mine).
27. For a revealing discussion of deictics in Beckett, see Angela Moorjani, "Beckett's Devious Deictics," in *Rethinking Beckett*, ed. Lance St. John Butler and R. J. Davis (Houndmills and London: Macmillan, 1990).
28. "Le Concentrisme," in *Disjecta*, 42 (italics mine).
29. "Dream of Fair to Middling Women," in *Disjecta*, 49.
30. Ruby Cohn, "Notes," in *Disjecta*, 170.
31. "Dream of Fair to Middling Women," 49.
32. Ibid. (italics mine).
33. *The Shorter Oxford English Dictionary* defines *dehiscence* (1828) as "gaping, opening by divergence of parts; in *Bot.* the bursting open of capsules, fruits, anthers, etc., in order to discharge their mature contents."
34. "Dream of Fair to Middling Women," in *Disjecta*, 49.
35. In some European languages the difference is also lexically marked, for example, *lingua/linguaggio; langue/langage;* and *lengua, idioma/lenguaje.*
36. "German Letter of 1937," in *Disjecta*, 172 (italics mine).
37. *The Unnamable*, 300.
38. "German Letter of 1937," 172.
39. Ruby Cohn, "Waiting," in *Samuel Beckett's "Waiting for Godot,"* 41–51 (quotation p. 46).
40. Beckett's "German Letter of 1937" deserves a full reading since it provides numerous suggestions on how to proceed in eroding the "terrible materiality of the word surface," as well as powerful insights on the nature of language, silence, and literature. See *Disjecta*, 170–73.
41. Ibid., 172.
42. *Molloy*, 121.
43. Samuel Beckett, *Waiting for Godot*, in *The Complete Dramatic Works* (London: Faber and Faber, 1986), 60.
44. In this context, it is interesting to recall what Beckett wrote to Axel Kaun in his "German Letter of 1937."
45. "German Letter of 1937," 172.
46. *Waiting for Godot*, 57, 63.
47. *The Unnamable*, 296 (italics mine).
48. Samuel Beckett, "Texts for Nothing, VIII," in *Collected Shorter Prose, 1945–1980* (London: John Calder, 1984), 96 (italics mine).
49. Samuel Beckett, *Collected Poems in English and French* (New York: Grove Press, 1977), 35.
50. *The Unnamable*, 309 (italics mine).
51. Beckett, *Collected Poems*, 44.
52. *Molloy*, 121 (italics mine).

53. *The Unnamable*, 299–300 (italics mine).
54. Samuel Beckett, *Cascando*, in *Collected Shorter Plays*, 140 (italics mine).
55. *Malone Dies*, 197.
56. I have discussed the relation of tropology and silence in my "Unwording Beyond Negation."
57. *The Unnamable*, 307.
58. Ruby Cohn and Enoch Brater have repeatedly highlighted the genre instability of Beckettian semiosis. See, in particular, Cohn's *Just Play: Beckett's Theater* (Princeton: Princeton University Press, 1980); and Brater's *Beyond Minimalism: Beckett's Late Style in the Theater* (New York: Oxford University Press, 1987).
59. "But it's entirely a matter of voices, no other image is appropriate" (*The Unnamable*, 325). At the time of the First Trilogy, the key metaphor of the voice had the power to deconstruct the compactness of messages; later on, in *Still* (1975) and *Stirrings Still* (1989), space-time metaphors of silence will replace the metaphor of the voice because contextualization becomes the semiotic means alluding to silence. The movement of tropes rather than the trope itself (voice vs. word) wages a war against logocentrism.
60. For a discussion of the role of an apophatic tradition in Beckett's works, see Shira Wolosky, "Samuel Beckett's Figural Evasions," in *Languages of the Unsayable*, ed. Sanford Budick and Wolfgang Iser (New York: Columbia University Press, 1989), 165–86.
61. These plays are included in the *Collected Shorter Plays*.
62. Samuel Beckett, *Ohio Impromptu*, in *Collected Shorter Plays*, 287.
63. Ibid., 285, 288.

Consorting with Spirits: The Arcane Craft of Beckett's Later Drama

H. Porter Abbott

This is an effort on two interrelated fronts. The first is to give some accounting of what seems to be an excess of invention in a fundamentally lyrical art. Beckett's extraordinary lyrical power rarely manifests itself in his later drama without an accompanying logistical complexity, a complexity that can at times be so great as to create an insuperable challenge to understanding. Why does he do this? The second issue is the status of the personal in this complex lyrical art. Enoch Brater has argued that Beckett in his later drama not only "relyricized the genre" but spoke to us in his own voice. Regardless of who acts these plays, it is Beckett who speaks.[1] Here the question I wish to pursue further is what is meant by the term "Beckett"?

In what follows, I shall focus on Beckett's 1979 play, *A Piece of Monologue*. Of all his work for the stage, this is arguably the most thorough-going in its suppression of dramatic business. Barely more than a staged monologue, it is a sustained, single-voiced lyric. Yet it is intricately complex. Moreover, it is a lyric in the third person. As such it provokes the two questions that I am asking: what is the role of all this strenuous originality in a basically lyrical piece? And if there is authorial self-referencing in its lyricism, what role does this inventive excess play in it?

THE ART OF THE LYRIC

Taken strictly as lyrical art, *A Piece of Monologue* is an evocation of loss that can be situated within the traditional modes of loss (the monody, the threnody, the elegy, the lament).[2] In that context, it is marked by its austere dedication to its mood. If it lacks the diversity and the consolatory gestures of philosophical transcendence that often characterize works in the elegiac tradition, it has in exchange a heightened intensity of focus, as if Beckett had gone back to the purer forms of the expression of grief (the dirge, the coronach). In the modern period, it is difficult to find anything quite so unrelieved. Swinburne, for example, who can come close to Beckett's constriction of emotional range, still trades on the conventional language of relief.

> Content thee, howsoe'er, whose days are done;
>   There lies not any troublous thing before,
>   Nor sight nor sound to war against thee more,
> For whom all winds are quiet as the sun,
>   All waters as the shore.

There is no similar perspectival movement outward in *A Piece of Monologue*. Its confinement is infernal. Beckett's monodist, in a brief gesture at an entr'acte, struggles to escape the intensity of focus to which he is condemned ("Move on to other matters. Try to move on. To other matters" [p. 268])[3] only to be drawn almost immediately back into his obsessive circling when he stumbles on the key word "*gone*" ("Or gone the will to move again. Gone. Faint cry in his ear"). At the end, he concedes that there "Never were other matters. Never two matters. Never but the one matter. The dead and the gone. The dying and the going" (p. 269).

This confinement of the narrative, together with the manner of its staging, make the play a black-and-white object of great density. Throughout, Beckett accentuates the exclusivity of "dying and going" by extracting all color from the staging and almost all reference to color from the monologue, leaving only the mordant shades: black, white, and grey. Photographs have been ripped from the wall and torn to pieces, leaving "grey void[s]" for the father and mother and a "grey blot" for the family. The vision of burial that recurs three times is a masterfully compressed evocation of bereavement: "Grey light. Rain pelting. Umbrellas round a grave. Seen from above. Streaming black canopies. Black ditch beneath. Rain bubbling in the black mud. Empty for the moment. That place beneath" (p. 268).

The oxymoron on which the monologue opens—"Birth was the death of him"—establishes this austere confinement of focus at the start. Instead of extending meaning outward, as would a paradox in the Joycean mode, it seeks instead some point of absolute compression in the "one matter" that is the play's subject. "Birth" (which begins the play) and "Gone" (which ends it) are fused by the action of the play into the single word *Begone*, a word that both binds and subordinates the word *be* to the word *gone*. If one hears the word *begin* in this word as well, it is equally subordinated.[4] The many echoes of this melding of opposites into one entity ("Born dead of night," "Dying on") and related puns like "Waiting on the rip word," in which the "untimely ripped" of Macduff's birth is blended with "rest in peace," are equally governed by the same gravitational pull. In its bare narrativizations, the birth scene itself is presented as an expiration in which the first breath marks not the beginning but the end of life: "Fade. Gone. Cry. Snuffed with breath of nostrils" (p. 269).[5] Even the word *matter* subordinates *mater* (both mother and the benignity of mother earth) to the dark side of the pun, imaged by the "black mud" of the cemetery.

This certainly is original art, yet in this aspect of its originality—its extraordinary focus and intensity—*A Piece of Monologue* is, as I noted above, readily compatible with the ancient lyrical tradition of the lament. Where the play departs, and departs radically, from the tradition is in the management of its dramatic and narrative material. Though one can to a certain degree thematize Beckett's innovations, making them conform to larger elegiac purposes, there is an excess of invention in this text (as there is in almost every postwar text by this author) that will not permit normalization in this way. This monologue, in particular, is at once so intricate and so compacted that there are hardly two commentaries that are not in conflict on one or more details of its literal content.

STRANGE LOOPS

The dramatic situation is this: A man stands in "faint diffuse light" by a lamp in a room with a pallet bed and delivers a monologue in the third person. And the narrative situation (what we learn from the monologue) is this: A man rises at nightfall as he has countless nights before, goes to the window, then gropes his way to the lamp, which he lights in a process using three successive matches, following which he turns to the eastern wall of his room (stage front) from which photographs of loved ones have long ago been ripped, and there he waits until the first word ("Birth") of the monologue we are at that very moment hearing takes shapes in his mouth.

With the first word of the monologue the narrative setting shifts to the night of his birth. "That first night" is a night that, with a few salient exceptions, is very like the night just described. It takes place in a room like the one we see, though with a brass bed in it rather than a pallet. This, by inference, is the bed in which he was born. Like the night just described, the action begins with a gaze out the western window, long after the sun has "sunk behind the larches." The gazer (again by inference) is the speaker himself, as if transported to the scene of his birth. The scene carries on to the lighting of the lamp, though this time by someone else and not with three matches but with a lighted "spill," and continues, as does the present night, through the dying of the lamp and the restoration of darkness. With the fading of the lamp comes the birth cry.

In other words, what seems to happen is that the sequence of acts in the present night, starting with the gaze out the window at nightfall and culminating in the first word ("Birth") of the monologue, functions as a kind of fuse that delivers up a vision of the night of birth. But this vision in its turn leads to a second, that of the funeral cited above, which is described in such general terms that it could be that of any of the speaker's "loved ones" as well as his own.[6] Moreover, the monologue that we hear goes on to describe in an abbreviated form two more repetitions of this complex triple loop: the actions in the present night, coupled with the monologue that begins by recapitulating them, leading to the nearly identical actions of the night of birth, followed by the vision of the funeral. It is possible that these are repetitions of action that take place one after another on the same night, the agent being a defective lamp, which smokes, even when the wick is turned low (p. 266), and fades and goes out, interrupting the monologue (and thus making it, truly, only a "piece" of monologue). But it is more likely that the repetitions are a kind of *reculer pour mieux sauter*, two micro versions of which have already interrupted the long first description of the present night. These repetitions express in their turn the repetitions that have been going on for what seem like "Thirty thousand nights," just as the birth night and the funeral express all births and all funerals.

Here, then, is how the monologue is structured in terms of its interconnected loops of narrative time, punctuated by brief interludes in which the speaker observes himself speaking.

Overture (lines 1–13:[7] "Birth was the death of him. . . . Wick turned low.")
Infancy, an overview of life "From funeral to funeral," concluding with the first description of the night of birth.
1st sequence (13–108)
   THIS NIGHT (13–80: "And now. This night. . . . Birth.") The sequence of nightly actions, bringing us to the moment in which the first word of the monologue is uttered. This is the longest sustained piece of consecutive narrative in the play. There are two quick recapitulations of the action so far, at lines 27 and 61, respectively. The concluding word, "Birth," comes at almost exactly the midpoint of the play.
   THE BIRTH NIGHT (80–97: "The slow fade up of a faint form. . . . Thirty thousand nights.") A fuller version of the night introduced in the overture. The key differences from the present night—the hands lighting

the lamp with a "spill" and the "Glimmer of brass bedrail"—are introduced, but the birth cry is muffled with the general statement, "Birth
was the death of him."

THE SPEAKER AT THE MOMENT (97–99: "Stands at edge of lamplight staring beyond. . . . Again and again gone.") In all particulars, the speaker
as we see him, standing and speaking.

THE FUNERAL (99–105: "Till dark slowly parts again. . . . Then fade.")
As the accompanying version of the birth night omitted the birth cry,
this first rendering of the funeral omits mention of the coffin.

THE SPEAKER AT THE MOMENT (105–8: "Dark whole again. . . . Making
do with his mouth.")

2d sequence (108–24)

THIS NIGHT (108–11: "Lights lamp as described. . . . Birth.") Very brief.

THE BIRTH NIGHT (111–15: "Parts the dark. . . . A cry. Stifled by nasal.")
The birth cry now included.

THE FUNERAL (115–17: "Dark parts. . . . Gone") As the accompanying
rendering of the birth night introduces the birth cry, this version of the
funeral now introduces a "Coffin out of frame."

THE SPEAKER AT THE MOMENT (117–24: "Move on to other matters. . . .
Then parted by cry as before.") This is the gesture of escape in which
the speaker seeks other matters only to be drawn back by the inevitable
resonances of his own words.

3d sequence (lines 124–64)

THIS NIGHT (124–31: "Where is he now? . . . Of lips on tongue.")

THE BIRTH NIGHT (132–41: "Fade up in outer dark of window. . . . Again
and again gone.") Here the brass bed is noted twice in a countdown
toward birth that closely echoes the countdown to the beginning of the
play: "Brass bedrail catching light. Thirty seconds. To swell the two and
a half billion odd. Fade. Gone. Cry. Snuffed with breath of nostrils."

THE FUNERAL (141–46: "Till whose grave? . . . Gone.") Completing the
accompanying version of the birth scene, the coffin now is "on its way,"
again following the same countdown: "Thirty seconds. Fade. Gone."

THE SPEAKER AT THE MOMENT (146–64: "Stands there staring beyond. . . . Alone gone.") Commenting generally on the ghost character
of what he consorts with night after night, and "Waiting on the rip
word," the speaker's self-description now coincides with the conclusion
we are at the moment experiencing. He carefully monitors the fading of
the light during the last thirty seconds.

As a design that accentuates the inescapability of loss, this complex structure can be seen as serving a fundamentally lyrical intention. A version of the dramatic monologue, it suggests through its relentless circularity a grief with no exit in a victim whose entire being is constituted by the experience of loss.

But to stress the lyrical intention of traditional art, however fiercely original its expression, as a full accounting of this design is to normalize a text that is bent on resisting any generic normalization. At the heart of this resistance is the ungraspable relation between the monologue itself and the narrative action it recounts. Seen as drama, this is a piece in which the entire dramatic action is the monologue, a character "Making do with his mouth" (p. 268). Seen as narrative, the utterance of this monologue is itself a piece of the narrative action it relates, action that both precedes the monologue and continues after it. The dramatic universe, in other words, contains the narrative universe, and the narrative universe contains the dramatic universe.

Further complicating this problem of ontogeny are the different realities within the narrative (the strange loops)[8] and the problem of knowing where and how the different realities come into being. At all three points in the monologue at which these additional loops begin, they are initiated not by the completion of the monologue but by the utterance of its first word "Birth":

Birth. Then slow fade up of a faint form. Out of the dark. A window.

Birth. Parts the dark. Slowly the window.

Birth. Parts lips and thrusts tongue between them. Tip of tongue. Feel soft touch of tongue on lips. Of lips on tongue. Fade up in outer dark of window.

If the vision of the past arises with the first word of the monologue, then this is action that is in some sense happening as the monologue continues, even while the words in the monologue are treating of other things (lighting the lamp with matches, staring at the eastern wall, and so on).

In other words, if we attend closely to the sequencing of events, then the demands put on our imagination are daunting. During the interludes in which the speaker reflects on himself as he is at the moment, he is described as both in the action and hearing himself speak at the same time: "Stands staring beyond half hearing what he's saying" (p. 268). This reinforces what seems inevitably to be the case: that we are asked to imagine all the levels of action—the action of the present night, the action of the night long past, the action of witnessing the funeral, the action of voicing the monologue—as coexisting. We are asked to do this even as the temporal distinctness of these actions is emphasized, both the "birth" of the monologue and the emergence of the vision of the past located very precisely in the action of "This night," and "This night" kept historically separate from "That first night." This synchronicity of normally incompatible time and space is, among other things, a travesty of divine omniscience, that is, the capacity to see all things in an eternal present, commonly attributed to God. As such, it chimes with other divine travesties: the discreating word *begone* and the creative goal, not of light, but of "Blest dark" (*let there be night*). But the fact remains that Beckett so constructed the play as to strain our mortal incapacity.

Strange loops are not uncommon in Beckett's theater. The first came when he superimposed the second act of *Godot* on the first, challenging us with a confluence of at least three different orders of time. *Play* shifts midway from one world to another, or at least one level of consciousness to another, then loops back and forth again when the play is repeated. The relations of the narrative loops in such plays as *Embers* and *Footfalls* have challenged Beckett's ablest interpreters. Why does he do this? Or, to ask it again, why should Beckett take a text that is so powerfully effective as lyrical art in its own right and overlay it with such an insistent challenge to our capacity fully to grasp what it is we are watching?

INCANTATION

The answer, I think, is that Beckett is doing magic. Ruby Cohn has noted how the repetitive pacing of May in *Footfalls* calls to mind the biblical description of the Devil who walks "up and down" and "to and fro in the earth." With this coloration of its principal action, *Footfalls* becomes a ritualistic effort of conjuring.[9] Such a reading fits the ambience of gothic settings and arcane practices that pervades the later drama of Beckett: its repetitive formulas and ritual acts, disembodied voices and sounds, ghostly visitations, prayers, strange rites carried on in the dark of night. In *Embers*, Henry calls up sounds and ghost presences through the power of his words. In *Not I*, a mouth seeks other magic words, ringing changes on its rush of verbiage, hoping to "hit on it in the end." In . . . *but the clouds* . . . , the face of the dead beloved is conjured through nightly ritual. In *Ohio Impromptu*, a sacred text is read aloud, the reading periodically interrupted with raps on the table. These dramas, as well as *Play, Eh Joe, That Time, Ghost Trio*, and *Nacht und Träume*, can all be seen as works of sorcery, clothed with the trappings of mysterious craft.

From this perspective, *Monologue*'s nightly repetition of acts in precisely the same order—gazing out of the western window, lighting the lamp with the magical three matches, turning to the eastern wall, waiting until the arrival of the word that brings in its wake the monologue—can be seen as a rite of conjuring that brings on the visions of birth and death. To see the play in this light is, in effect, to normalize it through conventions of the abnormal. It "explains" how the speaker can be present at his birth (as was Scrooge at his funeral), and how (as a hovering spirit) he can have the strangely elevated take on the umbrellas in the cemetery.

If this is an accurate reading, then it is also the case that the incantation is something to which the initiate is condemned, night after night (as is the case with so many of the rituals in Beckett). Moreover, though visions arise, achieving the final object of incantation is always in doubt. For, if the incantation is done right, such is the hope, the speaker will at last have finished "revolving it all" and will jump through death to a birth that is not, once again, a death in birth's clothing. In the infinitesimal fourth act of *Footfalls*, the possibility that such a jump has occurred is suggested by May's nonreappearance. This construction would strengthen the reading of the repetitions in *A Piece of Monologue* as a form of *reculer pour mieux sauter*, backing up in order to spring forward, to launch himself. At the end, he waits "on the rip word," which, as Rosemary Pountney reads it, is resignedly accepted as the start of the next inevitable repetition.[10] But it also expresses the faint hope that the incantation will finally succeed and that birth really will be birth this time.

Seeing the text as a representation of conjuring gives a special license to its complex unreadability. Our minds bent in the effort to grasp a fusion of stasis and motion, past and present, word and action, we are put through a cognitive warp, feeling in our synapses the exquisite failure of generic expectations without which magic doesn't happen. I would also argue, however, that magic for Beckett was more than a mode of normalization by abnormality, or a means by which he gave a special depth and complexity of effect to his lyrical enterprise. His work was closer to real sorcery than that.

THE REFLEXIVE LOOP

One of the stranger loops the young Beckett came across in the reading of his early twenties took shape suddenly, about fifty pages into *La prisonnière*, the sixth published volume of Proust's *A la recherche du temps perdu*.

> Elle retrouvait la parole, elle disait: "Mon" ou "Mon chéri" suivis l'un ou l'autre de mon nom de baptême, ce qui en donnant au narrateur le même prénom qu'à l'auteur de ce livre eût fait: "Mon Marcel," "Mon chéri Marcel."[11]

In a single light stroke, Marcel Proust dares us to read his novel autobiographically, a work for which, over five volumes, we have by now comfortably established a novelistic mind set. The stroke is very coy. It is not asserted but suggested in passing as a possibility.

Seventy pages further on, Proust does it once again, this time in a letter from Albertine addressed to "Mon chéri et cher Marcel" and that concludes, "Quelles idées vous faites-vous donc? Quel Marcel! Quel Marcel! Toute à vous, ton Albertine."[12] There is no explicit narratorial optioning at this point as there was in the first instance, but the name is still archly packaged. It appears in a text within the text (a letter composed, moreover, by an inveterate liar) and it is qualified in such a way as to underscore the problematical character of this business of naming: "Quel Marcel!" What a Marcel, indeed. What kind of a Marcel is this? How is he constituted? Why should Proust want to seem to thread his way into his work in this manner, suggesting some interconnection between the loop of fictive narrative and that of a life lived in what is usually called the real world? And how, in turn, might this glimpse of the autobiographical loop relate to the reflexivity of the conclusion of the *Recherche*, in which the long novel we have just been reading looks forward to what appears to be its birth, that is, to the birth of a novel by Marcel Proust?

This "barely suggested, seemingly accidental semihomonymy of the narrator-hero and the signatory"[13] has been a crux throughout the criticism of the *Recherche*. Here, too, the desire to normalize and have done with it has often been strong. Gérard Genette, in his landmark structuralist reading of the novel, made the aesthetic motive dominate by excluding autobiography and reading Proust's use of his first name as a symbolic representation of "the difficult experience of relating to oneself."[14] Though Beckett did not directly take up this crux in his own 1931 reading of Proust, his general emphasis was quite different from Genette's. For Beckett, Proust was a late romantic artist of the "inexplicable," one, moreover, who engaged in the "perpetual exfoliation of personality."[15] As such, Beckett's Proust would have counted on the sudden loss of bearings created by the intrusion of the author's given name. The coy maneuver of Proust's narrator aligns being with mystery and elusiveness, connects it with "the magic of literature,"[16] and sets it against the consecutive orderings of experience that constitute the accessible modes of biography and autobiography. In the same spirit, Beckett warned with regard to these comfortable and comforting modes that "There is no allusion in this book to the legendary life and death of Marcel Proust."[17]

Nicholas Zurbrugg has written well on the richly creative divergence of Beckett from Proust,[18] but in this instance it would seem that a Proustian seed was sown that grew and blossomed after the war. There are a number of points in Beckett's later drama where he appears to engage in an autobiographical dare much like Proust's. In *Not I*, the subject is "coming up to seventy," as was the author. In *Catastrophe*, P is pointedly given "clawlike" hands, "crippled," as Beckett's were, by "fibrous degeneration." In writing *Footfalls*, after considering the names Emily and Mary, Beckett settled on his mother's name, May. And, in his own version of Proust's foregrounding of the name Marcel, Beckett gives the name May an insistence through pauses and repetition.

> May—the child's given name—May: Not enough. The mother: What do you mean, May, not enough, what can you possibly mean, May, not enough? May: I mean, Mother, that I must hear the feet . . ."[19]

Then, in the play's third "act," the name May reappears anagrammatically as Amy, and again there is a pause to draw attention to the name: "and fixing Amy—the daughter's given name, as the reader will remember—raising her head and fixing Amy full in the eye" (p. 243).

These are very delicate touches, but they suggest that the fiction of which they are a part is porous, and that in some way a filament from the fictive realm can circle out into another kind of reality.[20] It is something like this effect, I believe, that Beckett sought in the reflexivity that has characterized his drama ever since Estragon looked out into the auditorium and decribed the "Inspiring prospects."[21] Here we can turn again to *A Piece of Monologue* and note (as many have) how, in the middle of the piece, as the speaker approaches the word "Birth," he not only adopts the phraseology of stage directions but appears to be describing with precision the onset (or birth) of the very performance we are observing.

> Still as the lamp by his side. Gown and socks white to take faint light. Once white. Hair white to take faint light. Foot of pallet just visible edge of frame. Once white to take faint light. Stands there staring beyond. Nothing. Empty dark. Till first word always the same. Night after night the same. Birth. (p. 267)

Similarly, with the conclusion (or death) of the performance, he notes "the light going now. Beginning to go."

In a play that carefully aligns scenes of birth and death (moving by three successive increments to the full birth cry as the coffin moves by similar increments into the earth), Beckett aligns as well the birth and death of speech and the birth and death of the performance we are observing. This final double step creates an opening into the non-fictive world, which Beckett, through the speaker, exploits carefully. The dark stillness "beyond" the eastern wall that he is presumed to face is where we sit when the play is performed.

> Nothing stirring. Faintly stirring. Thirty thousand nights of ghosts beyond. Beyond that black beyond. Ghost light. Ghost nights. Ghost rooms. Ghost graves. Ghost . . . he all but said ghost loved ones. Waiting on the rip word. Stands there staring beyond at the black veil lips quivering to half-heard words. (p. 269)

As such, it is a play seeking to exceed itself. It appropriates the audience. And, in our turn, participants in what Genette might call the dramatic paratext,[22] we become ghosts, both in the play and out of it, both ourselves and something else.

Beckett's drama thrives on effects of liminality like this. My argument is that, in an oeuvre that has been devoted to nothing so much as the apprehension of the force from which it originates (let's call it Beckett), these liminal spaces (if the phrase works) are where the magic transaction has a chance of happening.[23] This is an important sense in which Beckett's work, prose or drama, is "devised for company." The latter phrase is adapted from Beckett's prose work *Company*, which appeared the year after *A Piece of Monologue*.[24] On the face of it, the phrase has a bitter, solipsistic cast, as if it were constructed out of Hamm's lines in *Endgame:* "Then babble, babble, words, like the solitary child who turns himself into children, two, three, so as to be together, and whisper together, in the dark."[25] As if to reinforce this, *Company* ends with the single word "Alone," just as *A Piece of Monologue* ends with the two words "Alone gone."

Yet, given the fact that Beckett wrote all his life for audiences, coupled with the reflexive looping that doesn't let us ever forget this fact, these emphatic concluding assertions, like his use of the third person, take on the quality of what I have called elsewhere "radical displacement"—a denial so strong it denies itself.[26] Just as *begone* contains *be* in embryo, *alone* is almost *all one*. The point is that nothing is settled in Beckett. When his words are at their most emphatic ("Not I!") we cannot help but see glimmers of the counterstatement. So, too, this simple lyric is immensely complex. Its dogged singularities are in fact weddings, not only of concepts (like birth and death) but of entities (like actors and audiences, ghosts, loved ones, a playwright). Even at their most funereal, these weddings take place and with any luck lead to a birth. The final point, then, is that this alchemy is not simply what the plays are about. It actually happens, even when the playwright is dead and gone. And this is because it is not just play, it's magic.

NOTES

1. Enoch Brater, *Beyond Minimalism: Beckett's Late Style in the Theater* (New York: Oxford, 1987), 17.
2. *A Piece of Monologue* was put in its final form in 1979 when the actor David Warrilow asked Beckett for a play on the subject of death. The monologue, however, had already been in progress under the working title *Gone*, the seed for which appears to have been sown in a manuscript entitled "The Voice VERBATIM," which Beckett wrote in January 1977. See Charles Krance, "Beckett's *Encores*: Textual Genesis as *Still*-Life Performance," *Essays in Theatre* 8, 2 (May 1990): 122–23.
3. Page references for *A Piece of Monologue* are to Samuel Beckett, *The Collected Shorter Plays* (New York: Grove, 1984).
4. See Jane Alison Hale, *The Broken Window: Beckett's Dramatic Perspective* (West Lafayette: Purdue University Press, 1987), 127–28; and Brater, *Beyond Minimalism*, 116.
5. Commenting on the first phrasing of this event, "stifled by nasal," Beckett told the Fletchers that it describes "The nasal consonant in 'gone.' " See Beryl S. Fletcher and John Fletcher, *A Student's Guide to the Plays of Samuel Beckett* (London: Faber, 1985), 244. In the context of the birth night, however, this phrase and the later "Snuffed with breath of nostrils" must also refer literally to the onset of regular breathing once the baby's first cry has ceased. Connotatively, the phrasing makes this stillness of peaceful nose-breathing a death that follows upon the last sound from the old life in the

womb, the birth cry, or, in this inversion of our normal way of viewing it, an agonized death cry. Of course, the sentiment expressed by all cries in this work is "Gone."

6. Linda Ben-Zvi reads the funeral scene as the increasingly unavoidable "approaching death of the speaker" (pp. 11–14) in a play that focuses "less on a replaying of the past than on the experience of the present and future" (p. 12). Kristin Morrison reads the play as the speaker's last night, representing his effort "to evade something which he is coming to understand very well: the imminence of his own death" (p. 354). See Linda Ben-Zvi, "The Schizmatic Self in 'A Piece of Monologue,' " *Journal of Beckett Studies* 7 (Spring 1982): 7–17; and Kristin Morrison, "The Rip Word in *A Piece of Monologue*," *Modern Drama* 25, 3 (September 1982): 349–54.

My view is different. My guess is that, among other reasons, Beckett repeated the funeral scene three times because three individuals have been specified as gone or going: father, mother, speaker. But, however one explains it, it is important to keep in mind that the speaker anticipates his death in the first lines of the monologue and elsewhere yearningly seeks the "blest dark." As for the future, the problem is that it is indistinguishable from the past and the present, each being comprised of just the "one matter." This is another implicit oxymoron: facing east, the speaker heads repeatedly into the past.

7. These and subsequent numbers refer to lines of prose in *The Collected Shorter Plays*.

8. The term *strange loop* is taken with considerable license from Douglas Hofstadter's *Gödel, Escher, Bach: An Eternal Golden Braid* (New York: Basic Books, 1979). Hofstadter devised the idea of a strange loop to explain the relation between the determinate (bio/neurological) and the "higher" activities of our brains: thought, hope, agency, consciousness. But the term seems tailor-made for the kind of loops I am describing, and since I hope to show that they, too, bear on the mystery of self-consciousness, I feel comfortable with my appropriation.

9. Ruby Cohn, *Just Play: Beckett's Theater* (Princeton: Princeton University Press, 1980), 136.

10. Rosemary Pountney, *Theatre of Shadows: Samuel Beckett's Drama, 1956–1976* (Gerrards Cross: Colin Smythe, 1988), 217.

11. Marcel Proust, *A la recherche du temps perdu*, vol. 3 (Paris: Robert Laffont, 1987), 72. "Then she would find her tongue and say: 'My _____' or 'My darling _____' followed by my Christian name, which, if we give the narrator the same name as the author of this book, would be 'My Marcel,' or 'My darling Marcel.' " See *Remembrance of Things Past*, vol. 3, trans. C. K. Scott Moncrieff and Terence Kilmartin (New York: Vintage, 1982), 69.

12. *A la recherche*, 133. " 'My darling dear Marcel. . . . The ideas you get into

your head! What a Marcel! What a Marcel! Always and ever your Albertine' " (*Remembrance*, 153–54).

13. Gérard Genette, *Narrative Discourse: An Essay in Method*, trans. Jane E. Lewin (Ithaca: Cornell University Press, 1980), 249.

14. Ibid. "We know," Genette writes in a footnote, "that the only two occurrences of this first name in the *Recherche* are late . . . and that the first is not without reservation. But it seems to me that this is not enough for us to reject it. If we were to contest everything that is said only once. . . . On the other hand, naming the hero Marcel is obviously not identifying him with Proust; but this partial and fragile coincidence is highly symbolic" (p. 249n). In a spirited response, David Ellison argues: "I do not believe much is gained or solved if we affirm, with Genette and Germaine Brée, that the first-person narration in the *Recherche* is the result of a conscious esthetic choice rather than the sign of confession or 'confidence directe.' This hypothesis amounts to isolating the text in the realm of an abstract, self-sufficient fictional space where existential force is simply replaced by the free play of forms. What Genette, Brée, and many other readers of Proust note in passing rather than examine deeply is the *perversity* of saying *je* when one may or may not, may and may not 'mean what one says' " (David R. Ellison, *The Reading of Proust* [Baltimore: Johns Hopkins University Press, 1984], 139).

15. Samuel Beckett, *Proust* (New York: Grove, 1957), 13.

16. Ibid., 63.

17. Ibid., "Foreword."

18. Nicholas Zurbrugg, *Beckett and Proust* (Gerrards Cross: Colin Smythe, 1988).

19. *Collected Shorter Plays*, 241.

20. I am tempted to see in the repetitions of May's name in *Footfalls* a very personal incantation: "May . . . May . . . May . . . May . . . May: I mean, Mother . . ."

21. Samuel Beckett, *Waiting for Godot* (New York: Grove, 1954), 10.

22. For a full development of the theory of the paratext, see Gérard Genette, *Seuils* (Paris: Seuil, 1987).

23. For a parallel argument on the linguistic space created by Beckett's bilingualism, see Ann Beer, "Beckett's 'Autography' and the Company of Languages," *Southern Review* 27, 4 (Autumn 1991): 771–91.

24. Samuel Beckett, *Company* (New York: Grove, 1980), 8.

25. Samuel Beckett, *Endgame* (New York: Grove, 1958), 70.

26. "A Poetics of Radical Displacement: Samuel Beckett Coming Up to Seventy," *Texas Studies in Literature and Language* 17, 1 (Spring 1975): 219–38.

All My Sons After the Fall: Arthur Miller and the Rage for Order

Hersh Zeifman

In the introduction to the first volume of his *Collected Plays*, Arthur Miller commented: "The very impulse to write, I think, springs from an inner chaos crying for order . . . ,"[1] an image he later expanded in his essay "The Shadows of the Gods": " 'There is a hidden order in the world . . .' [T]he great writer [is] the destroyer of chaos, a man privy to the councils of the hidden gods. . . . "[2] "Oh! Blessed rage for order . . . ," wrote Wallace Stevens, "The maker's rage to order words. . . . "[3] This rage for order, for an anodyne to his "help-lessness before the chaos of existence,"[4] is the driving force behind all of Miller's plays, the fuel of both their passion and their urgency. And nowhere is this more evident than in *All My Sons*, the 1947 play that brought Miller his first Broadway success, a play so tightly constructed that it is practically straitjacketed by "order."

Formally, the play's order stems from its relentless Ibsenite real-ism, a mimesis celebrating linearity, chronology, causality: the ghosts of the past—what Miller once termed "the birds coming home to roost"[5]—return to haunt the present and to shape its future. The intense realism of *All My Sons* is immediately evidenced in its minutely detailed setting: the backyard of the Keller home on the outskirts of a midwestern town. Miller obeys every possible unity in this early play, including those not even dreamt of in Aristotle's philosophy. Thus, the setting, for example, remains constant throughout all three acts, while the events of the play unfold during the course of a single August Sunday—one long day's journey into night. And, to complete this orderly neoclassical rigor, there is, most crucially of all, unity of action: the play centers on an ideological struggle between father and son, a literally life-and-death struggle of ethics and values.

The quest for order is dramatized in the play, then, not only formally but thematically: the conflict between Chris Keller and his father Joe is precisely a conflict between order and chaos. "*All My Sons,*" Miller has stated, "is about the conflict between private and public morality . . . the destruction of the hermetic seal around the family. And the conflict between being a father and being a citizen. . . ."[6] For Joe Keller, family is everything. To preserve his family—specifically the family manufacturing business, which he was building to pass on to his sons—he knowingly shipped defective cylinder heads to the Air Force during the Second World War, resulting in the crash of twenty-one American P-40s and the deaths of their pilots. As Miller has written,

> Joe Keller's trouble . . . is not that he cannot tell right from wrong but that his cast of mind cannot admit that he, personally, has any viable connection with his world, his universe, or his society. . . . The fortress which *All My Sons* lays siege to is the fortress of unrelatedness.[7]

The spokesman in the play for relatedness, for a connection with the larger family of humanity, is Joe's son Chris. As his name suggests, Chris is a metaphoric Christ,[8] a secular saint espousing universal love for all God's children (twice we are told in the play that Chris "likes everybody").[9] As his neighbor Sue rather sardonically comments, "Chris makes people want to be better that it's possible to be. He does that to people" (p. 93). "Chris, a man can't be a Jesus in this world!" (p.

125) Joe cries out in anguished self-defense at the play's climax. But a Jesus in this world is precisely what the idealist Chris demands, as Joe instinctively acknowledges. When Chris responds to Joe's confession of guilt that closes Act II with the words "What must I do, Jesus God, what must I do?," Joe's reply, "Chris . . . My Chris . . ." (p. 116), is both plea and whispered prayer.

Joe's justification for his crime is the primacy of family. "I'm his father and he's my son," he informs his wife Kate, "and if there's something bigger than that I'll put a bullet in my head!" (p. 120). For Chris, of course, there is something bigger than that; to believe otherwise is to abandon civilization to the beasts, to ethical chaos. As Miller has commented, "The fish is in the water but the water's in the fish. You can't extricate individuals from society. . . ."[10] However much he chooses to rationalize his crime, Joe is not divorced from his society, from the world at large: he has responsibilities to that world, to himself as a social and therefore a *human* being. "What the hell are you?" (p. 116) Chris demands of his father at the height of their confrontation—the key question in all of Miller's plays. Joe's ultimate answer is to walk offstage and put a bullet in his head, thereby both acknowledging his guilt and conceding the validity of Chris's moral vision.

The conflict over relatedness in *All My Sons* is enacted, as we have seen, in the Kellers' backyard: "*The stage is hedged on right and left by tall, closely planted poplars which lend the yard a secluded atmosphere*" (p. 58). Setting thus symbolizes the play's ideological struggle: solipsistically cultivating his own garden, Joe thinks he can build a kind of wall around his family, insulating them from the world outside. But the claims of that outside world keep intruding, as evidenced by the play's central visual symbol, the presence in the garden of the stump of an apple tree. The tree had been planted as a memorial to the Kellers' younger son, Larry, reported missing in action three years previously. During the early morning hours of this fateful Sunday of the play's action, the tree has been toppled by a violent storm. This very day the Kellers will learn for certain that Larry is dead, having committed suicide after discovering his father's treachery. The broken tree symbolizing Larry's death thus acts as a powerful indictment of

Joe's blinkered morality: Larry killed himself because the pilots Joe sent to their deaths were, in a larger context, *all* his "sons."

In the original production of *All My Sons*, Miller was puzzled by his first glimpse of the set—specifically by a low bump in the middle of the grassy garden over which the actors were constantly tripping. "What is the point of it?" Miller asked the play's designer, Mordecai Gorelik. Gorelik replied,

> You have written a graveyard play. . . . The play is taking place in a ceme-tery where their son is buried, and he is also their buried conscience reaching up to them out of the earth. Even if it inconveniences [the actors] it will keep reminding them what the hell all this acting is really *about*. The bump stays![11]

It was shrewd of Gorelik to note the symbolic significance of setting in this intensely realistic play, but the backyard functions as more than simply a metaphoric grave for this precursor to Sam Shepard's buried child. For the presence of the tree, along with various plants and a small trellised arbor, reminds us that the backyard is specifically a garden, and the fact that it's an apple tree points to the symbolic nature of that garden.

The yard of the Kellers' home is thus a Garden of Eden, but not in the sense so fiercely maintained by Joe of a paradisal family haven. "It's lovely here," Chris's fiancée, Ann, comments as she looks around the garden early in the play. "The air is sweet" (p. 83). So said Duncan, similarly deceived, as he approached Macbeth's castle.[12] Joe's garden is Eden after the fall, a place of sin, and when Joe enters in Act II and "takes a little box of apples from under the bench," breaking one in half before passing it to Ann and Chris (p. 96), the source of that sin is clearly identified. Larry's memorial tree, then, functions as both the symbol of Joe's sin and the sign of his potential redemption. For, by dying in expiation of Joe's sin, Larry enacts the truth of Chris's assertion. The tree has become the cross, a mute but constant reminder that one must indeed be a Jesus in this world.

In his autobiography, *Timebends*, Miller reiterated the profound or-der being dramatized in *All My Sons*.

Whenever the hand of the distant past reaches out of its grave, it is always somehow absurd as well as amazing, and we tend to resist belief in it, for it seems rather magically to reveal some unreadable hidden order behind the amoral chaos of events as we rationally perceive them. But that emergence, of course, is the point of *All My Sons*—that there are times when things do indeed cohere.[13]

Yet, for many critics, things do *not* cohere in *All My Sons*. The play's order is seen as somehow spurious, both in form and in content. Formally, the play's creaky contrivances—a climactic letter from beyond the grave; the denouement propelled by a slip of the tongue; the sudden blurting out of long-buried truths for maximum dramatic effect—smack of the worst excesses of the well-made play, of soap opera: "All My Children" rather than *All My Sons*. And thematically, while Joe Keller's guilt is painstakingly spelled out for the audience, what about Chris's guilt? Miller appears to have stacked the deck, allowing Chris to hold all the moral cards and to exult in playing them. As Ruby Cohn has noted, Chris, with his "prim moral stance, pontificates in abstractions."[14] This makes Chris, in many ways, a difficult character to admire. His idealism can easily come across as smug self-righteousness, as nothing more than adolescent whining.

In "The Shadows of the Gods," Miller claimed that a play needed to "pursue the ultimate development of the very questions it asks. But for such a pursuit, the viewpoint of the adolescent is not enough."[15] It is a criticism, not unfairly, that could be turned against Miller's own play, for Chris does seem adolescent in his simplistic approach to complex moral issues. Whenever I teach the play, I always ask my students how old they think Chris is, and their answer is invariably in his late teens or early twenties. It comes as something of a shock, then, to discover that, on his first appearance, we are informed in the stage directions (those "boring" lines in italics that students usually skip) that Chris is thirty-two (p. 64). Arthur Miller was born in 1915; in 1947, when *All My Sons* was first produced, he was thirty-two. The fact that Chris is made to be Miller's exact age strongly reinforces the sense that he functions in the play as the dramatist's alter ego, his impassioned voice, Miller's voice. And, because Miller identifies so strongly with Chris, the question of

Chris's own possible moral failings remains essentially unexamined.[16] It would take Miller seventeen years to examine Chris's complicity and guilt, to expose the spuriousness of the apparent order in *All My Sons*, in effect to rewrite the play under a different title: *After the Fall*.

All rewriting is an attempt to wrest order out of disorder, and a dramatist's rewriting of a previously produced play only emphasizes the point. What was presumably once viewed as complete, a finalized order, is now perceived as incomplete, a kind of disorder. Unlike his contemporary, Tennessee Williams, say—or, to cite the example of a more recent American dramatist, Lanford Wilson—Miller is not especially known for tinkering with the text of a play once it has been produced. There are some exceptions to this generalization—the two-act version of *A View from the Bridge*, for instance, or the revised text of *The Archbishop's Ceiling*, or *After the Fall* itself, which has been published in two very different texts and which Miller further extensively revised for the 1984 off-Broadway revival with Frank Langella—but as a rule Miller tends to leave well (or ill) enough alone: there is no Miller equivalent of Williams's *Battle of Angels* transformed into *Orpheus Descending* transformed into *The Fugitive Kind*.

When I suggest, then, that *After the Fall* is a "rewriting" of *All My Sons*, I'm not referring to a literal, line-by-line reworking of the text but to a more general, ideological revision—the kind Adrienne Rich spells "re-vision" and defines as "the act of looking back, of seeing with fresh eyes, of entering an old text from a new critical direction. . . ."[17] For over the years it is precisely ideology that has shifted in Miller. The beginnings of that shift were apparent as early as 1957, when Miller wrote in his introduction to the first volume of his *Collected Plays:*

> The assumption—or presumption—behind these plays is that life has meaning. I would now add, as their momentary commentator, that what they meant to me at the time of writing is not in each instance the same as what they mean to me now in the light of further experience.[18]

When he came to write *After the Fall*, first produced in 1964, Miller continued to believe that life had meaning—but the nature of that meaning had altered radically from the meaning suggested by *All My Sons*. Miller was now older, and perhaps wiser, and "the light of further experience" shines brightly through the later play. *After the Fall*, unlike *All My Sons*, is not a drama written by a young man.

In *The Anxiety of Influence*, Harold Bloom theorized that all strong poets in effect "misread" their major precursors, "so as to clear imaginative space for themselves."[19] What Miller himself once proclaimed literally about the relation between the American writer and his biological father—"The writer in America is supplanting somebody, correcting him, making up for his errors or failures, and in the process he is creating a new world"[20]—Bloom proclaimed metaphorically about the relation between son and literary father. *After the Fall* offers a particularly agonized variant of this theory, for how much more intense the shadow of the anxiety of influence must be when the "ghostly father" against whom the writer is rebelling is his own earlier self. Of the six "revisionary ratios" Bloom analyzes in his study, the one he terms "kenosis" seems most applicable to the kind of rewriting we encounter in *After the Fall*. "[K]enosis," Bloom notes, "is a movement toward discontinuity with the precursor. I take the word from St. Paul, where it means the humbling or emptying out of Jesus by himself, when he accepts reduction from divine to human status."[21]

Although I'm deliberately interpreting Bloom more literally than he intended, the "reduction from divine to human status" seems to me to capture precisely the revisionist strategy of *After the Fall*, a strategy that extends to the very form of the play. For replacing the realistic landscape of *All My Sons* is an expressionistic soulscape: "The action takes place in the mind, thought, and memory of Quentin."[22] After *All My Sons*, realism began to strike Miller as a kind of trap. "[O]ur inability to break more than the surfaces of realism," he concluded in 1957, "reflected our inability—playwrights and audiences—to agree upon the pantheon of forces and values which must lie behind the realistic surfaces of life."[23] *All My Sons*, he later noted, "was my only tightly made play among seven or eight of a far looser and more vagrantly poetic form; now I hoped to open up the side of my vision that was, so I imagined, a path into my own chaos."[24] The paradox here is startling: the ordered realism of *All My Sons* results in what is now perceived as a false order; genuine order can be achieved only through chaos, through a theatrical form that, superficially at least, evokes disorder. The structure of *After the Fall* is thus deliberately confusing, a fluid, seemingly alogical stream-of-consciousness that mimics not the objective patterning of divinity but the subjective free-for-all of the human psyche.

A more significant use of *kenosis*, however, can be seen by analyzing the reduction from divine to human in the content of Miller's play. *After the Fall*, like *All My Sons*, features an authorial spokesman whose age (and, in this instance, specific and often notorious life experiences) identifies him as Miller's alter ego. Quentin, the stage directions inform us, is "a man in his forties" (p. 128), Miller's age at the time of writing. Also, like *All My Sons*, *After the Fall* begins with the hero's proposed marriage, the questionable appropriateness of which acts as the catalyst that sets the whole play in motion. The twice-divorced Quentin has recently met in Germany a woman, Holga, whom he both loves and is afraid to love. For, given his past, what kind of commitment can he make to her? "I am bewildered by the death of love," Quentin confesses to us, "And my responsibility for it" (p. 190). It is this notion of Quentin's complicity, as Miller states in his foreword to the play, that renders the play at heart a trial: "the trial of a man by his own conscience, his own values, his own deeds."[25] *All My Sons* was likewise a trial, the trial of Joe Keller and the false values he believed in. The essential difference in *After the Fall* is that now it is Chris who is on trial. Quentin is Chris finally grown up (chronologically and, more important, ethically), looking back on his life—looking back, in effect, on *All My Sons*—and cringing at his former youth and naïveté.

And I look back at when there seemed to be a kind of plan, some duty in the sky . . . and the world so wonderfully threatened by injustices I was born to correct! How fine! Remember? When there were good people and bad people? And how easy it was to tell! . . . Like some kind of paradise compared to this. . . . Until I begin to look at it. . . . God, when I think of what I believed, I want to hide!

Quentin then continues this speech by offering a specific example of his former innocence, shocked by his advanced age at the time: "Yes, but I wasn't all that young! You would think a man of thirty-two . . ." (p. 149). Significantly, when wishing to "freeze" Quentin in an image of false innocence, Miller chose the exact age of Chris Keller.

In a direct reversal of *All My Sons*, then, Quentin prosecutes himself for the identical crime that previously allowed Chris to become the *prosecutor:* the myth of his own innocence and goodness. Thus the ontological question hurled accusingly at a father by his son in *All My Sons*, the question that exposes Joe's guilt, is now hurled at the son: "What are you," Quentin's father demands of him, "a stranger?" (p. 193). That is precisely what Quentin is; it is impossible to be anything else. Quentin is not Chris(t), not a creature of infinite love and self-sacrifice, for no such creature exists on this earth—although many of those who loved him over the years tried to make him into one. "I bless you, Quentin!" (p. 201), the doomed Maggie whispers to him, "[Y]ou're like a god!" (p. 198). Quentin knows, however, that he is not a god, despite the temptation to play the part. Thus, spreading his arms "in crucifixion" between two light fixtures on his wall, Quentin momentarily accedes to the temptation, only to lower his arms in disgust. "What the hell am I trying to do," he berates himself, "love *everybody?*" (p. 202). This was specifically Chris's temptation. As Miller suggests in his foreword to *After the Fall*, it is a temptation universally seductive.

> through Quentin's agony in this play there runs the everlasting temptation of Innocence, that deep desire to return to when, it seems, he was in fact without blame. To that elusive time, which persists in all our minds, when somehow everything was part of us and we so pleasurably at one with others . . . "26

The myth of blamelessness, of uncomplicated relatedness, dies hard, but die it must or else it destroys us. As Miller concludes in *Timebends*, "innocence kills."27

In *All My Sons*, Joe Keller's guilt consisted ultimately of thinking that he was a "separate person," that he could divorce the concerns of his family from those of the world at large. In *After the Fall*, Quentin's innocence consists of thinking that it was ever possible to be other than a "separate person. "We are all separate people" (p. 233), Quentin confesses to Maggie, and that is our crime. If we don't kill literally (like Joe), then we kill symbolically or allow others to kill. For, when the chips are down, when it's a matter of self-preservation, we choose ourselves. We sacrifice others, consciously or unconsciously, so that we may live (*After the Fall* was originally subtitled *The Survivor*).[28] Thus, when Maggie attempts to cast Quentin as Jesus opposite her Lazarus, as the god who will raise her from the dead, he refuses. "Whoever goes to save another person with the lie of limitless love," Quentin proclaims, "throws a shadow on the face of God" (p. 233). This is the bleak truth Quentin is forced to acknowledge as he sifts through the countless memories of betrayal that constitute his life. His role—the role of all humanity—is not that of the savior Jesus but of the betrayer Judas. "[I]n whose name do you ever turn your back . . . ," Quentin concludes, "but in your own? In Quentin's name! Always in your own blood-covered name you turn your back!" (p. 240).

Quentin's insight is dramatized most powerfully in the play's central visual symbol, the blasted stone tower of a German concentration camp that dominates the entire stage, its windows "like eyes," and its reinforcing rods spreading "like broken tentacles" (p. 127). During the course of the play, the tower lights up at various key moments of betrayal. "The concentration camp," Miller has noted, "is the final expression of human separateness and its ultimate consequence."[29] The central symbol of *All My Sons*, the apple tree, evoked simultaneously a postlapsarian world and the promise of its redemption. Paradise can be regained, the tree suggested, by means of the brotherhood of man. Through Chris, Miller identified with "all my sons"—both primal innocence (son as child) and the restoration of that innocence (Son as Christian Savior). In the revisionist *After the Fall*, however, the concentration camp tower evokes a postlapsarian world beyond redemption, in which paradise can never be regained because it never truly existed. "Who can be innocent again on this mountain of skulls?" Quentin wonders. "I tell you what I know! My brothers died here . . . but my brothers built this place; our hearts have cut these stones!" (p. 241). Through Quentin, Miller no longer identifies with "all my sons" but with "all my brothers"; the benign brotherhood of man is in reality the blood-drenched brotherhood of Cain and Abel.

After such knowledge, what forgiveness? Or, to rephrase the question in Quentin's words, "When you've finally become a separate person, what the hell is there?" (p. 168). Joe Keller killed himself because he learned that we are not separate people; must Quentin now kill himself because he's learned that we are? *"After the Fall* would have been altogether different," Miller once stated in an interview, "if by some means the hero was killed, or shot himself. Then we would have been in business."[30] Unlike his Faulknerian namesake, however, Miller's Quentin does not "love death above all," nor is he "incapable of love."[31] Miller deliberately denies Quentin both Joe's evasion through suicide and Chris's evasion through innocence. The painful realization he has struggled with throughout the play must be acknowledged.

> To know, and even happily that we meet unblessed; not in some garden of wax fruit and painted trees, that lie of Eden, but after, after the Fall, after many, many deaths. Is the knowing all?" (p. 241)

The path Quentin ultimately chooses is infinitely more difficult than either Joe's or Chris's, and infinitely more courageous: to take the hideously deformed face of one's life in one's arms and finally embrace it. The closing word in the play is Quentin's "Hello" (p. 242), the same word with which he opened it (p. 128)—and thus a beginning not an ending. That first hello, addressed to his own psyche, was tentative and frightened. His last hello, now addressed to Holga—still tentative, still frightened—nevertheless bears the promise of an affirmation of life, of a new and hopeful love—but east of the lie of Eden, long after the Fall.

By electing, in effect, to rewrite *All My Sons* in this unusual way, Miller was presumably attempting finally to bring order to what had clearly become for him disorder. Ironically, however, many critics have found in *After the Fall* even greater evidence of disorder than in the earlier play. *After the Fall* has been variously attacked for its verbal pretentiousness and infelicities, its cheap settling of old scores, its misogyny, its trivializing of the Holocaust, its prolixity, its lack of theatrical conflict, its metaphysical shallowness—and, most damning of all because most circular, the adolescence of its central character. According to Richard Gilman, for example,

> Miller has succeeded in conveying no meaning whatsoever, but only an endless sophomoric revery about meaning. . . . Quentin-Miller's observations are . . . unutterably pompous and flaccid . . . compos[ing] a rhetoric of . . . hopeless banality and adolescent mutterings . . .[32]

Miller, so the charge goes, has once again stacked the deck. Quentin may hold very different cards from those held by Chris, but he plays them in the same ostentatious, self-righteous way. As Christopher Bigsby has so elegantly concluded, "The man who strikes his chest in confession may derive his satisfaction not so much from his admission of guilt as from the exquisite nature of the blow."[33] Such criticism is, unfortunately, not without merit: where Chris once reveled in his innocence, it is difficult not to see Quentin now reveling in his guilt. And is it, in fact, genuine guilt? According to Ruby Cohn, "Though Quentin assures us that innocence is impossible, his final confession of guilt is a disguised self-justification . . ."[34] Miller's rage for order, then, may finally be as elusive (or as doomed) as all playwrights' engagements in that simulacrum of divinity, the creation of the world and other business. Or perhaps our judgment is simply premature, for Miller may one day complete the circle and surprise us with yet another implicit acknowledgment of the suddenly provisional nature of a theatrical order once presumably attained: a reordered, revisionist rewriting of *After the Fall*.

NOTES

1. Arthur Miller, "Introduction," in *Collected Plays, Vol. 1* (New York: Viking, 1957), 38.

2. Arthur Miller, "The Shadow of the Gods," *Harper's* 217 (August 1958), reprinted in *The Theater Essays of Arthur Miller*, ed. Robert A. Martin (Harmondsworth: Penguin, 1978), 180.

3. Wallace Stevens, "The Idea of Order at Key West," in *The Collected Poems of Wallace Stevens* (New York: Knopf, 1954), 130.

4. Miller, "Shadows," 179.

5. In a conversation with Christopher Bigsby, Miller commented: "[Ibsen] was carrying the Greeks into nineteenth-century Europe, principally because they were both obsessed with the birds coming home to roost: the effect of the past . . ." See Christopher Bigsby, ed., *Arthur Miller and Company* (London: Methuen, 1990), 49.

6. Miller to Harry Rasky, "Arthur Miller on Home Ground," CBC television documentary, 1979.

7. Miller, "Introduction," 19.

8. Christian imagery in Miller's plays is always metaphoric. As Leonard Moss notes, "Miller interprets Old and New Testament ethical concepts in a wholly secular manner." See Leonard Moss, *Arthur Miller* (New York: Twayne, 1967), 94.

9. Arthur Miller, *All My Sons*, in *Collected Plays*, Vol. 1, 75, 91. All further page references will be cited in the text.

10. Bigsby, ed., *Miller and Company*, 80.

11. Arthur Miller, *Timebends: A Life* (New York: Grove Press, 1987), 275. For a discussion of the metaphoric possibilities of Miller's set in *All My Sons*, see Enoch Brater, "Miller's Realism and *Death of a Salesman*," in *Arthur Miller: New Perspectives*, ed. Robert A. Martin (Englewood Cliffs: Prentice-Hall, 1982), 116–18.

12. "This castle hath a pleasant seat, the air / Nimbly and sweetly recommends itself / Unto our gentle senses." See William Shakespeare, *Macbeth*, in *Shakespeare: The Complete Works*, ed. G. B. Harrison (New York: Harcourt, 1968), I.vi.1–3.

13. Miller, *Timebends*, 134–35.

14. Ruby Cohn, "The Articulate Victims of Arthur Miller," in *Dialogue in American Drama* (Bloomington: Indiana University Press, 1971), 70.

15. Miller, "Shadows," 192.

16. Christopher Bigsby regards the issue of Chris's moral failings not as a criticism *of* the play but rather as a criticism *within* the play. Miller, according to Bigsby, has always been supremely aware of Chris's "flaw." Bigsby argues that *All My Sons*, like Ibsen's *The Wild Duck*, thus mounts a two-pronged attack: "It is a play equally about the corrupting power of greed and the destructiveness of an idealism untinged with humanity" (Christopher Bigsby, ed., *File on Miller* [London: Methuen, 1987], 17)—an argument I find eloquent but ultimately unconvincing. Elsewhere in his

writings, Bigsby concedes that this issue is only a "submerged theme" in the play (C. W. E. Bigsby, *A Critical Introduction to Twentieth-Century American Drama*, vol. 2 [Cambridge: Cambridge University Press, 1984], 168), one that "doesn't seem entirely worked out" (Bigsby, *Miller and Company*, 48).

17. Adrienne Rich, "When We Dead Awaken: Writing as Re-Vision," in *On Lies, Secrets, and Silence* (New York: Norton, 1979), 35.

18. Miller, "Introduction," 8.

19. Harold Bloom, *The Anxiety of Influence* (New York: Oxford University Press, 1973), 5.

20. Bigsby, *Miller and Company*, 15.

21. Bloom, *Anxiety*, 14. See also the chapter on *kenosis* (pp. 77–92).

22. Arthur Miller, *After the Fall*, in *Collected Plays, Vol. 2* (New York: Viking, 1981), 127. All further page references will be cited in the text.

23. Miller, "Introduction," 46.

24. Miller, *Timebends*, 276.

25. Arthur Miller, "Foreword to *After the Fall*," *Saturday Evening Post* 237 (1 February 1964), reprinted in Martin, *Theater Essays*, 257.

26. Miller, "Foreword," 256.

27. Miller, *Timebends*, 527.

28. Moss, *Arthur Miller*, 83.

29. Olga Carlisle and Rose Styron, "Arthur Miller: An Interview," *Paris Review* 10 (Summer 1966), reprinted in Martin, *Theater Essays*, 289.

30. Ibid., 287.

31. William Faulkner, "Appendix," in *The Sound and the Fury* (New York: Vintage, 1956), 9, 10.

32. Richard Gilman, "Still Falling" [review of 1964 Lincoln Center production of *After the Fall*], in *Common and Uncommon Masks: Writings on Theatre, 1961–1970* (New York: Random House, 1971), 153–54.

33. C. W. E. Bigsby, "The Fall and After—Arthur Miller's Confession," *Modern Drama* 10 (1967–68): 134.

34. Cohn, "Articulate Victims," 89.

"The Garden is a Mess": Maternal Space in Bowles, Glaspell, Robins

ELIN DIAMOND

Gertrude Eastman Cuevas's garden somewhere on the coast of Southern California. The garden is a mess, with ragged cactus plants and broken ornaments scattered about.

[stage directions, I.i, *In the Summer House*, Jane Bowles, 1953]

The high modernist and postmodern impulse in performance stresses the flatness of the image, the volumetrics of space in contradistinction to realism's perspectival depth, its seductive regimen of viewing and feeling. In realism, so the critical story goes, the plot's linearity and the character's interiority produce spectatorial mastery, a far cry from the unchronicled body knowledge of postmodern performance. But this is a sorry binary. Ibsenite realism, the beginning of modernism in drama, always worked variations on the regime of mastery. The curtained inner room within Hedda Gabler's drawing room, the interior space that draws the eye to a point of origin, both affirms and mocks the traditions of perspectival painting to which realism is heir, for the vanishing point evaporates even as the eye strains, the inner room yields no causal logic. It is rather a space of nondiscursive negativity, dimensionless and hallucinatory, an uncharted space where, to paraphrase Judge Brack, Hedda does what people don't do.

Like the hysteria that turns a physiological body into an erotogenic one, realist rooms gradually lose their specific dimensionality, the discernible symbolic boundaries of gender and class, and become instead symptomatic spaces bearing signs that taxonomize not the empirical real but rather the Freudian territory of psychic reality—of contradiction, division, fragmentation. Although Freud continued to use archaeological metaphors for heuristic purposes, the idea of the psyche as layered, as that which, when dug into enough, would reveal truth, was one that he abandoned before he wrote his *"fragment* of an analysis" of Dora in 1899 (published in 1905). In working on *The Interpretation of Dreams* (1900), Freud discovered that the constructions of the psyche, like that of the dream, could not be figured as an essay, or even a Chinese box, but as a rebus, a depthless picture-puzzle of words and images with no coherence, no representational unity. The rebus, a modernist object, abstracted and obscure, breaks with a perspectival realism so often structured by secrets and their telling. If the rebus has a structure, it is best defined by Derrida's notion of "spacing," that which "divides the present from what it is"[1]—suggesting another scene—although not a truer or a deeper one. Even in Ibsen we sense this odd spacing of teleological time in which, as the play marches forward, fragmented bits of other scenes, the play's rebus, come into view and divide the present from "what it is."

If we look back nostalgically to the coherent bourgeois interiors of nineteenth-century western culture, the notion of the psychic fragment—Hedda's puppetlike head peeking out from behind the curtain before she closes herself off permanently—bespeaks a failure of the humanistic models of cognition and mastery. Looking ahead into the twentieth century, that fragment becomes objectified, presentational, an alienating index of spatiality, as in Picasso's "analytical" cubism or, more suitable to the illogical dimensionality of the rebus, Boccioni's now destroyed futurist sculpture, "Fusion of a Head and Window."[2] But this mechanistic, antihumanist body so beloved of Futurists has a special valence in *Hedda Gabler*, and indeed in all modernist experimentation, and that is gender. In early modernism, the "beast in the jungle" that could not be repressed was the feminine, for if the "new woman" did not embrace her gender, the social boundaries so crucial to bourgeois hegemony were imperiled. Whether she was the "angel in the house" who defined a nonmercantilist private interior, the leisured lady whose identity kept working-class women visible as ungendered effects of labor, or the malingering hysteric against whom "true" feminine health could be defined, women had to take some role in the gender story.

Unfortunately, the latter condition, hysteria, problematizes all social fictions. A disease a least as old as Galen, hysteria seemed pervasive among bourgeois women in the great metropolises of Europe and the United States from the mid-nineteenth century through the First World War. According to the popular press, hysteria erupted in suffragette demonstrations, in modernist manifestoes, and in the terrifying colors and images on the walls of art galleries.[3] Inscribed in these social hysterias was the deadly message Freud learned to read in his female patients and came to analyze later: the girl-child's assumption of heterosexual femininity was, in the most "normal" of developments, a fraught and problematic journey. Beneath her complex symptomatology the hysteric asks the questions that most people learn to repress: "Am I a man or am I a woman?" With this question she disturbs, for both genders, subjectivity, identity, and desire, as well as the social and political categories they underpin.

One such social category is, of course, motherhood. In rejecting femininity, the hysteric lashes out at her mother (Dora dismisses hers) and refuses to be one. It is no coincidence that Hedda is both unsatisfyingly married and secretly pregnant; nor is it surprising that in the first London production of *Hedda* lines concerning the pregnancy were excised. And in her memoirs of her Ibsen years the American Elizabeth Robins, actress/playwright, feminist, suffragist, and leading exponent of the Ibsen revolution in England, omitted all references to the pregnancy in her analysis of the play. Of course, Victorian physicians, including Freud, recommended marriage and motherhood as ways of forestalling the neurotic self-absorption of hysteria. In response, early feminists tried to disentangle sexuality from motherhood, for maternity, like marriage, was already coded in the patriarchal story as that which destroyed sexuality and desire. For the "new woman" marriage was the threshold of prison, maternity the permanent condition of incarceration. Yet the increasing visibility of unwed mothers among industrial workers, in U.S. as well as British cities, the highly publicized instances of infanticide by desperate working-class women, and the preoccupation, from the turn of the century through the 1950s, with mothering as the crucial element in producing successful American men, brought into dangerous alignment hysteria—a disease, after all, of the "hysteron" or womb—and maternity.

Certain U.S. women dramatists, I will argue, explore this troubled maternity, in its social and political aspects, with impressive vigor. Interestingly, the garden, that symbol of feminine enclosure, of nature tamed, of postlapsarian redemption, becomes in their plays the space of maternity gone bad. My focus will be on Jane Bowles's *In the Summer House* (1953),[4] particularly Joanne Akalaitis's production of it in August 1993, but my discussion will include Elizabeth Robins's *Alan's Wife* (1893) and Susan Glaspell's *The Verge* (1921). For these American dramatists the maternal garden was "a mess"—a space that encroached upon domestic interiors, that troubled gender relations, that, more subtly, produced a "spacing" in seemingly realist dialogue and characterization by dividing "the present from what it [seemed to be]." In referring to this spacing as the play's rebus, I want to recall that the word derives from the Latin *res*, for "thing." The rebus discloses words, not in their meaningfulness (though meaning is never fully suspended) but in their materiality. The materiality I am tracing here is the maternal signifier across various theater texts, but my larger project concerns theater in the cultural matrix. For Freud the rebus was a provocative challenge to interpretation. How might we read the rebus?

UR-GARDENS IN ROBINS AND GLASPELL

In May 1893, when Elizabeth Robins was to appear in repertory performances of Ibsen's major plays in London, she performed in a one-acter, which she cowrote (anonymously) with Florence Bell, entitled *Alan's Wife*. Subtitled "a dramatic study in three scenes," the text lacked the symmetry and balance of the Ibsenite structure Robins claimed to admire and focused instead on the convergence of "new woman" sensibilities—social independence, sexual assertiveness— and cultural proscriptions of same. Exploiting the rage for medico-criminal naturalism, *Alan's Wife* dramatizes an infanticide carried out by Jean Creyke, an exuberant young woman in a Northern English village who can't stand to raise her deformed son after her young husband, her glorious swaggering "master," dies in a mill accident. Like all Ibsenites, Robins found Nietzsche's cultural poetics both inspiring and dramatically usable. In this brief "study" of female criminality, she pits her glorious nature-loving strong ones—Jean and Alan—against the Christian conformism and mean mindedness of the village curate, Jean's mother, and, ultimately, her incarcerators. Arrested for the act, she goes willingly to prison and to her execution, refusing in the last scene to speak—symbolic of her rejection of the discourse of penance or redemption but also effecting a curious spacing in the performance. In the Robins text, stage directions supplant speech; action is suspended between page and stage, not fully realizable in either medium.[5]

The first scene rewrites the classic naturalism of lower-class life with an unusual signifying geometry. The stage is bisected by a "village street," and at a right angle to the street is the side of the Creyke cottage, leaving a triangular space at the center of the stage where Jean's mother sits, where a female neighbor stops to chat, and where Jean will serve Alan's hot meal when he comes home from the mill. As a female space of nature and nurturance, the garden also becomes the space of trauma when the mutilated male is brought home on a stretcher, and when, implicitly, the fetus of the pregnant Jean is similarly mutilated. Yet we understand that if Jeans's garden/body is defiled it is not by tragic fate but by an already guilty nature—her nonconformity, her outspokenness, and most of all her erotic identification with the sensuous Alan. In the popular Victorian imagination an overindulgent eroticism was typical of malingering hysterics. As a mother who kills her child, Jean becomes punishable by a culture that has little tolerance for female independence. As a corollary, the mother-child connection, far from sustaining Jean in her loneliness, perversely incites her to murder. A half-century later, social psychologists will say that mothers, by virtue of being mothers, can barely control their murderous instincts. But in the 1890s, the "angel in the house" ideology had by no means exhausted its influence. *Alan's Wife* disgusted its reviewers and the play was withdrawn after only two performances.

By 1921, in Susan Glaspell's *The Verge* at the Provincetown Playhouse, the garden had become a scientifically controlled environment and the social psychology of motherhood had become the object of complicated scrutiny. As Barbara Ehrenreich and Deirdre English have written, "scientific motherhood" in the 1920s and 1930s was "to bring the home into harmony with industrial conditions," in other words, to inculcate, through mothering, "obedience, punctuality and good citizenship" in the future work force of the United States before it "ever heard of trade unions or socialism."[6] In the 1920s, the Rockefeller Foundation spent more than 7 million dollars in the founding of institutes nationwide devoted to the standardization of child rearing. Women were not to be trusted in this management, however; rather they were expected to follow to the letter the advice of experts in the crucial rearing of "the little child" (p. 209). As a not unimportant epiphenomenon of this hierarchy of knowledge and service, the "new woman" and the "woman question" faded as disturbances to patriarchal authority. With the granting of universal suffrage to women in the United States, feminist advocacy soon lost its edge. But in Glaspell's botanical laboratory that edge—and maternity itself—is reconfigured in the experimental Edge Vine, one of the Claire Archer's efforts at smashing the "forms moulded for us," to achieve an "outness—and otherness."[7]

Radically refunctioning the scientist/expert as a creative woman who mothers plants, not American children, Glaspell was, however, unable to rewrite the gender script. As Claire moves farther "out" with her sui generis Breath of Life, as she is forced to confront her conventional daughter (raised by her sister to adopt traditionally gendered views), as she attempts to forge a love affair with the one man she believes understands her, her thoughts become increasingly erratic. As was the case for countless real and fictional female hysterics, a "nerve specialist" is brought in who confirms her husband Harry's diagnosis: "You're sick, Claire. There's no denying it" (p. 92). And, as in Robins's *Alan's Wife*, the incipiently criminal woman—the woman whose Nietzschean creativity/negativity puts her at odds with the mercantilist progressivism of her husband, her sister, and the gender script of true womanhood—becomes an actual criminal. Claire chokes her would-be lover and ends the play with her body reduced to mechanical jerks while she sings the Christian hymn she has mocked throughout the play, "Nearer My God to Thee."

If *The Verge* seems to capitulate to "fallen-woman" plots, Glaspell takes Claire's "sickness" into innovative areas, effecting a spacing of the Ibsenite dialectic (Nietzschean independence versus socioreligious/gender conformity). Consider Claire's obsession with discursive limitation—"[Adelaide] always smothers it with the word for it" (p. 91)—and her own "hysterical" discourse, her movement into poetic language, which seems directed toward, or is solicited by, an unknown but powerful Other. Like her Provincetown colleague, Eugene O'Neill, Glaspell explores expressionistic settings—the laboratory, the tower—paying special attention to inner and outer areas, the orifices in ceiling and floor. Finally, the sexuality of Clair herself unravels the Ibsenite dialectic, almost to the point of incoherence. Taking pains to individuate the males in Claire's life, Glaspell also reduces them to a banality of phallic desire: Tom, Dick, and Harry. The killing of Tom, who, for Claire, signifies and thus stultifies beauty, is translated into a "gift"—but destined for whom?

Here Glaspell prefigures the absolute expenditure of Beckett's female fictions, particularly Mouth in *Not I*, who attempts through agonizing ellipses to satisfy and reject the juridical discourse of an Other. In the last moments of *The Verge*, as she jerks her head from left to right ("a cross") while speaking the lines of the Christian hymn, Claire involves us not in some spiritual awakening but in a failed interpellation, her inability to take a position in the socio-symbolic network. Claire's otherness is, in realist terms, the ideological position of anyone labeled sick, but only when Glaspell spaces the structure of dialectical realism is she able to signify beyond "[her] own dead things" the dead plot structures that "block the way" (p. 77). Most crucial is the signifier of Claire's eccentric garden where what she cultivates has no forebears or heirs, no recognizable form or function, where the growing space exceeds the limits of knowledge and mimes instead the "long and flowing pattern" that ultimately swallows and negates.

"IN THE SUMMER HOUSE" IN THE FIFTIES

For creations without forebears or heirs Tennessee Williams had a special affection. At the first production of *In the Summer House*, at the University of Michigan's Lydia Mendelssohn Theater in Ann Arbor, May 1953, Williams saw

> a piece of dramatic literature that stands altogether alone, without antecedents and without descendants, unless they spring from the one and only Jane Bowles. It is not only the most original play I have ever read, I think it also is the oddest and funniest and one of the most touching. Its human perceptions are both profound and delicate; its dramatic poetry is both elusive and gripping. It is one of those very rare plays which are not tested by the theater but by which the theater is tested.[8]

Of course, critics in the early fifties, like their counterparts in the nineties, rarely respond favorably to plays that test them. Fiercely nonconformist, Bowles, a relatively "out" lesbian, startled everyone with her unapologetic focus on intimacy between women and in her darkly humorous exploration of the pathologies of maternity. From its opening in Ann Arbor to its stunted Broadway run in November 1953, the critics were either enraged or annoyed, and their tropes had a familiar ring: "a morbid [Victorian code word for "hysterical"] study of . . . psychic difficulties whose . . . chief weakness is that all the important characters were, in varying degrees, mentally deranged . . . the mother is inhumanly ambitious [read: afflicted with "penis envy"], brittle and superficial. The daughter is drawn cruelly by the author—a doltish, lumpy and dull girl . . ."[9] We will consider more of this "expert" testimony in a moment.

In the opening of *In the Summer House*, Gertrude Eastman Cuevas, knitting on the balcony of her old beachfront house "somewhere in Southern California," gazes across a wide garden strewn with "ragged cactus plants and broken ornaments" to summon her daughter Molly, who sits sequestered in a small, vine-covered summer house. The space that divides and connects this mother and daughter will be the play's main thematic thread, but that thread unravels quickly. Realist dialogue and characterization are encroached upon by signifiers of psychic space: the unstated fears and aggressions that, recurrently in Bowles's work, are the effects of intimacy. She gives Gertrude too many motives, or too few. Because she is devoted to her father's joy-killing credo of "idealism, backbone, and ambition" (p. 280), because she is anxious about her moribund relations with the inert Molly, and because she is worried about money, Gertrude declares her inclination to take a second Hispanic husband, Mr. Solares, who comes on stage bringing picnic food and an entourage of female relatives including his sister Fula Lopez and her daughter Frederica. The slovenly good spirits and spontaneous affection of the Mexicans—Bowles's racism is painfully unselfconscious—contrast obviously to Molly's and Gertrude's anomie. Refracting the latter, too, are Mrs. Constable and her daughter Vivien, both loquacious and "nervous," Vivien attaching herself immediately to Gertrude and invading, without being asked, Molly's summer house in order to get away from her overprotective mother. The only significant male in the play, a young man from St. Louis called Lionel, is fleeing the mercantilist demands of his family. He grows attached to the laconic Molly because she only half listens to him.

Bringing the three mother-daughter pairs together with Lionel in a chaotic first scene, Bowles soon moves them all to the beach where, by the end of scene two, Vivien has fallen from, leaped from, or been pushed by Molly from the ocean cliffs. In the third scene, a double wedding celebration in the garden for Gertrude and Molly (in which no grooms appear until the end), Molly declares her love for Gertrude, begs her to stay, and, as the now-alcoholic Mrs. Constable snores in the grass nearby, is rebuffed.[10] In Act II less happens, but the structure becomes more conventional.

Lionel and Molly work in and live above The Lobster Bowl, an anonymous, seedy bar and restaurant. Two letters arrive, one from Gertrude announcing that she hates married life in Mexico and hinting at a permanent reunion with Molly, the other from Lionel's brother inviting him to work in St. Louis. As far back as the well-made play extends, letters from "outside" divert and provoke action: indeed, the act ends with Molly pushed to choose between Gertrude and Lionel. Bowles wrote and rewrote this act, unable to settle on Molly's decision.[11] In one version, Molly commits suicide, in another she stays with Gertrude, and in still another she runs to Lionel and the conventional safety he represents. As we will note later, the printed text uses this last version, leaving Gertrude a broken figure of pain and defeat, now facing a long night's journey into loneliness and isolation.

The 1950s was a decade that featured powerful mothers. Mary Tyrone in Eugene O'Neill's *Long Day's Journey Into Night* (1956), semi-invalided from a morphine addiction, recalls the grand guignol melodrama of nineteenth- and early twentieth-century bourgeois wives and mothers who took to their beds from undiagnosable ills and pains (the common description of hysteria) and drained their families of patience, love, and eventually money. At the end of the decade, Lorraine Hansberry's *A Raisin in the Sun* (1959) provided a wholly different maternal image. Lena Younger, ever supportive of family and unity and integrity, is the force that moves them all to confront racism and an uncertain future. In the last moments of the play, she returns to her empty apartment to grab a scrawny plant that she has tended throughout, a metonym for an unseen garden, a sign of continuity and growth.

While Mary Tyrone and Lena Younger are both believable fictions and super-real icons, Bowles's Gertrude Eastman Cuevas, with her Anglo-Hispanic name, is deliberately contradictory. *Cueva* is Spanish for *cave*, and Eastman would suggest to any American spectator the multi-million-dollar Eastman Kodak Company (founded in 1892), a testimony not only to successful robber-baron industrialism (Eastman's was the first U.S. firm to mass produce a standardized product) but to a technology that replaces the subjective imprecision of mimesis (representation) with a scientifically precise copy (reproduction). When Plato used the cave metaphor in *The Republic*, it was to debunk what he believed were the delusional mirroring powers of mimesis. But the cave is a slippery metaphor, signifying something both internal and open, as in the maternal womb. In Luce Irigaray's contemporary formulation, Plato's cave allegory amounts to a violent repression of maternal origins. The feminine womb (which she provocatively calls "Plato's hystera") is the site not only of human reproduction but also of spectacular representation, a "scene of reflection" producing both real and "fake offspring."[12] Thus Irigaray doesn't merely overturn masculine mimesis with feminine maternity, but she claims mimesis and maternity as features of a complex female materiality. Plato's idealism, she argues, is rooted in his turn away from, his fearful forgetting of, this multivalent female body.

Gertrude's respect for idealism and ambition, and her distaste for the earthy, affectionate Mexicans ("I don't like pleasures. I like idealism, and backbone, and ambition. I take after my father"), suggest she would also like to forget the maternal. Indeed, Molly, her "own flesh and blood . . . saps [her] vitality" (p. 208). Then, too, while Eastman Cuevas, her masculine family names, invoke two quite different versions of mimesis, Gertrude is also a tawdry version of her Shakespearean namesake: both are lured by phallic privilege rather than by maternal identification. Bowles's Gertrude "takes after" her father, but as a woman, she, like *Hamlet*'s Gertrude, has power (or financial security) only through marriage. That Gertrude Eastman Cuevas's scheme falls miserably short of her expectations reiterates the contradictory thwartedness Bowles builds into both her name and her situation.

Her situation: Bowles's realism in this play would seem to have little to do with the snapshots of American life generated by the Eastman Kodak Brownies that in the 1950s were finding their way into every American home. But, if we think of these photos as both material objects and bits of a rebus, a nonrepresentational picture-puzzle, we come close to Bowles's spacing in the play, her ability to suggest a dividedness within the present. As director JoAnne Akalaitis puts it, [the play] resists the traditional forms of storytelling so familiar in the American theatre. It, instead, forms a fabric like a surrealistic painting that provides an emotional ambience for the story of a daughter's struggle with her mother that can be ferociously felt and highly ridiculous at the same time.[13]

Before turning to Akalaitis's production, I want to suggest that some of this felt ferocity is attributable to Bowles's deadly accurate sense of the misogyny of the 1950s, which seeps into the characterization and language of the play and produces her uniquely undecidable ("spaced"-out) entities. If in the writing of Gertrude's opening monologue-cum-dialogue Bowles prefigures Beckett's Winnie (*Happy Days*, 1961) and Pinter's Meg (*The Birthday Party*, 1959), Bowles's vision is ultimately quite different, for she presents maternity and femininity with a sense of its social-psychic history. Gertrude, Mrs. Constable, Fula, Molly, Vivien and Frederica spring not from the male imaginary but from female (un)consciousness shaped in part by the social discourses of her time.

Let's recall the professional discourse on mothers and mothering in the 1950s. Ehrenreich and English note that factory-inspired mothering gave way to the demands of "an economy more and more dependent on individual consumption—of cars, housing and domestic goods" (p. 212). Permissiveness now became the best line for child rearing, helping to inculcate in both parents and children the pleasure of buying. To sustain the permissive environment mothers had to provide "unquestioning, spontaneous, warm, all-enfolding love. This was not the measured love of the scientific mother, the austere love of the morally righteous mother, or the long-suffering love of the martyred mother" (p. 220). In the 1950s, mothers were expected to find, in mothering itself, their hearts' desire: "mother and child [were expected to] enjoy each other, fulfilling one another's needs perfectly, instinctively" (p. 221–22). American women, tending toward penis envy (the psychiatric code word for "too ambitious"), were now told to quit work and fulfill themselves in domesticity; if they felt unfulfilled, they, not the domestic ideal, were to blame. Indeed, by mid-century psychiatrists were witnessing abundant symptoms of distress in children, and they were quick to blame mother. But, having stressed the instinctual side to mothering, they were forced to conclude that some women—perhaps all women—had bad instincts, were in fact instinctually perverse. In *Maternal Care and Mental Health*, first published 1951, John Bowlby described the most devastating kind of pervert, the rejecting mother.[14] She was responsible for the "deprived child" who, in ever-increasing numbers, had become "a source of social infection as real and serious as carriers of diphtheria and typhoid" (p. 230). The rejecting mother had an even darker twin, the overprotective mother, who back in 1943 was already being targeted for destroying the virility of American males. The offspring of these demon mothers had predictable symptoms. Rejecting mothers produced passive, insecure, frightened children; overprotective mothers, who ranged from dominant to submissive, created either tyrannical children or ones that were too docile (p. 232).

With uncanny accuracy Bowles offers carefully distorted, affectionate, even loving representations of both the rejecting and the overprotective mother, Gertrude Eastman Cuevas and Mrs. Constable, respectively, as well as their "abnormal" offspring: the inert, fearful Molly, product of both rejection and domination; and the uncontrollable Vivien, the result of submissive overprotection. Bowles even provides fragments of the psychobabble of the 1950s, itself reminiscent of nineteenth-century Victorian doctors. "I am the nervous type," Mrs. Constable announces (p. 225). Vivien, to Gertrude's dismay, never uses "controls": "When I feel myself going up I just go on up until I hit the ceiling. I'm like that" (p. 226). Describing another character, Inez, Lionel speaks for both mid-1950s psychiatrists and Victorian nerve doctors in describing the inherent contradictions of females: "Inez is a grown-up woman. A kind of sturdy rock-of-Gibralter type but very high strung and nervous too. Every now and then she blows up" (p. 234).[15] At the end of the play, when the conventional realist plot calls for life-changing revelations, Lionel becomes the voice of truth, which also reiterates the testimony of experts about domineering mothers. "You're using her," he tells Gertrude, "You need Molly. You don't love her. You're using her. . . . Let her go, if you love her at all, let her go away . . ." (p. 284). Anyone remembering struggles with her or his own mother would find these words affecting. My point is that, if Bowles opens up accesses to emotion for late-twentieth-century spectators, it is because she retains, as in the rebus, signifiers of *the real* of cultural discourse even as she rejects the motivational logic of realist plotting. What remains is as real and as disturbing as dreams. The rebuslike play defies a stable, penetrable interiority (the rebus has no inside/outside); it is, rather, permeable, spacious, what JoAnne Akalaitis calls a "landscape."

BOWLES WITH AKALAITIS

In her program notes, Akalaitis writes that *In the Summer House* "resists traditional forms of storytelling." The Vivian Beaumont Theater, site of Akalaitis's production in August 1993, did even more: it "knocked the play out of the realm of family drama and into [an] outdoor landscape." A smaller theater might have sunk the play into the "bathos" of American naturalism and stifled the "rhythms, dynamics, and emotional logic" of *In the Summer House*, which is "not at all naturalistic."[16] A founding member of the experimental performance company Mabou Mines, Akalaitis has directed, among many others, ground-breaking productions of Franz Xaver Kroetz's *Request Concert* and *Through the Leaves*, works not unlike Bowles's in their mixture of bleak domestic anguish and comedy. In those plays, however, the interiors of rooms, however sketchily built, enclose the action.[17] Bowles sets both acts outside of private rooms, and the Beaumont Theater, with its extremely wide proscenium stage, allowed designer George Tsypin the freedom to explore what outdoor or public spaces might become. Between Molly's summer house (downstage corner) and Gertrude's high balcony, Tsypin replaced Bowles's "ragged cactus plants and broken ornaments" with a large ornamented pillar fallen off its pedestal and, directly across, an enormous, grotesquely mishapen tree, trunk bent double to the ground and tubular dead limbs stretching like roots over the walking space of the stage. This stage image is recalled long after it materially disappears. In Act II, Mrs. Constable confesses to Molly that neither her dead daughter nor her husband loved her, nor did she love them: "My heart had fake roots . . . when the strain was over, they dried up . . . they shriveled and snapped" (p. 264). With rootlessness writ large at the outset—with the signs of *both* classical order and Mother Nature in "a mess"—Tsypin's summer house and beach house seemed to hover between substance and invisibility. We see Molly in her retreat through a wall of gauze, and Gertrude's house lacks even an illusionistic interior. The huge scrim filling the upper stage area with its purplish hills and neon blues of ocean and sky (through which, thanks to Jennifer Tipton's lighting, we seem to see for miles) subtly makes another thematic point. Molly hates the sea, and Gertrude loves it: taking our seats during a pleasing but monotonous soundtrack of softly crashing waves invites us into both emotions.[18]

The rebuslike, dreamlike nature of the play inspired Philip Glass's plaintive score for violin and viola, a surreal contrast to the rousing bandstand renditions of Mexican love songs performed by Frederica, Quintina, Esperanza, and Alta Gracia. Akalaitis's signature contribution to the play-as-rebus was to choreograph scenes as shapes.[19] At the beach, the characters sitting on brightly colored beachchairs form a perfect horizontal line across the wide stage (all except Molly who maintains the diagonal with her mother). At the beginning of Act I, scene iii, with both mother and daughter in wedding dress, under a banner declaring FELICIDAD the full company comes together in a phalanx pattern and performs a brief stomping dance, the referent for which, only parodically, is a nuptial celebration. With their expressionless faces and staccato body movements, the dancers seem possessed by rhythms, by drives that they cannot cognitively grasp. When Freud was first convinced that the hysterical paralysis of his patients had no organic basis, he explained their symptoms with the concept of "hysterical conversion," in which the feelings attached to an unremembered trauma are withheld from consciousness and diverted into bodily innervations. In hysteria, the physiological body is in effect supplanted by an erotogenic body, and it is this body Freud learned to listen to and interpret. Akalaitis's actors had for the duration of the dance hystericized bodies, that is, bodies driven by desires, terrors, and reminiscences that are inexpressible through discourse. The dance created a moment of pure ritual (the underside of all weddings) when, to paraphrase a line from Bowles's brilliant story, "Camp Cataract," life seemed to separate from the self. Put another way, the dance produced a nonrealist space in which drive-ridden, death-driven "life" became momentarily visible.

Although this astonishing image fades and the semisolid framework of hidden psychologies and self-absorbed characterization reforms, its "roots" in realism have been severed. Through choreography, through abstracted, almost vanishing sets, through a pruned script, Akalaitis produces a "rebus painting" in which boundaries between mind and Other, inner and outer, blur, where, as Virginia Woolf put it, "the ordinary appears ringed by the strange."[20] Using an amalgam of different Bowles texts, Akalaitis makes the death of Vivien ambiguous, thus giving Molly not one ghastly secret but a spectrum of inexpressible feelings including (but not limited to) jealousy and hate. Most importantly, she removed lines that Judith Anderson, playing Gertrude in the original production, demanded she be provided with in order to motivate her feelings about Molly's escape at the end of the play. According to Paul Bowles, a psychiatrist was brought in before the New York premiere. Apparently speaking for the penis-envy paradigm, he "kept wanting to know more about Gertrude's father."[21] Hence, Jane Bowles gave Anderson what she wanted: an Electra complex. Her Gertrude ends the play not unlike O'Neill's Mary Tyrone, her focus deflected from the living child she has lost to a reverie of her own childhood: "When I was a little girl. . . ." In her 1993 production, Akalaitis used an earlier Bowles script in which Molly runs out into the night, perhaps to Lionel, perhaps not, and Gertrude ends by reminding the inebriated Mrs. Constable that the summer house "was made of wood." Gertrude's messy garden with its large cathected objects is the "true" space of her maternal life. For Bowles, that space was neither more precious nor more mysterious than wood.

"I wish Ms. Akalaitis had more interest in elucidating the mysteries [of the play]. [She] emphasizes all that is surrealistic, pathological and outsized about *In the Summer House* . . . but not [its] everyday reality."[22] This amazing remark by the *New York Times* reviewer lacks even the self-consciousness of Brooks Atkinson who wondered, in his 1953 review, whether his "feeling of flatness" after the play was not due to his inability to appreciate Bowles's "chiaroscuro style."[23] Actually I agree with Atkinson, although, forty years later, I find this "flatness" both painful and exhilarating, a kind of permission to dive into the wreck, to explore spaces that are unlovely and unresolvable, to, in effect, read the rebus.

NOTES

1. Jacques Derrida, "Difference," in Alan Bass, trans., *Margins of Philosophy* (Chicago: University of Chicago Press, 1982), 13.
2. See Marjorie Perloff, *The Futurist Moment: Avant Garde, Avant Guerre, and the Language of Rupture* (Chicago: University of Chicago Press, 1986), 53.
3. See Janet Lyon, "Militant Discourse, Strange Bedfellows: Suffragettes and Vorticists Before the War," *Differences* 4, 2 (Summer 1992): 100–133.
4. Jane Bowles, *In the Summer House*, in *My Sister's Hand in Mine* (New York: Ecco Press 1978), 207. All references are to this edition.
5. See my "Mimesis, Mimicry, and the 'True-Real,'" *Modern Drama* 32, 1 (March 1989): 58–72.
6. Barbara Ehrenreich and Deirdre English, *For Her Own Good: 150 Years of the Experts' Advice to Women* (New York: Anchor Books, 1979), 207ff. All references are to this edition.
7. Susan Glaspell, *The Verge*, in C. W. E. Bigsby, ed., *Plays by Susan Glaspell* (Cambridge: Cambridge University Press, 1991), 64. All references are to this edition.
8. Cited in Millicent Dillon, *A Little Original Sin: The Life and Work of Jane Bowles* (New York: Holt, Rinehart and Winston, 1981), 227. All references are to this edition.
9. Cited in Dillion, *Original Sin*, 227. If penis envy as a legitimate category has been subverted in feminist psychoanalytic theory, it still has currency in psychoanalytic thought; it is derived from Freud's essays on female sexuality from "On the Sexual Theories of Children" (1908) through "Female Sexuality" (1931). For Freud, penis envy combined different elements of female sexuality: castration, resentment toward the mother for failing to provide a penis, and the wish for a (preferably) male child. Mid-century psychoanalytic thought emphasized self-denial as the key to feminine satisfaction (see Helene Deutsch, *The Psychology of Women* [New York: Bantam Books, 1973] as an antidote to congenital penis envy. Self-denial would at least allow women to have pleasure in heterosexual coitus. Holding on to girlhood penis envy (refusing self-denial) was thought to produce domineering mothers and overly ambitious women.
10. See Gayle Austin's important insights on Molly and Gertrude as brides

together in *Feminist Theories for Dramatic Criticism* (Ann Arbor: University of Michigan Press, 1990), 7off.

11. See Dillon's account of Bowles's writing and revisions, in *Original Sin*, 226–35.

12. Luce Irigaray, *Speculum of the Other Woman*, trans. Gillian C. Gill (Ithaca: Cornell University Press, 1985), 255.

13. Program insert for her production of *In the Summer House*, Vivian Beaumont Theater of Lincoln Center, New York. The production ran 1–22 August 1993.

14. Though Bowlby's book was enormously influential, his intent in its writing was not to demonize mothers but to record the effects of isolation on World War II war orphans, hospitalized children, and those who had been boarded in rural areas to protect them from air raids. Bowlby discovered that such infants were withdrawn, had lower IQs, and showed signs of autism. The problem, argue Ehrenreich and English, is that he extrapolated from his data a theory of home care. When citing reasons why families fall apart, he included "fulltime employment of the mother" along with "death of a parent" and "social calamity—war, famine" (Ehrenreich and English, *For Her Own Good*, 230). Bowlby's book provoked a volume of professional commentary; see, for example, *Deprivation of Maternal Care: A Reassessment of Its Effects* (New York: Shocken, 1966) by child psychiatrists Dane Prugh and Robert Harlow.

15. Inez is important for other reasons. Not introduced until Act II, she is both engagingly self-sufficient and a drudge. Through her Bowles tries out alternative forms of female identification/mimesis, as when Inez suggests to Molly: "Ever try modeling yourself after someone? . . . You just pick the right model and you watch how they act. I never modeled myself after anyone, but there were two or three who modeled after me" (p. 266). This is also a parody of ego-psychology doctrine as it filtered into the popular press.

16. JoAnne Akalaitis was kind enough to discuss the play with me in a phone conversation on 21 September 1993.

17. Ruby Cohn's long-standing support and admiration for the work of Mabou Mines (the group no longer exists as such, although former members frequently work together on projects) inspired me to write on Akalaitis's *In the Summer House* for this collection of essays in her honor.

18. The cast included, in the main roles, Dianne Wiest (Gertrude), Frances Conroy (Mrs. Constable), Alina Arenal (Molly), Kali Rocha (Vivien), Alma Martinez (Mrs. Lopez), Jaime Tirelli (Mr. Solares), Liev Schreiber (Lionel), Sheila Tousey (Inez), Karina Arroyave (Frederica), Mary Magdalena Hernandez (Esperanza), Carmen de la Paz (Alta Gracia), and Carmen Rosaria (Quintina).

19. Akalaitis is drawn to the image of horizontal, frontal presentation of her characters—as in her production of *Woyzeck* (Public Theater, New York, October 1992–January 1993), to cite just one example. In that production, too, she gathered her company into a stomping dance but this one in the French-Canadian folk style with fiddle accompaniment. In our conversation, Akalaitis said she saw no connection between the choreographies; she certainly hadn't been thinking of *Woyzeck* when she directed *In the Summer House*.

20. Virginia Woolf, "The Ghost Stories," in Leon Edel, ed., *Henry James: A Collection of Criticism* (Englewood Cliffs, N.J.: Prentice-Hall, 1963), 52–53.

21. Cited in Dillon, *Original Sin*, 231.

22. David Richards, "*In the Summer House* Preserves Its Riddles," *New York Times*, 8 August 1993.

23. Cited in Dillon, *Original Sin*, 227.

their own entrapment. To be known is a badge of public recognition. Not to be known, not to be recognized, produces fears of anonymity, phobias of self-extinction. Yet to be known can also be felt as a source of weakness and prompt feelings of transparency, which end in a compulsive fear of being watched and persecuted. In an age of universal surveillance, covert wars and political conspiracy, that delusion is not always a delusion. There still remains a sneaking suspicion that it can be true. What finds its full and flowing force in fantasy often has its basis in unpalatable fact. Technologies of watching are as never before.

Paranoia has always had a long tradition in the history of religious cults and their persecution by the state. But the most recent secular starting point of a schizoid culture in which paranoia and celebrity have combined in unlikely fusion was the breakdown of consensus that began in the 1960s with the Civil Rights movement, political assassination, uprisings in American cities, and the conflicts over the Vietnam War. About the assassinations of King and the Kennedys conspiracy theories still abound. Some of the better ones cannot be disproved and as the events recede in time probably never will. In the American theater these monumental events have been conspicuous largely by their absence. Because they have been acted out as live social dramas, instantly reported by press and television and then constantly recycled, stage drama has found them too preformed. The same is not true of film or fiction where they have featured more widely as open-ended narratives of detection. The assassination of John Kennedy and the Watergate cover-up have both been "dramatized" for the cinema and fueled in the 1970s the revival of American film noir as a genre now acquiring political overtones. The novels of Robert Stone and others have obliquely charted the descent of American politics into an open-ended paranoia of secret surveillance wars, a force field taken to extremes in the paranoid fictions of Don DeLillo. In the 1980s these culminate in *Libra*, DeLillo's chilling fictional reinvention of the life of Lee Harvey Oswald. DeLillo's work is the compelling side of the fictive recreation of history. The less serious is the Hollywood mythlogizing of the recent past, which finds more expression in Oliver Stone's stylish but simplistic moral melodrama, *JFK*.

Of course, there has been important geopolitical drama with topical references. *The Archbishop's Ceiling, Principia Scriptoriae,* and *Death and the Maiden* spring immediately to mind. Most of it, however, is not set in the United States, and the documentary element in such work is always downplayed. It sits uneasily with the history of the American theater with its endless renewals of melodrama in different guises and also with the ludic turn in much of the new playwriting. Here much dramatic writing since 1970 defines itself in a unique manner by playing reflexively upon the performative culture of its age. It is a bold play on playfulness, upon the fix of game playing, a theatrical gloss in the mind-set of performance. Whereas the American novel oscillates between naturalistic precision and transcendental fabulation—for what else is *Gravity's Rainbow?*—the new drama has developed a more unified form. It is not under the same pressure as narrative writing to come to terms with what Adorno once called the cult of information, and hence, iconoclastically, to subvert that cult through an aesthetic "modern" moment. If, arguably, American theater is not as ambitious in this respect as the fiction of the period, it is equally as powerful. Its characters invent their roles with daring existential ingenuity. They seem to orchestrate, or better still improvise, their performances with great panache on the verge of despair. In the process performance is no longer a Stanislavskian conceit for revealing the "inner" self or revealing character. It becomes the nature of character itself.

I perform, therefore I am. This is not only the key to the players' brittle identity. It also explains their constant desperation at the prospect of its loss. To cease performing is to cease being. That element of desperation that we find in *Geography of a Horse Dreamer, Action, The House of Blue Leaves,* and *American Buffalo* has its source in the material motives of everyday life, in the need to survive amid adversity. But these motives quickly become lost as the means of enacting them take over. Characters start out wishing to achieve material goals but end by desperately aiming for visceral impact by any means. Meanwhile their captive audience of fellow performers onstage usually ignores them. Sometimes the listening is partial, a token listening in which performer and watcher fail to connect. At other times reflexive performers are forced to act themselves out entirely in a vacuum, as Hoss, the fading rock star, does in Shepard's *Tooth of Crime*. They go through their evanescent skills of performance, but the audience is no longer there. Or, if it is there, it is not *all* there. Its attention is elsewhere. Everyone performs, but no one listens. The legacy of Beckett and Pinter is ever clear. To commune is also to evade. But American writing differs. The evasion somehow is never accepted. It is defiantly opposed and the fading powers of persuasion must be renewed with even greater intensity. Thus, performers feel they have to be excessive in order to be heard. The key to performance lies in the imagined subtleties of that excess. Here the Goffmanesque presentation of self in everyday life becomes hyperreal, deranged. Overemphasis is normal. Excess is diurnal. The wired personas who perform seem not to trust the senses of their spectators to be anything less than impaired.

The watershed for the new drama was, as suggested, the Vietnam War. The political loss of innocence it engendered was real enough, but the countercultural celebration of that loss was hyperreal. The loss quickly became a living myth, a convenient legend of the Fall out of which all kinds of casual pathos could spring. The reflexive nature of modernity had started to become less a form of insight and more, at times, a sickness-unto-death, the plaything of what Tom Wolfe called "the Me Generation." At the same time the brutality of the war had started to enter into domestic life. In American fiction, Stone turns the hilarious, utopian journal of the Kesey commune by Tom Wolfe, *The Electric Kool-Aid Acid Test*, into a paranoid, dystopian parable of drug running in *Dog Soldiers*. A more moderate but similar transition can be seen in Michael Weller's drama, between the good-natured Chekhovian iconoclasm of the college generation of *Moonchildren* in 1970 and the paranoid drug visions that end *Fishing* five years later. In Sam Shepard the cosy, fantasizing 1960s beach party of *Icarus's Children* atrophies into the solipsistic 1970s anticommune of *Action* with its paranoid drug monologues delivered over a disastrous Christmas dinner in a cabin in the wilderness. Ideals of community deteriorate quickly into paranoia and conspiracy as Watergate becomes a double-edged sword, suggesting the discovery of conspiracies that are only the tip of the iceberg. Yet the paranoid mind cannot cope with the enormity of its own delusions and seeks solace elsewhere. A few years later, narcotic visions of human happiness collapse into pipe dreams of celebrity as the Hollywood studios reassert their global power in the age of Ronald Reagan. Yet the Vietnam legacy sticks. To paraphrase Yeats, all is changed and changed utterly. David Rabe, the most powerful of all American playwrights to deal with Vietnam, makes the point with some irony in *Sticks and Bones* where the reality of Vietnam is stronger in the pathos of the blind David's homecoming than the world reentered, a world that is hyperreal and drowned in the clichés of television. The veteran's family, Rick, Ozzie, and Harriet, is thus based, with macabre humor, on the family of a postwar TV sit-com and is itself bound up in the world of television. Vietnam, as senseless battlefield becomes continuing nightmare, evokes not the surreal world Coppola later made of it in *Apocalypse Now* but the lost world of mimesis. Stateside, by comparison, the world to which David returns has become a hyperreal artifact constructed by electronic culture.

The one play that marks this transitional point with searing and unparalleled power is John Guare's *The House of Blue Leaves*. It is worth noting that, although Guare had the first act performed in Connecticut in 1966, it was not until 1971 that the completed play opened in New York. On Guare's own account, seeing productions of Strindberg and Feydeau in London, with Laurence Olivier in both, crystallized his dramatic vision. One cannot help but think that the upheaval and tumult of the United States in the intervening five years was just as important. This is tragicomedy at its zaniest and its darkest. But, unlike Chekhov, there is no clear transition of mood. The zanier it becomes, the darker it becomes, and vice versa. Its tragicomic mood hinges on dependency, the dependence of the Shaughnessy household on the forms of celebrity in the world at large. Artie dreams of doing music scores for Hollywood movies; his girlfriend Bunny rushes to greet the Pope's cavalcade on his peace visit to New York. The "celebrity" of the Pope might after all stop the war in Vietnam, which is threatening to take away their son Ronnie. Ronnie himself has other ideas. He takes the sinister option that so obsessed the American psyche after Kennedy's assassination and plans to throw a bomb at His Holiness, his potential savior. His plan farcically misfires, and the bomb blows up a much lesser version of celebrity, Corinna, the one-picture movie actress whom Artie mistakenly regards as his ticket to Hollywood. For the crazed family trapped in their apartment in Queens, there are two options: to latch onto the world of celebrity or take revenge on it and destroy it. But the world of celebrity, as Ronnie finds out, is too big to destroy. Instead it is the desperate and vulnerable family that self-destructs. Deprived of his arrested son and his dream of Hollywood, Artie strangles Bananas, his schizophrenic wife, who has withdrawn into her own world and only moves out of it to kiss the Pope whenever he appears on her TV screen.

Earlier, the deranged but strangely moving elision of paranoia and celebrity by Bananas, in her vision of cruising Broadway in their old green Buick, encapsulates the dilemma of the whole family. The dream-wish to join the famous turns into a nightmare of insanity in a world still trying to recover from the death of JFK: "Four corners. Four people. One on each corner. All waving for taxis. Cardinal Spellman. Jackie Kennedy. Bob Hope. President Johnson. All carrying suitcases. Taxi! Taxi! I stop in the middle of the street—in the middle of Broadway—and I get out of my Green Latrine and I yell, 'Get in, I'm a gypsy, a gypsy cab. I'll take you where you all want to go. Don't you all know each other? Get in! Get in!' "[1] But Bananas merely sets the famous against her and each other: they all come to blows in the chaos of the Manhattan traffic before each gets into a separate cab and deserts her. One already feels the weight of the mythic reference here. Without the defining presence of the absent JFK, the center cannot hold; things fall apart.

In true American tradition, Guare's play discounts the happy-family scenario of the American Dream. But, unlike Arthur Miller, economic failure and the breakdown of intimacy seem secondary. What counts as recognition is fame; but fame is a fantasy, a desperate telephone call to Billy Einhorn, Artie's boyhood friend, now a well-known movie director living in Bel Air. The apartment in Queens is where the action is not. Artie's songs in the living room with piano accompaniment are an act of desperation. They are not the inspired lyrics of a popular musical, for Guare's play is an antimusical. Artie is singing songs to an audience that is not there but, like Beckett's

Godot, is eternally awaited. Yet Einhorn, the shrewd movie director, resists Artie's play for belated fame by reassuring him that what he does have is the solidity of the common person. He is a necessary part of the necessary audience of Hollywood in a reliable place like Queens, and he should stay there. For Billy, Queens is real and Hollywood depends on it. For Artie, Queens is unreal, and neither he nor Hollywood has any need of it. It is a delusion that eventually destroys him. He is mentally between worlds, wired for fame and nourishing fantasies but physically stuck in his family apartment where murdering is a false and tragic compensation.

The double take of celebrity occurs again in the opening of Guare's *Landscape of the Body*. A man and a woman on a New England ferry pass the Kennedy compound at Hyannisport and remark on its famous inhabitants. Suddenly their personas are revealed as Marvin Holohan, a New York detective, and Betty Yearn, a woman he wrongly suspects of brutally murdering her son. Their concrete identities place them at the more sordid end of human psychodrama. Fame for Betty could only be vicious notoriety and for Holohan the buzz of making a dubious but spectacular arrest. Fame for Betty so far in her life has consisted of brief appearances in soft-porn movies. Both are pale shadows of the spectacular, locked in mutual distrust and surveying the squalor of life all around them.

During the Vietnam War the plight of a divided America created a dilemma for the emerging counterculture. Utopia provided a spur to the unlimited pursuit of freedom, yet politics created a deep fear of being under surveillance by an omnipotent technocratic state. The counterculture permitted everything, but the technocratic state permitted nothing. The ideological paradox was never resolved and created a radical devaluation of values, which led to the disintegration of the counterculture. Existing moralities were deemed corrupt, yet the euphoria of utopian action was supposed to make all morality redundant anyway. The result was the felt absence of a true moral censor in a polarized society. The counterculture quickly discovered that no amount of sexual freedom, avant-gardism, narcotics, or street revolt could deliver lasting utopia. As Christopher Lasch

observed in *The Culture of Narcissism*, the more ecstatically performative self-dramatizations of the counterculture easily fed back
into the mainstream of American life. Sexuality, narcissism, and psychodrama became commodified as sellable items of consumer culture
and the electronic media, items sold, that is, as pleasure without
guilt, action without moral limit. But the lack of a credible morality
remains a felt absence at a level not always conscious during this
period, seldom explicit. It is to this predicament that American
drama explosively responds.

In this response to the devaluation of values, paranoia is central. As
a deluded perception, literally, of the nearby Other who stands outside
and theatens the self but may yet be part of the self, paranoia occupies
an extreme place in the pantheon of human guilt. Paranoid behavior
invokes a radical displacement of a guilt that derives from intense
feelings of worthlessness onto the imagined conspiratorial actions of
others, often invisible. Paranoic guilt comes not so much from the
violation of constraining rules but from the absence of any credible
rules based on moral principles that obviate worthlessness. The subject
feels he or she is operating in a vacuum and, to compensate, invents an
imaginary world of threatening presences. The euphoria in which
everything is permitted rapidly deteriorates into the isolation in which
the bruised ego feels itself permanently under attack. Delusions of
grandeur turn into scenarios of fear, betrayal, and mistrust.

Here celebrity plays a specific and surprising role. It becomes a
psychic compulsion to pure being, a means of warding off the nothingness of anonymity. For to be anonymous now means to be alone. It is
this anonymity that Hoss fears most of all in Shepard's *The Tooth of
Crime*, in which Crow, the upstart, makes a play for the rock star's
crown. To lose the audience about whom he is already paranoid is a fate
worse than death. Hoss plays a deadly game he knows he must win,
but in his paranoid state the world now seems dominated by universal
game playing from which there is no escape. His suicide is informed by
this particular phobia. Even winning against Crow would bring no end
to the agnostic game playing that is the only means of survival. The
paranoia of Hoss is both the fear of being watched and of not being
watched, of being turned into stone by millions of prying eyes, on the

one hand, but on the other being rendered extinct by not being watched at all. He is "stuck in his image" and no longer has a residual self on which he can fall back.

The petrified image of Hoss is underpinned by the number of records he continues to sell. Image in that sense is not all. Symbolic capital is underwritten by economic capital. Here the counterculture seems not an adversary but a subversive extension of a culture of risk that is at the center of things American. This comes out clearly in the plays of David Mamet, where the dilemmas of American capitalism are not moral but tactical. In *American Buffalo* and *Glengarry Glen Ross* Mamet's characters are not so much outsiders as thieves with one foot firmly planted in the "legality" of the market. Donny's resale shop can equally resell items that have been legitimately purchased and goods that are stolen property. In their fly-by-night real-estate office, Shelley Levene and Ricky Roma are trying to sell gullible clients worthless land, which nonetheless bears a legal title. In both plays there are prices and conditions but few rules and no morality. In the service of profit, anything goes. Yet the free play of the market to which rules are secondary creates its own forms of fear and terror, above all of the failure of nerve in the art of duplicity. Can Levene and Roma sustain their masquerades until they close their deals? Can Teach convince Donny that his planned robbery will not only succeed but bring in something of value? Can anyone in the vortex of agnostic free-fall trust anyone else? The culture of risk prompts the adrenalin to flow in vivid performance, but it confronts its players with a void from which their bad faith just—and only just—diverts their attention. They cannot question too closely the absence of value that underpins their world. Yet that absence always shadows them.

Mamet has been criticized, at times rightly, for his misogyny and his obsession with male bonding. But his best work rolls back both these criticisms. Significantly, it is *House of Games*, a feature film, not a stage play, that has produced his most credible female protagonist, and much depends here on the outstanding performance of Lindsay Crouse. In his best drama, particularly *American Buffalo*, *Glengarry Glen Ross*, and *Sexual Perversity in Chicago*, the male fear of women is not evaded but clinically dissected in a clear ambience of homoerotic attraction. Freud's rather one-sided view of paranoia as a form of repressed homosexuality in which the subject obsessively fears the watching that might expose his libido, certainly finds some vindication in Mamet's dramaturgy. Central to this is the act of seduction. For these plays are not merely about the risks of capital, they are equally about the risks of seduction, and at key moments the two are powerfully elided. In *Sexual Perversity* the heterosexual boasting of Bernie and Danny contains a fear of sexual inadequacy increased by the more relaxed and possibly erotic relationship between Deborah and Joan. The sexual ambiguities here, one might conjecture, are ones that lend themselves powerfully to all-female casting, thus belying the false image of machismo that often distorts responses to the play. In *American Buffalo,* where the women, Grace and Ruthie, are never present but are still a sexual threat, the homoerotic element is clearer. Teach and Bobby are rival suitors for Donny's approval, hoping to prove themselves through robbery. In this vein, when things go seriously wrong, the paranoid Teach angrily describes himself as Donny's "nigger" and his "wife," derogatory terms of submission that reveal the sharp edge of his self-hatred but also his ambiguous sexual role. Yet for Mamet sexual seduction is no more a true possession of the body than the power of money is a true possession of the goods purchased. They always have a stand-in value, and the objects they may fleetingly possess always elude them. The coin desired by Donny and his thieves, with its predatory image of the hunted buffalo, has no authenticated value. It is what predators make of it.

On the surface, Teach's bravado displays a wide spectrum of male American values: the shunning of fear, the discounting of risk, the reckless readiness to go in with a gun. But on a deeper level, one recalls Sartre's reading of Genet's larceny as the erotic risk and fear of being caught in the act, of the secret desire to be caught in the act. Hence Teach's strange lack of attention to detail in the plan that Donny soon teases out of him. The constant fear of being watched, the overwrought suspicion of cruising police cars, the paranoia of a pure sound—whether it be a ringing telephone or a noise in the street—reveal Teach's suspicion as an extreme symptom of unacknowledged guilt. It is a guilt that in his closed world of male bonding cannot be acknowledged, for robbery is never a moral issue, only a tactical one. The bravado of the planned act will bring, he hopes, recognition, respect, and passing celebrity. But the secret fear of being caught brings back repressed guilt. Mamet's dramatic power is based on the swift, unpredictable oscillation between these two extremes. The play's dramatic tension is based on the audience never being sure which of the two extremes will finally play itself out.

Mamet inverts the common relationship between paranoia and celebrity. Celebrity here seems to be local, while paranoia is universal. Thus, Teach seems to fear everything around him but wants recognition as a successful thief from his small circle of friends. In the real-estate office of *Glengarry Glen Ross* the ambience is similarly close and obsessive. The top salesman's prize is a Cadillac. The limit of material ambition matches the trivial aspirations of the salesmen to that of their clients. But the downside is starker. Since failure means being fired, the atmosphere of distrust is all-pervasive. The prided possession of the American highway is no match for the cutthroat competition that ends in robbery. Shelley Levene shows us how the performance of deceit has become almost Pavlovian in his operation, a second nature to all the salesmen. But the more effective Ricky Roma shows us the true power of seduction. His "closing of the deal" with James Lingk has all the boldness of a lover on a one-night stand, and the boldness lies in the outrage of language. Lingk succumbs to the pitch, which is the opposite of the hard sell. Roma assures him over drinks that all is fate and all is permitted in human affairs, that all forms of outrage, once done, should bear no guilt.

> When you *die* you're going to regret the things you don't do. You think you're *queer*. I'm going to tell you something: we're *all* queer. You think you're a *thief*. So *what?* You get befuddled by middle-class morality. . . ? Get *shut* of it. Shut it out. You cheated on your wife. . . ? You *did* it, live with it (*Pause*) You fuck little girls, so *be* it.[2]

The monologue at the end of Act I, to which Lingk listens with a passive fascination, is one of the most remarkable speeches Mamet has ever composed for the stage.

We soon discover that Roma's pitch, his closing of the deal, is not only an act of seduction through the lure of extreme amorality. It is also an act of cuckoldry. When Lingk returns to annul the contract, it is at his wife's prompting, and in his despairing hesitation he seems stranded between spouse and seducer. This dimension of the drama has, ironically enough, been brought out most fully in James Foley's recent film adaptation of the play, scripted by Mamet himself. The playing of Al Pacino as Roma against Jonathan Pryce as Lingk uses the intimacy of the movie camera to great effect in deepening the sexual ambiguity of Lingk's initial submission and his later refusal. In his performance here and in the London stage production of *American Buffalo*, Pacino's inventive power suggests that he, and not Joe Mantegna, is the quintessential Mamet protagonist. He is not simply duplicitous, abrasive, and streetwise. He is also predatory and para-noid. His Teach is the hunter who fears being hunted and trusts no one. His Roma trusts no one, even while the inflections of his voice and the postures of his body language suggest that he is willing to trust anyone. The very definition of trust proves to be illusory and circular. You trust your friends, but your friends are only friends because they are the people you trust. In an existential world there is no a priori that guarantees trust or loyalty. Yet these are the very things Mamet's characters strive for even as they betray them. It gives an emotional edge to their desperation, their life of risk, and a dra-matic edge to Mamet's tragicomedy.

Shepard and Rabe share with Mamet the device of the storyteller as unreliable narrator. But the usage is slightly altered. For Mamet the story is an integral part of the pitch, of the intended act of possession, which promises more than it can deliver. In Shepard's work it is the narcotic vision or the unreliable memory, while in Rabe it becomes, as often as not, a poisonous narrative of self-hood. All three are variants of a controlled paranoia in which, finally, truth and fantasy are not to be distinguished, in which the elation of the story contains the hidden fear that it might be revealed as an untruth. For Shepard's great tragicomic narrators, Hoss in *The Tooth of Crime*, Rabbit in *Angel City*, Shooter in *Action*, Lee in *True West*, and May and Eddie in *Fool for Love*, storytelling strives for a mythic aura to innoculate the frail and defensive self. Words speak louder than action for fear that action may speak louder than words. In Rabe's dramatic parable of paranoia and celebrity, *Hurlyburly*, his drug-taking Hollywood habitués analyze themselves and each other to death in the language of a California psychobabble that communicates nothing and also does nothing to prevent the horror of the violent deed. In the end, action in fact does speak louder than words, but language is already at a megawatt pitch. Shepard and Rabe have the capacity to show us the finality of action out of control despite the abundant inventiveness of the language that surrounds it. In the best American drama, language shares the same excitement as action yet works in dissonant counterpoint to it. Unlike Pinter, where it often acts to prevent action from going out of control, where it has an elliptical function of containment, here it cannot prevent the destiny outside itself. Language is no longer fate but incites a fate that it cannot control.

Where does fate lie? Usually it lies buried in the quicksand of celebrity. *Celebrity* connotes both a state of being and an act of celebration. Its etymology lies in the religious ritual of a solemn ceremony, the act of the celebrant. But its current usage has long been more profane. In electronic culture it implies a utopian freezing of time in which the transient process of celebrating becomes an artificial state of being—like Hoss, Shepard's rock star, who complains of being "stuck in his image." Hoss is a celebrity, but he wonders for how long this state of grace will continue. The lure of fame means that he wishes the status of celebrity to outlive the rituals of celebration, of which he is no longer capable. But, without celebration, celebrity is divorced of its underpinning and turns into a trap. While Artie Shaughnessy is endlessly celebrating the celebrity status he will never attain, Hoss is a celebrity who has given up celebrating but refuses to admit that the end is near. He acts like Richard II toward his crown, taking it seriously only when it becomes endangered. But the point is more clearly made by those not important enough to have a crown in the first place, those on the margins of celebrity, stranded between the banality of everyday life and the lure of fame.

Here celebrity, like paranoia, becomes an ordering principle vital to American life because it promises coherence in the midst of social chaos. To be be widely known is an ordering principle, like the delusion of a universal conspiracy. These, of course, are very different ordering principles from the one de Tocqueville thought would govern the chaotic energies of the American nation, namely, diverse beliefs in the one indivisible God necessary to unite in the imagination all that was destined to stay divided in daily life. In ludic drama, however, God is absent from the stage. The theater's contemporary legacy is not theology but rationalism and the aesthetic legacy of the moderns. It could be argued that paranoia is their most poisoned offshoot. In recent years the paranoid reaction of the American religious cult against all forms of rationalism, and the counterparanoia of the secular state, have resulted in the gruesome horrors of the Jamestown and Waco massacres. But contemporary theater deals in the dramatic space of spiritual solitude not the collective hysteria that Miller captured so well in *The Crucible*. At its most extreme, it is a theatrical space we might want to call "home alone," in which home is a loose domestic space to be defended against exterior and potentially catastrophic forces. Celebrity is the extreme utopia for those who feel home alone, where the desire for fame transforms "home alone" into the illusory center of the universe. In this heavenly state of the paranoid mind, adoration radiates inward instead of suspicion radiating outward.

The brilliance of this double inversion is at its strongest in Shepard. Hoss wants, paradoxically, to be at the center of a world he has retreated from and fears. Rabbit's quest for celebrity in *Angel City* ends in the catastrophe scenarios of the overreaching paranoid, the upstart movie mogul who can no longer distinguish between disastrous movies and disaster movies. The lesson is clear. If apocalypse does not exist, it has to be invented. But two tendencies can be found in the drama of the 1980s that were not so pronounced in the previous decade. The battle of the sexes becomes more fiercely Strindbergian, while the "home" becomes more exclusively feminine, as in *'night, Mother*, or else exclusively more masculine. The weak masculine "homes" of *True West, Hurlyburly,* and Marlane Meyer's *Kingfish* are ones in which the absence of women remains a haunting presence. The male home is disorderly, makeshift, undomesticated, a very brittle defense against external horrors and internal self-destruction.

Meanwhile the sex wars take place elsewhere. Those of *Fool for Love* are set in a motel room on the edge of the California desert, and the agonistic contest of May and Eddie is a bruising episode in a cycle of repetition in which, with Eddie's eternal return, the past is never resolved and the future remains uncertain. Meanwhile the fight and flight at the start of *A Lie of the Mind* are already in a space within memory that forgoes most naturalistic contours. The trauma of Jake's violent beating of Beth is evoked in a bleak phone booth on a highway, a bare hospital room, and a seedy motel room. The strength of Shepard's staging in the first act of the play lies, in his own words, "in the impression of infinite space, going off to nowhere."[3] The first three overlapping scenes, which are played on different areas of the same set, disperse the spatial enclosures of "domestic" violence only to intensify its dramatic effect.

Moreover, Shepard raises more boldly the question of appearance and reality in the paranoid mind-set of the jealous male. Jake sees Beth's acting schedule as an attempt to achieve sex and celebrity by taking shortcuts, to live out her rehearsed love-performance as if it were more real than her everyday life. He is insanely jealous of her acting persona and hostile to the performance culture he reads into it: "A job is where you don't have fun. You don't dick around tryin' to pretend you're somebody else."[4] It is a single instance of the paranoid confusion of appearance and reality set against the background of a dual family saga that is dramatically more conventional. The dramatic introduction of the inept male agonizing over injury inflicted by male on female is echoed in Eddie's panic response to Phil's early-morning entry at the start of *Hurlyburly*. Yet there is one vital difference. In Rabe's play the paranoid mind-set, which fails to distinguish acting theatrically from acting in everyday life, permeates not just one scene but the whole play. Here the distance from women, who are usually just "passing through," acts to fuel the fears and fantasies of the all-male household in Hollywood. They all make their living by means of peripheral roles in mass-produced fantasies. Phil, the small-time actor endlessly hustling for TV movies, acts out in life the villainous role for which he hopes to be cast in his next cop thriller. He is stuck, like Hoss, in his image, but his image exists largely in his imagination, like a form of anticipatory casting that seldom comes to fruition. He acts out the role of the tough guy for which he usually fails to be chosen. Just as Eddie in *Fool for Love* is a stunt artist, a stand-in for celebrity, so Phil's life becomes an everyday rehearsal for the TV part he fails to clinch.

Hurlyburly brings paranoia all the way back home. It is male, and yet it is domestic, a self-created masculine entrapment that breeds on the phobia of the outside, a dependence upon the culture of celebrity in which true recognition is always withheld. Eddie and Phil function erratically as surrogate spouses for one another, mulling over the uncertain worlds of women and celebrity, with which they can never come to terms, in a language of self-analysis that is empty of meaning. The talk is addictive, and yet it is also the result of another kind of addiction, the predictable toking and snorting that accompany instant coffee and moldy snowballs for breakfast. A histrionic language of self-discovery that is meant to be reflective becomes a narcotic excess that is wired and expressive. Performance here is bold and bad. Confession and accusation degenerate into an abstract illiteracy but still strike inane poses as matters of life and death. In the open-plan space of the canyon dwelling, run wild with vegetation, psychodrama rules. It is a tragicomic tour-de-force in which the uneasy laughter of the audience verges on a shudder of collective apprehension. It senses very quickly that no amount of psychobabble can disperse the violence that is in the air. It has failed to stop Phil's beating of Susan. It will fail to stop Phil from throwing Bonnie from a moving car. It will fail to stop the narcotic Eddie from failing to recognize the unpredictable nature of his friend's brutality.

> Nobody's going to take substantial losses over what are totally peripheral, totally transient elements. You know, we're all just background in one another's life. Cardboard cutouts bumping around in this vague, you know, hurlyburly, this spin-off of what was once prime time life; so don't hassle me about this interpersonal fuck-up on the highway, okay?[5]

Eventually the hurlyburly will fail to stop Phil from taking his own life. For the failure of language to resolve paranoia and self-obsession acts as a positive incitement to violent acts. It is no wonder that Darlene, Eddie's bemused lover, exclaims: "I can't stand this goddamn semantic insanity anymore . . ."[6] The insanity vibrates until the bitter end, like an electric charge in the atmosphere, and there is clear dramatic irony in the men's bird-brained dismissal of Freud as an answer to their many problems. The talking cure, after all, has now become an incitement to hate.

Hurlyburly, like True West, American Buffalo, and Geography of a Horse Dreamer, suggests a new and very bleak kind of male dramatic space, an interior space without women in which the barriers to the outside world become as much mental as physical. It is a space without permanence or continuity. Ultimately it self-destructs. Mamet's drama ends in the miasma of distrust, True West in the wrecking of the absent mother's home, and Hurlyburly in Phil's suicide. The destruction is not total. Life is salvaged from the wreckage and goes on, but the discordant strings of male intimacy have snapped, and this damage is irreversible. All, moreover, are instances of the wider failures of celebrity amid the dubious triumphs of a paranoia that proclaims the ruin it has created as pure self-made apocalypse, as do-it-yourself catastrophe. The failure of Lee and Austin, in True West, to swap roles without violating the physical space in which they operate shows us the limits of free will side by side with the impulse to think that the freedom of the will has no limit at all. But the aborted role reversal of the two brothers reveals something far deeper. It unveils the kinetic impulse to violent injury as the actual truth of male American society as a whole, a reflexive truth become a self-fulfilling prophecy, which then destroys its deranged free-lance prophets. Thus do the tragicomic males of American drama painfully reveal themselves, and we know not whether to laugh or cry. They give us narcotic dream-visions of doom, then proceed to hang themselves with their own rope.

NOTES

1. John Guare, The House of Blue Leaves (New York: Viking, 1972), 53.
2. David Mamet, Glengarry Glen Ross (New York: Grove Press, 1984), 47.

The Dramaturgy of the Dream Play: Monologues by Breuer, Chaikin, Shepard

BILL COCO

"This is a strange repose, to be asleep
With eyes wide open; standing, speaking, moving,
And yet so fast asleep."
—Sebastian in Shakespeare's *The Tempest*

In a program note for *The Ghost Sonata*, which was performed under the title *The Spook Sonata* by the Provincetown Players in New York in January 1924, Eugene O'Neill made one of his greatest and most explicit tributes to the playwright whose dramatic writing had inspired his career—August Strindberg.[1] In a sanatorium in 1912–13, while he was recovering from tuberculosis, O'Neill had taken up reading, among others, the plays of Strindberg, and this encounter with the Swedish dramatist changed his life. Thereafter, he would dedicate himself to writing for the stage. So the performance of *The Ghost Sonata* a decade later at the Provincetown was indeed a performance of tribute. O'Neill's brief essay, which he provided for the playbill, celebrates the presence of Strindberg as "the precursor of all modernity in our present theatre." For O'Neill, Strindberg had shown what a playwright could do; by pushing to its limits the vision of naturalism, he said, Strindberg broke through into a new world, which O'Neill saw as that of "super-naturalism," where "we 'wipe out and pass on' to some as yet unrealized region where our souls, maddened by loneliness and the ignoble inarticulateness of flesh, are slowly evolving their new language of kinship."[2]

O'Neill's engagement with Strindberg and the possibilities introduced within his dramaturgy coincided, as we know, with the birth of the first notable experimental theater in America, the Provincetown Players. The group lasted from 1915 to 1927 and inaugurated for the American stage the first phase of a tradition of experiment that remains one of the central achievements of the American theater. Continuing that tradition in the 1960s, another phase of experimentalism was initiated along the margins of the American theater with productions that remain among the most important in contemporary theatrical art.

In surveying the significant plays in the American experimental theater over the past few decades, it is enlightening to see how significantly the shadow of Strindberg continues to fall over our dramatic productions. (I am not speaking here of the main line of American playwriting that runs from Albee to Kushner, in which Strindbergian themes and images abound, but rather of that more narrowly focused world of experimentation within a small theatrical ensemble.) The styles of contemporary experimentalism are, of course, significantly different from what the Provincetown Players knew—we have vastly more sophisticated technologies of light and sound, and our performers have assimilated the stage practice of a range of Europeans; they have created their own methods out of the investigations of the Living Theater and others.

And yet, if one looks to the very core of these contemporary experiments, or many of them, one may perceive deeply resonant affinities with Strindberg's theater, particularly with respect to *A Dream Play*. In fact, I believe we may go further and say that at the heart of the work of some of the most significant contemporary American experiments there lie paradigms of dramatic coherence and exploration that we may read as prophetic in Strindberg's work for the stage.

In what follows I am going to sketch an examination of two of what I take to be the most important events in the American experimental theater of the mid-1980s and try to suggest how at the core of these dramatic conceptions Strindberg may be seen, in O'Neill's phrase, as a "precursor" of our "modernity." I am not arguing that Strindberg is there as a direct influence. In fact, I believe that he is not. But more to the point, in my way of reading these works, is the degree to which the *possibilities* of theatrical form and dramatic practice established by Strindberg, especially as he spelled them out in the prefatory notes and in the structure of *A Dream Play*, can be seen as fundamental theatrical paradigms with which our most daring experimentalists still engage. I will first examine a performance piece of 1983 entitled *Hajj* by Lee Breuer of the Mabou Mines theater collective; and then I will discuss the most recent play written by Sam Shepard and Joseph Chaikin, *The War in Heaven*, a performance piece for radio, which premiered in 1985. In both cases I will try to suggest how in an essential way an aspect of *Dream Play* dramaturgy inheres in the very fabric of these two experiments with the form of dramatic monologue.

Strindberg writes in his preface or "Explanatory Note" to *A Dream Play*: "The characters split, double, redouble, evaporate, condense, scatter, and converge."[3] In a letter to his German translator Emil Schering he elaborates on this idea: "Human beings appear at several points and are sketched, the sketches flow together; the same person splits into several persons only to form into one again."[4]

In Lee Breuer's dramatic monologue entitled *Hajj*, a single Performer, a woman, stages in her imagination a journey to her dead father's grave. *Hajj* is the Arabic word for the pilgrimage or journey each Muslim is expected to make at least once in a lifetime to Mecca, the place from which flows the spiritual understanding of life. For the nameless woman in Breuer's *Hajj*, her hajj, her journey, is both toward a place, that is, her father's grave, and toward an understanding of her father that constitutes a final settling of accounts. Her motive, she tells us, is to cleanse herself of pride—the ineluctable driving force of all spiritual search.

On the tiny stage before us is the woman, kneeling, seated at her low makeup table with her back to us. She will not turn around until late in the performance. Above the playing area hang streamers from a central point that drape over the space to suggest a tent. Framing the large triptych mirror upstage is an Arabic-like arch of tilework emblazoned with the words of the hajj in Arabic characters. The Performer begins by gazing upon her mirrors, exquisite perfume bottles, and cups of exotic creams and oils. Her eyes move across the bottles and her glance appears to set in motion the quiet, celestial tinkling of many prayer bells. This vibrating world carries her modest dressing room into a space of inner voices and memories. The bottles and mirrors and cups are instruments of her identity, for she is an actress, and she is making up her face as she speaks cryptically about money. Later she will tell us that "Love is money Alex / money, love."[5] But for now we only hear references to cash deals and agreements. Talk of money turns to talk of love, as she closes her initial speech with the line, "I love you / Daddy . . ."[6] She is here to settle a large debt, her retribution.

Up to this point we have seen her only from the back, but we can read her face reflected in the three large mirrors set upon her table, and on a large video screen above the mirrors. Soon still other mirrorlike frames will show us her face from additional angles, coming in from the sides, and each will contribute to a faceted portrait of the woman's face, though her back is still to us. The images on the video screens are conveyed by way of three unseen, live video cameras offstage, which follow the movements of her face. These many images of the woman's face will give way to others, as the cameras zoom in on her lips, for example, or catch other details of her face at the makeup table. Then, in a significant transformation, her face will blend into that of her child, who shares a deep resemblance to her and even could be herself at that young age, and later into that of her father who looks like both of them.

In a kind of dramatic subplot, there will be pictures of a truck moving across a desolate winter landscape that could be the Yugoslavia of her father's origin and at the same time the American Midwest, where he settled and later shot himself with a gun before the daughter could repay a large sum of money he lent to her, an emblem of the greater debt she owes him. Through the journeys in Yugoslavia, through Europe, and on to Midwestern America, she tells us, they always slept together, father and daughter, in a space in the truck that he recreated as her room at home.

As little by little we learn the story of her spiritual and monetary debt to her father, the prismatic imagery of her portraiture—made of the mirrors and images of her on the video screens—becomes the visual substance of the performance, which is meant to echo the intricate chambers of memory and association she is calling up. This visual fantasia, which projects her face, the son's face, and the father's as aspects of one face, reaches its climax toward the end of the performance when we see that her long séance at the dressing table is but a prologue to her ceremonial donning of a mask. In a lightning-bolt shift, she takes up from the floor a patchwork quilt that has accompanied her all through her life's journey. She throws it around herself with authority and makes a momentous turn toward us for the first time, statuesque and robed like a Japanese *onnagata*, very late now in the performance.

The mask is revealed to be that of the father, and we see daughter and son and father fused in the live person before us. In the mask, she moves quickly into a different mode, and shifts from the elusive, idiomatic speech of the early part of the play to a documentary sketch of the father's life. As the words become more prosaic, her movement becomes dancelike, until she abruptly strips off the mask at the end of her pilgrimage: "Here in the dark box of my throat I bring you back to life."[7] Peeling off one half of her father's face, we see hers and his in a Bergman *Persona*–like climactic fusion. She peels it, even tears it, from her face at this, the end of her journey to the grave of his consciousness.

In her concluding verses, the woman commits herself to an understanding of her debt to her father.

In my body, Alexander
Your charmed bones
Take on a certain glow

You can't leave me; that plan has a flaw
We'll never sort each other's atoms out
We are under sentence of a Boyle's law
For hope's dispersal in chambers of doubt.[8]

These words of closure, it seems to me, sum up the performance and suggest as well an underground passage to Strindberg's idea about the nature of character. "We'll never sort each other's atoms out." Character is seen here, as it is in Strindberg's preface, not as a substance of parts but as a kaleidoscopic identity, with bones of one body vibrating within the bones of another, giving off a glow that is both personality and identity.

In the staging and in the very conception of *Hajj*, with its polyphonic imagery, picturing the woman from so many angles followed by this same image metamorphosing into that of child and father, we have an explicit contemporary version of the ways in which character can "split, double, redouble, evaporate, condense, scatter." And, when the woman takes on the father's mask and performs her dance, all the characters converge in her, in one. As Strindberg says in the Schering letter, "Human beings appear at several points and are sketched, the sketches flow together; the same person splits into several persons only to form into one again." In Lee Breuer's Performer we have a contemporary instance of the prismatic characters of Strindberg converging once more into the prism itself.

Perhaps the most intriguing and controversial notion that Strindberg presents in his preface to *A Dream Play* is that of the dreamer. Who is the dreamer? Strindberg himself? The audience watching the play? Or a third consciousness that Strindberg interposes between us and him? Probably the issue can't be settled, and no doubt Strindberg imagines the dreamer as partaking of all three levels. It is this complex weave of various strands of consciousness that seems to be at the heart of our unsettling experience of the play, which is to say its effectiveness as a dream experience in the theater.

In the execution of this dream effect, it is perhaps the figure of the

Daughter of Indra who holds the key. She is, after all, nearly unique in the modern drama: she partakes of divinity and yet she is also, for the time of the play, of the human world. The capacity she possesses, which is that of a double consciousness, human and divine, has its cost in terms of character. As Agnes we do know her in an early way, but in her judgments of the world and her speeches to her invisible father she is in essence only a voice—she is a characterless character, an alien who struggles with the human in human experience.

In their collaboration of 1985, Joseph Chaikin and Sam Shepard have explored just such a condition and character—a "characterless character" who also is a spiritual being caught in a human world. In a letter to Chaikin, very early in the collaboration, Shepard wrote about a dramatic idea that had been forming in his mind.

> Something's been coming to me lately about this whole question of being *lost*. It only makes sense to me in relation to an idea of one's identity being shattered under severe personal circumstances—in a state of crisis where everything that I've previously identified with in myself suddenly falls away. A shock state, I guess you might call it.

Two weeks earlier he had written to Chaikin about the possibilities of a similar scene.

> The whole question of characters is unavoidable and maybe we should actually begin there . . . Maybe there is a *characterless* character—in other words a kind of lost soul hunting through various attitudes and inner lives for a suitable character—one that not only functions in this world but one which is really "himself."[9]

The outcome of this idea was a monologue play for radio, *The War in Heaven*, which is subtitled *Angel's Monologue*. Coauthored and developed through improvisation by Chaikin and Shepard, the performance on radio was spoken by Chaikin with music composed and played by Shepard. It is the third in a series of collaborative pieces by the two artists, the earlier works being *Tongues* and *Savage/Love*, and I believe that of the three it is the most supple and distinguished. Now, while it charts new territory for both artists, and while it is one of the most successful and daring presentations in American avant-garde theater of the 1980s, there are ways in which it also looks back to Strindberg—particularly to the character of Indra's Daughter, who in some ways can be seen as a unique precursor of the Angel whose monologue comprises *The War in Heaven*.

The appeal and the mystery of the Daughter of Indra derive from her reality within the play as a "characterless character" (Shepard's phrase). She is even without a name, and her personality is without color or quality. In fact, it is her very namelessness and absence of character that enable her to sustain the grave task that falls to her by Indra's command. The monologue called *The War in Heaven* is made up of phrases and sentence fragments, spoken in a light, airy, even childlike voice, which then can grow ominous and introspective. From the elusive reports given by the Angel in the course of the monologue, it would appear that the war in heaven led to the the exile of the Angel, who now is trapped in an earthly life. The Angel is charged with living on earth, and thus is neither of the heavens nor truly a human being. As he moves about, he shuttles between antagonistic laments and a pleasurable celebration of his estate.

Like Indra's Daughter, he is both participant and observer all in one, and the theatrical tension of the piece derives precisely from the double life that comprises such a fallen condition. We observe in the course of the play the war within the Angel himself, as he, like the Daughter of Indra, struggles through the experience of human emotions. He tells us that he died the day he was born and became an Angel. "Since then," he goes on,

> there are no days
> there is no time
> I am here
> by mistake.[10]

Before the war, he says,

I felt I had a destination

I was moving
toward something
I thought I understood

there was an order
that was clear to me
a lawful order

Then we were invaded
all the domains were shattered
connections
were broken
we were sent
in a thousand directions.[11]

He crashed to earth, and this led to his present stage, of both confusion and pleasure in the world.

Immediately his complaint gives way and we hear him taking on the emotions of earthly existence. He experiences grief, and what he calls a sense of "beginning." And then, just as quickly, in an appeal that echoes that of Indra's Daughter, he asks to be taken back.

Every minute I'm here
something's changing in me
something's diminishing
my power slips away

I'll perish
if I stay tied up like this
I will
I'll perish

Then you'll be without me

Turn me loose
Turn me loose.[12]

He is tied up in humanity.

Again and again, he spirals through the same three modes: of recollection of harmony before the war, of intense experience of a human kind, and of calls to a higher power to set him free. As he ventures even more deeply into the world of human emotion, we never get the sense of a person of experience whose plight gives rise to these emotions; we simply receive a report of the outcome. It is as though all the dialogue scenes of *A Dream Play* were excised, and there remained only the speeches of the Daughter to herself and to her father.

The Angel speaks of earth, of love, of hate, and of war on earth. Then he tells of a "soul" whom he sees, then sex, sometimes soul and sex together, and sometimes no soul at all. He then descends down the orders of being to animals, to birds, and finally he seems to move back to an ancient time. At the end he is triumphant, as he reaches a human experience that does bring accord. It is the experience of music, music that allows him to escape into a celestial harmony even while being in the world. Yet, just as he reaches this high plane where the war of being is dissolved, he falls, and there the monologue abruptly ends, looping back to a repetition of the opening nine lines of the monologue. As much as the Angel might resemble Indra's Daughter, his end is not hers. She is able to rise with wisdom toward the clouds and the father of her beginning. The Chaikin/Shepard Angel is condemned in the return to his beginning—the day he was born, which was the day he died, and became the first Angel he is.

What I have identified as some of the underground passages that exist between these two works and *A Dream Play* are worthy of our attention, it seems to me, not in order to demonstrate that the avant-garde road leads back to Strindberg. Rather, a pursuit of the Strindbergian thread that runs through these works suggests how closely we remain in Strindberg's debt and, just as much, the distance that separates him from us. The video cameras and screens in *Hajj*, for example, and the disembodied vocalism that the radio allows Chaikin and Shepard—these technologies permit notions of character only envisioned by Strindberg to be articulated, even within the monologue form, in a manner he could not have dreamt of. But there are deeper differences.

If we set our two experiments beside A Dream Play, they all are thrown into relief. And, in contrast, the Dream Play seems large and operatic in a nineteenth-century way, nearly Wagnerian, with its multitude of spaces, images, and characters, and in its whole sense of vast projection. Set next to this vision, Hajj and The War in Heaven seem like miniatures, chamber works—yet far more compressed than Strindberg's own Chamber Plays. Further, Breuer, Chaikin, and Shepard focus upon the spiritual lives of discrete individual selves. The world outside is pared away and we know or see that world only as it is imprinted upon the lonely or isolated self whose inner confrontation animates the play. Both experiments pursue intricate chamber harmonies within the narrow limits of a single imagination in contrast to Strindberg's vast symphonic orchestration, which conjures an entire universe outside the self.

The lushness and profusion of A Dream Play are all the more fully revealed when we see how the two plays examined here partake of an American tradition of lyrical poetry in which the large issues of life and mind are compressed within a small form. They are at one with the intense verse of the inner self that runs from Emily Dickinson and Walt Whitman, through Hart Crane, to Wallace Stevens, Sylvia Plath, Robert Lowell, John Ashbery (think only of one title, by John Ashbery, Self Portrait in a Convex Mirror), Allen Ginsberg, and up to the present. Where Strindberg is epic, even when pursuing a domestic theme, the Americans are lyrical, finding within the single voice the dimension and the scope that Strindberg calls upon an entire imagined world to portray.

Finally, seen in the light of American lyricism, Strindberg's Dream Play appears to stand Janus-like at the crossroads, looking back toward the teeming life and large forms of the nineteenth-century imagination and forward toward the internal, contemporary exploration of the self in forms at once more concentrated and confined.

Of course, it was this very fullness in Strindberg that so appealed to Eugene O'Neill when he took up reading the plays in his hospital bed more than eighty years ago. As I have tried to suggest here, this very prodigious invention in Strindberg, this richness of form and of reference, continues to illuminate an entire generation of contemporary experiment. It reminds us of Strindberg yet again, as O'Neill saw him, a precursor of our own modernity.

NOTES

1. The lines quoted in the epigraph (from Shakespeare's *The Tempest,* II.i.204–6) are cited in August Strindberg, *Open Letters to the Intimate Theatre,* trans. Walter Johnson (Seattle: University of Washington Press, 1966), 204.
2. From Eugene O'Neill, "Strindberg and Our Theatre," in *American Playwrights on Drama,* ed. Horst Frenz (New York: Hill and Wang, 1965), 1–2 (first published in *Provincetown Playbill,* no. 1, season 1923–24).
3. From "An Explanatory Note" for *A Dream Play,* in August Strindberg, *A Dream Play and Four Chamber Plays,* trans. Walter Johnson (New York: Norton, 1975), 19.
4. From Walter Johnson, "Introduction to 'A Dream Play,'" in Strindberg, *A Dream Play and Four Chamber Plays,* 3.
5. From *Hajj,* in Lee Breuer, *Sister Suzie Cinema: The Collected Poems and Performances, 1976–1986* (New York: Theatre Communications Group, 1987), 116.
6. Ibid., 109.
7. Ibid., 122.
8. Ibid.
9. Sam Shepard, in letters to Chaikin, 29 October, 1983, and 15 October, 1983, in *Joseph Chaikin and Sam Shepard, Letters and Texts, 1972–1984,* ed. Barry Daniels (New York: New American Library, 1989), 128, 123.
10. From Joseph Chaikin and Sam Shepard, *The War in Heaven,* in *A Lie of the Mind, A Play in Three Acts by Sam Shepard* [followed by] *The War in Heaven: Angel's Monologue by Joseph Chaikin and Sam Shepard* (New York: New American Library, 1987), 137.
11. Ibid., 139.
12. Ibid., 140–41.

"Codes from a Mixed-up Machine": The Disintegrating Actor in Beckett, Shepard, and, Surprisingly, Shakespeare

GERRY MCCARTHY

In May 1993 the first international conference on the work of Sam Shepard was held in Brussels. The attendance was largely from the United States and the discussion of Shepard as a (greatly contested) cultural icon was fascinating as much for the incongruity of the location in a distant European capital as for the vehemence with which it was conducted. If culture loomed large in the proceedings, performance came to dominate them. Joe Chaikin performed a solo piece, *The War in Heaven,* on which he and Shepard had been collaborating from 1981 to 1984 when the actor suffered a serious stroke followed by aphasia, from which he had made only a partial recovery. The fragility of the performance was deeply affecting, even disturbing, and the manifest difficulty encountered by a great actor now struggling to overcome the limitations of his body was at one and the same time fearful and enlightening. For Chaikin the effort of making the words concentrated the resources of mind, nerve, and muscle. The control of voice was a prodigious effort, yet he pitched accurately a fifth in the refrains of the piece. But at what a cost. The struggle to bring together the elements of the performance was easily discernible, in Chaikin himself, but also in his audience. It was the most apparent demonstration of the process of empathy that I can recall.

Chaikin demonstrated a point that too easily escapes even the sophisticated attendance at such a conference: that the meaning of dramatic art cannot be divorced from the nature as well as the occasion of its performance. Whatever the cultural and ideological significance of the enactment, enactment there must be, and the actor is the initial or primary locus of knowledge of the play. The lesson of Chaikin's performance was that, reduced as he was to the very materiality of performing (the grain in the wood, as it were, lying beneath the polished effect, almost at the point of collapse), the sense of his acting was shared by the audience. No more was needed, at least in the expressed opinions of those present. It would have been wonderful to have seen Chaikin restored, and the performance would have been more agile, more resonant, but it could not have been in its essentials more complete.

Chaikin's performance made clear the identification of actor and audience in the crystallization of a knowledge, in Beckett's phrase from *Endgame*, what "they're at."

> *Hamm:* I wonder (*Pause.*) Imagine if a rational being came back to earth, wouldn't he be liable to get ideas into his head if he observed us long enough. (*Voice of rational being.*) Ah, good, now I see what it is, yes, now I understand what they're at![1]

The question naturally arises as to what the audience "knew" and how they did so. When the performance teetered on the edge of disintegration, this was known to the spectators, who in their turn strained to assemble its elements, joining in the struggle of the performer to hold the act together. It struck me at the time that this was, stripped of grace and elegance, the essence of the acting performance. It also connected with a series of thoughts on the appeal of a variety of dysfunction in the work of dramatists, not least Shepard himself, but also notably Samuel Beckett, and its relationship to audience experience, the reception of drama and the particular epistemology of performance.

In Shepard's *Motel Chronicles* there is an extended narrative describing the cerebral hemorrhage, treatment, and progress of a patient. This may describe the illness of a member of Shepard's family.

We began to time our visits according to the drug schedule she was on. Early in the morning she was at her best. Her energy was highest. She could sit up while we fed her. It was the first real food she'd had since the surgery. We'd put a spoonful of food in her mouth but she wouldn't chew. The food would just sit there. We'd tell her to chew. She'd wait a long time just staring with the food hanging in her mouth. We'd keep telling her to chew. She'd start chewing methodically as though the jaw was obeying instructions from some distant authority with no connection to the act of eating. When the food was reduced to almost liquid state she'd keep chewing. We'd tell her to swallow. She'd keep chewing. The food would pour out the sides of her mouth. We'd tell her to swallow. She'd stop chewing and stare. She'd swallow and grimace. We'd start all over with a new spoonful. She seemed to recognize us now and started to speak in a little girl voice. The words would come out in short blurts like the codes from a mixed-up machine.[2]

The connection between this and Shepard's *A Lie of the Mind* may well be suspected, a play that depicts brain damage and aphasia and is dedicated to the memory of L. P. Beyond the poignancy of the personal inspiration of the play, I suspect the writer is drawn by the magnetism of a human experience that lies paradoxically close to the medium of drama and its inherent power of expression. Why should Shepard or any dramatist create characters or require performances that are in any way dis-abled? Does not the dramatist naturally desire a fluent actor to deliver his or her speeches? Certainly the uncomprehending reception of Chekhov in England at the beginning of the century was the result of a prevailing sense that the dramatist should write speeches, properly arranged, and not the disordered ramblings of characters who seemed to be off their heads: codes from a mixed-up machine. The knowledge that the characters were Russian, and therefore foreign, was of some assistance to the London critics at the time.

From early in his writing Shepard has shown an instinct for the medium of performance and a specific interest in the function or dysfunction of the mixed-up machine. Writing for Chaikin in the days of the Open Theater, he created a short performance piece, *Teleported Man*,[3] in which the actor describes the disintegration of mind and body in the teleported effect. This is dangerous, mirroring conflicting sensations of mind and body that can often overcome the actor and disorder the performance. The image of the character teleported out of his body comes perilously close to the experience of stage fright, in which the mass and balance of the body feel unfamiliar and unmanageable. Many actors will describe extreme stage fright as a species of out-of-body experience during which the mind looks on helplessly at the body isolated and vulnerable in stage space. This is the stuff that nightmares are made of. The machine is mixed up and the actor loses control over it.

In Shepard's *Action* the ordering of the internal experience of the actor is developed further within a cast that is imperfectly coordinated. Not only is the body dangerously autonomous, but the memories of the actions played out onstage are evanescent, and the structure of the events imperfect. Shepard writes the play agonizingly close to the experience of playing prepared activities, learned into the muscles, which can proceed hypnotically while the mind inquires about the further progress of the action. The machine gets mixed up, functioning of itself, much as the patient in *Motel Chronicles* chews automatically "as though the jaw was obeying instructions from a distant authority." At one point in *Action* Jeep gets "stuck" and demands from his partner Shooter "a reason for moving . . . a justification for me to find myself somewhere else?" Shooter then dictates to him the moves of an activity. Once his hands are busy gutting a fish he feels better.

> JEEP: I'm getting better now. Even in the middle of all this violence. . . . I'm in a better position now. Now, I've got something to do. . . . I

can even imagine how horrifying it would be to be doing all this, and it doesn't touch me. It's like I'm dismissed.[4]

When Shepard wrote *A Lie of the Mind* he had entered a period in which his work began to assume a more familiar form: the period of the "family plays." If, as Edward Albee has claimed, every writer must make a statement about the times and a statement about the medium in which he works, then Shepard would appear to be turning away from "art," and his overt dramatic experimentation, toward "the world" and a more familiar gallery of characters and a more recognizable set of relationships. The reflection of the times, however, contains a further development of Shepard's exploration of the nature of performance.

Shepard takes the disjunctions of *Action* and develops them within a more clearly recognizable social and political framework. Jake has savagely beaten his wife Beth to the point where he believes her dead. She is, in fact, brain damaged, aphasic. In the course of the play she gradually recovers her speech and painfully and imperfectly reconstructs, or rather reinvents, the elements of her world. After the attack Jake is damaged, sick and exhausted physically, mentally shocked. His sister considers him "crazy, just plain crazy," while his mother hints at childhood brain damage. Shepard on one level creates a network of relationships within a dysfunctional family; on another he uses that social group to address the function of mind in the actor. If, for example, each of the central characters is "deluded" and at some point sees a relative as the other (in Act I Jake speaks to his sister Sally as Beth, and the play concludes with Beth weirdly costumed, preparing for her "marriage" to Jake's brother Frankie), the issue is not alone the destiny of the family and these relationships but the audience's actual involvement in the mental constructs Shepard employs. The playwright foregrounds the processes whereby meanings are made in the theater and highlights the metaphorical power of these overt constructions to create the experience of the forms of life.[5]

Throughout *A Lie of the Mind*, Shepard forces players back to the first steps in the creation of the role, that is, the search for its physical form. The central effect and focal point of the play is the mixed-up machine, the actress playing Beth, whose meanings cannot initially be decoded, though they are intensely felt by an audience. Her first words, as the stage direction requires, are heard in blackout.

She tries to speak, but no words come, just short punctuated sounds at the end of her exhales.
Beth: Saah - thah - Jaah - saah - saah -[6]

These are indeed the codes from the mixed-up machine of the *Motel Chronicle* story. They cannot initially be deciphered, especially in the theater where they must dissolve with the passing moment. As the words are painfully formed the actor's meaning is sensed despite its lack of a specific, completed articulation. This is, of course, a matter of the context of the speech: known to the performer but as yet not elaborated to the audience. To pick up on some current terminology, is this a dis-abled performance, or a differently abled performance?

Beth: You gant take in me. You gant take me back.
Mike: I'm not going to take you anywhere. We'll stay right here until you're better.
Beth: Who fell me?
Mike: Don't worry about that.
Beth: Who fell me? Iza - Iza - name? Iza name to come. Itz - Itz - Inza name. Aall - aall - all - a love. A love.[7]

The search for meaning is experienced by actress and spectator alike as a physical struggle with language whose structures are dismembered in the forms Shepard observes in the aphasic subject. The substitution of "fell" for "hit" or "knock down" is a characteristic malformation, as is the inability of the subject to proceed through a syntactic sequence. Finally, the homonymic collision between "aall," "all," and "a love" extends the pattern of synchronic and diachronic collapse to the basic building block of language, the phoneme.[8]

As a statement on the world, on the fragility of personal relationships, and on the disintegration of the family and the national framework, the play is rich in material, but underpinning this lies Shepard's statement on his art and his continued experimentation with the medium of acting. The lie of the mind in the title points to the struggle for meaning, which goes on within the action of the play and between different roles but also within the mental constructs that make up the acting performance. The struggles are occasioned by a daring discontinuity in the construction of the performances: memory, which is lost; identifications, which are inconsistent; pictures in the mind, which have the value of actual experience; and so forth. If the representations that arise in the mind can afford specifically the pictures that deceive Jake, they also are the images that allow the invention of the conclusion, despite the desperate protests of Frankie, Jake's brother.

> Jake: (To Beth, very simple) These things—in my head—lie to me. Everything lies. But you. You stay. You are true. I know you now. You are true. I love you more than this life. You stay. You stay with him. He's my brother.[9]

Here, at the climax of the play, Shepard brings Jake finally face to face with Beth. It is notable that both these key roles are played close to some point of physical or mental breakdown or disorder. Beth is carried by her brother to Jake who in turn is hauled to his feet to play out a rehearsed confession ("We had it all memorized!"). The stage directions indicate the physical nature of the performance:

> Mike carries Beth across the set to the porch and down steps to Jake who remains on his knees facing audience. He sets Beth down on her feet, facing Jake, and forces her to look at Jake.
> Mike: (Holding Beth in place) Now look at him! Look at him! Isn't that the man you love? Isn't that him? Isn't that the one you say is dead?
> (Beth shakes her head.)
> Mike: (Shaking her by the shoulders) Look at him! (to Jake) Get up on your feet. Stand up!
> (Mike grabs Jake by the collar still holding Beth. Jake struggles to stand.)
> Get up on your feet and tell her what you're gonna say. Tell her everything we talked about in the shed. Go ahead and tell her now. Go ahead!
> (Pause as Jake stands there, trying to maintain a vertical position. He stares at Beth. He tries to form the words but falters on them.)
> Jake: (Softly) I - I - I - I love you more than this earth.[10]

A Lie of the Mind goes much further than exploiting the affective power of various types of mental strain and disorder. It uses the forms and pathology of brain damage and the etiology of the condition to ground performances in their muscular origins. The consequence is a foregrounding of the relationship between the actor's self and the physical and mental experiences of acting.

In this Shepard shares a contemporary sensitivity to the phenomenon of neuropathology, which has clearly interested other contemporary dramatists. Pinter dedicates his *A Kind of Alaska* to Oliver Sacks, the New York psychiatrist and neurologist whose *Awakenings* was his source. Peter Brook has treated the same writer's *The Man Who Mistook His Wife for a Hat*, which has also been the source of an opera by Michael Nyman. Edward Albee has confessed to an interest in general reading in the area, and his radio play, *Listening*, bears this out.

Beckett manifestly draws the forms of some of his work from a similar area. His *Not I* may well be related to the distress caused by the stroke his mother suffered near her suburban Dublin home (Croker's Acres, a real place, is mentioned in the text). Although the play makes little apparent concession to the world as we observe it daily, the art of its conception marvellously captures the forms of life sensed in the disordered neurology of the aphasic stroke victim.

The exigency of Beckett's staging here, as in most of his plays, effects a severe restriction of the acting performance. In *Not I* there is a compression effect as the play, an almost uninterrupted stream of monologue, must be delivered very rapidly. The actress who plays Mouth is in black, and only her mouth is illuminated, a difficult and precise operation with a pin spot. The problem of lighting, and the proximity of a microphone to relay the voice, means that the player must not move during the thirteen to fifteen minutes of the performance.[11]

To compression is added repression. Unlike the relatively greater naturalism of Shepard's disintegrating performances, Beckett does not represent an observed collapse, nor the particular symptomatology of a mental or cerebral condition. Mouth must narrate, overheard by the scarcely visible auditor figure, the account of a blackout, after which the sufferer slowly regained consciousness and then the power of speech: the aphasia is not assumed by the actress but is experienced by an alleged third person, "she." As the play develops, it becomes clear that what "she" experiences describes the actuality of the performer's position and experiences as she struggles to sustain the enormous physical and mental difficulties of the role. Describing the agony of aphasic disconnection, the actress conceives herself at the brink of an equivalent breakdown. The "Not I" of the title is the negative of the positive "I" of the performer herself.

Beckett requires an extraordinary combination of effects. The actress must execute a performance of rare athleticism, and at the same time conceive the potential disorder of her own body and mind. The very pressure of the speed of performance, and the frightening similarity of the images she constructs in her mind to her actual experience, requires that, despite the feat of her delivery, she create the experience of her mind disjoining from the various efforts of speech that she is actually making. The better she achieves the task, the closer it brings her to a realization of the experience and therefore to the threat of a breakdown.

> just all part of the same wish to . . . torment . . . though actually in point of fact . . . not in the least . . . not a twinge . . . so far . . . ha! . . . so far . . . this other thought then . . . oh long after . . . sudden flash . . . very foolish really but so like her . . . in a way . . . that she might do well to . . . groan . . . writhe she could not . . . as if in actual . . . agony . . . but could not . . . could not bring herself . . . some flaw in her make-up . . . or the machine . . . more likely the machine . . . so disconnected . . . never got the message . . . or powerless to respond . . . like numbed . . . couldn't make the sound . . . not any sound . . . no sound of any kind . . . no screaming for help should she feel so inclined . . . scream . . . .[12]

And at this point the performer twice screams, and listens, and concludes in the resonant silence of the theater: "no . . . spared that . . . all silent as the grave . . ." Of course, we are not spared that—nor, since she goes through the excruciation of this performance for us, is the actress. The "machine" of Not I "fails to get the message it is so disconnected." This play mercilessly makes the actress contemplate the connections, the articulation, and the "piecing together" (the phrase is there in the text) of the acting performance. One might accuse Beckett of cruelty. Why this tampering with the actor's security? Why reflect the performance back onto the actor? Why risk disintegration, when, as the play reveals, integration is the primary task of the performer?

Mixing up the machine threatens a disintegration, which, as every actor knows, can be avoided only through the correct and careful preparation of performance and the proper concentration on appropriate through-lines. Ultimately, the actor must be able to rely on the body, trust that it has learned the physical forms that must be played, and that the mind can engage securely with determined objectives. Experience of the self must not lead to unwanted introspection and an undue awareness of the functionality of the autonomic and sensory-motor nervous systems, and thereafter to the confusion of the self: the self as knowing and the self as known. On the other hand, the closer Shepard and Beckett draw the actor to possible collapse, the nearer the actor approaches to the total engagement of the self in the symbolic act. This prompts the question as to whether this is a risky and dangerous no man's land of acting or the stuff that acting is always made of. Does not all acting mobilize similarly calculated resources and engage the actor in tasks that require concentration and courage to hold the performance together? If integration is indeed the crux of performance, this might explain the contemporary theater's attraction to crucial instances of breakdown, and even aphasia, never a promising subject for spoken drama.

In classical acting, and with Shakespeare, in particular, as an example, there is a precisely equivalent concern with the stability and integration of acting. The discussion of playing in *Hamlet* stresses the "suiting" of speech and physical form,[13] and one may remember that the actor astounds Hamlet with an ability to bring together a series of behaviors in one integrated whole—and all for nothing, for Hecuba. And this, like *Not I*, is a narrative piece, with Aeneas relating to Dido the fall of Troy, and no discussion of feeling arising from characterization by any sort of imaginative leap.[14] The actor, we may remember, assembles a performance, "his whole function suiting with forms to his conceit." This is the integration of mind and body that is the condition for the engagement and realization of the self, the reason that the actor should weep for an abstract such as Hecuba.

The power of acting is plain at the point where its means are taxed to the limits of expresssion. In Shakespeare one need hardly expect the classic aphasia of modern neurology; the diminution of the role is rather associated with human agency and thus forms part of the moral economy of the play.[15] Nevertheless, a physical deficit is exploited in a number of roles, and among these the most evident disintegration is the consequence of a crude and brutal aphasia: the butchering of Lavinia in *Titus Andronicus*.[16] The theatrical power of the bleeding victim is conceivably too crude for the taste of many, but this ignores the way in which Shakespeare exploits the mute performer as the ravished Lavinia meets her uncle, Marcus Andronicus. The dramatic idea concerns knowledge in performance and depends on the operations of empathy. The speech set for Marcus is in fact a dialogue of a particularly dramatic character. To remove speech from Lavinia produces an agonizing negotiation of the meaning of the scene, first expressed in the interplay of bodies, aphasiac on one side and agnosiac on the other: imperfectly expressed meaning in tension with uncompleted knowledge. The speech charts the physical exchange between the two—Lavinia's initial flight, Marcus's shocked pause, then the pressed question:

> Speak, gentle niece, what stern ungentle hands
> Hath lopped and hewed and made thy body bare
> Of her two branches . . .[17]

The physical form of the exchange creates the shared but unspecifiable knowledge of the events that have taken place. Words only confirm a prior realization. The method is clear. Speech on one side interrogates mute breath on the other, and the whole is grounded in a physical rhythm notated in the text with unusual clarity.

> Why dost not speak to me?
> Alas, a crimson river of warm blood,

> Like to a bubbling fountain stirred with wind,
> Doth rise and fall between thy rosed lips,
> Coming and going with they honeyed breath.[18]

The power of the scene derives from the tacit sharing of the knowledge of Lavinia's ravishment and from the disintegrative effect on either player, struggling to read the physical codes (in Shepard's phrase) and construct the meaning of the exchange. Marcus "knows" Lavinia's distress physically, but he cannot resolve the tension between this embodied knowledge and the breakdown of speech. This disjunction creates the actual bodily tensions that sustain the virtual world of the play. This scene is written for the interplay of bodies.

> Shall I speak for thee? Shall I say 'tis so?
> O, that I knew thy heart, and knew the beast,
> That I might rail at him to ease my mind![19]

As in Shepard and Beckett, the physical and mental coordination of the acting performance is crucial to its effect. The actual state of the self is the source of its symbolic power in the play.[20]

In *All's Well That Ends Well*, there is an unusual moment, which concludes a particularly disintegrative scene. The braggart Paroles is tricked by his friends into believing that he has been captured by the enemy on the battlefield, which is the last place he purposed to be. Blindfolded, he is cross-examined in gibberish with the aid of an "interpreter" and betrays his fellows to the assumed enemy. As the lingua franca has broken down, the actor must plead and bargain in dialogue with tormentors he cannot understand. (It is not unusual for actors in workshops to use similar techniques, sometimes to quite disturbing ends.) The actor is thrust to the limits of the powers of language, which he has manipulated with such specious ease hitherto. When the deception is revealed, one by one the company leaves the scene and the speechless Paroles. The last humiliation comes from a common soldier.

> Fare ye well, sir.
> I am for France too; we shall speak of you there.

The effect is to strip the actor of the character he has played: Paroles, words. Left alone on stage, the actor is given a short address to the audience.

> Yet I am thankful. If my heart were great
> 'Twould burst at this. Captain I'll be no more,
> But I will eat and drink and sleep as soft
> As captain shall. Simply the thing I am
> Shall make me live.[21]

At this moment the actor is revealed in the absolute simplicity of "the thing he is" before he exits to construct an altogether meaner performance than before. This is a controlled destruction (or reduction) of the elaborated performance, stripping down the governing parameters to a direct exchange with the audience, which then sets the terms for the substitution of a new framework. To take Shepard's phrase, here the codes break down and we see the machinery for what it is.

Only shallow people, Oscar Wilde wrote, fail to judge by appearances. Acting is not pretending, the making of false claims. It is a matter of seeming, and seeming is the source of its symbolic function. Actual performances give rise to virtual impressions and are the source of a complex knowledge. Both virtual and actual experience are known to the actor, and in integrating the two the actor himself and his audience experience the human self reconstructing itself, from moment to moment, in all its dangerous instability (a process that is seen magisterially in Shakespearean tragedy).

All performance runs the risk of collapse. That is its nature and the source of its power. It is also the explanation of a certain tyranny exercised over the actor by the text and the task of memory. The consequence can be an implicit avoidance of risk, by the memorizing and recall of text as past performance, or the repetition of rehearsed readings. The routine, reiterated performance is without interest, for its elements were never sufficiently isolated nor creatively assembled to enable the mind to direct itself freely outward and away from the complex task that the body absorbs. The actor is secure in the recall of the text, for it is viewed as a past event being replicated in the present, and specific attention is directed to the markers that establish the unfolding of the role. Under these circumstances the integration of the role is illusory, for the objectivity necessary to the playing of the part is blurred, and its physical sense is generalized.

It is only the performance, which is composed of discrete "functions," to take Shakespeare's term, integrated painstakingly in rehearsal (and time after time afresh in performance), which is capable of generating the "conceit" specifically manifesting the attention and objectivity of the actor. It is in the rhythm of this actual thought process that the forms of the play are manifest. Then and only then does one glimpse what I would term the primary function of acting: the symbolic reintegration of the personality.[22]

If such a reintegration is always required in performances (for equally it is the case in the reintegration of mind and body in the dancer or musician), then it is to be expected that the actor will be impelled toward some possibility of breakdown. Toward the end of his life, Samuel Beckett, suffering the effects of a stroke, created a last piece, *comment dire* (in French, literally, 'How do you say . . .'), which reflects the typical Beckettian attempt to assemble the impossible utterance. The critic and scholar, Ruby Cohn, one of Beckett's close friends, asked if he had considered making a translation, thinking that it might be played by Joe Chaikin. The suggestion was a tentative one, but the single sheet was eventually delivered to Cohn and Chaikin with the title, *what is the word*.[23] It was written, we know, at a point when the writer and the eventual performer were literally at the limits of their ability to control the physical means of expression. The fifty-two lines of the French text contain one noun, *folie*, madness.

NOTES

1. Samuel Beckett, *Endgame* (London: Faber and Faber, 1958), 27.
2. Sam Shepard, *Motel Chronicles and Hawk Moon* (London: Faber and Faber, 1985), 111. In 1979, O-Lan Shepard's mother, Scarlett Johnson Dark, suffered a stroke and aphasia. See Joseph Chaikin and Sam Shepard, *Letters and Texts, 1972–1984*, ed. Barry Daniels (New York: Plume, 1990), 153. In November 1979, Shepard replied to Chaikin's inquiries about her prog-

ress: "Scarlett's doing very well, considering the trauma she's undergone. She's having to relearn everything from the ground up. Walking, speech, sight, all her muscle controls. It's quite amazing for all of us. Having her at home seems to be a big help. She's going through what they call 'aphasia,' which is a kind of gap in language comprehension. In other words, she may recognize an object but not be able to name it or call it another name. I think you described going through this in one of your stays in the hospital. Her emotions are like a little child, and she goes in and out of a wide range of feelings in a very short time" (pp. 69–70). This invaluable collection contains much material that reflects directly on the issues I consider in this essay.

3. Published first in Sam Shepard, Hawk Moon (New York: PAJ, 1981); reprinted in Shepard, Motel Chronicles and Hawk Moon, 185–86. I have discussed this piece and Shepard's Action elsewhere. See Re-reading Shepard, ed. Leonard Willcox (London: Macmillan, 1993), 59–62.

4. Sam Shepard, Action, in Angel City, Curse of the Starving Class, and Other Plays (London: Faber and Faber, 1978), 143.

5. A letter Shepard wrote to Chaikin during the period of their collaboration on The War in Heaven attests to Shepard's direct interest in the forms of life that are created in certain of his plays: "Something's been coming to me lately about this whole question of being lost. It only makes sense to me in relation to an idea of one's identity being shattered under severe personal circumstances—in a state of crisis where everything that I've previously identified with in myself falls away. A shock state, I guess you might call it. I don't think it makes much difference what the shock itself is—whether it's a trauma to do with a loved one or a physical accident or whatever—the resulting emptiness or aloneness is what interests me. Particularly to do with questions like home? family? the identification of others over time?" (Chaikin and Shepard, Letters and Texts, 1972–1984), 128.

6. Sam Shepard, A Lie of the Mind (London: Methuen, 1987), 4.

7. Ibid., 6.

8. I am grateful for a question posed by Andrew Sofer at the University of Michigan (at a lecture that formed the basis of this article) as to my views on the metonymic and metaphorical operations of language revealed in aphasia. As I think he suspects, both are applied by Shepard in what appears to be a profound impulse toward the deconstruction of the acting performance.

9. Shepard, A Lie of the Mind, 128–29.

10. Ibid., 125–26.

11. I have discussed the practical problems of performing this play and their relationship to its interpretation in "On the Meaning of Performance in Samuel Beckett's Not I," in Modern Drama 33, 4 (December 1990): 445–60.

See also Enoch Brater, *Beyond Minimalism: Beckett's Late Style in the Theater* (New York: Oxford University Press, 1987), 18–36.

12. Samuel Beckett, *Not I* (London: Faber and Faber, 1973), 8–9.

13. The elements that are "unsuited" in the aphasic examples given earlier.

14. I mean here to make clear that there is no suggestion of any sort of psychological naturalism, such as is frequently practiced in the contemporary theater, in which the reflection of the assumed character's supposed psychological makeup is imaginatively adopted by the actor. In this sense the actor would weep for Hecuba because she *is* a member of his family and the symbol of the despoiling of his home: Stanislavsky's hypothetical "if": "You know now that our work on a play begins with the use of *if* as a lever to lift us out of everyday life onto the plane of imagination. The play, the parts in it, are the invention of the author's imagination, a whole series of *ifs* and given circumstances thought up by him. There is no such thing as actuality on the stage. Art is a product of the imagination as the work of the dramatist should be. The aim of the actor should be to use his imagination to turn the play into a theatrical reality. In this process imagination plays the largest part." See Constantin Stanislavsky, *An Actor Prepares*, trans. Elisabeth Reynolds Hapgood (London: Bles, 1937), 54. One recognizes the problem that Stanislavsky here deals with, but he (or his translator) is clearly in difficulty wielding terms like *actuality* and *reality*. The lesson of Shepard and Beckett is that there is very much an actuality on the stage, and it is for that actuality that they compose their roles not for some "theatrical reality" of the actor's imagination.

15. It is notable that Shepard makes aphasia the consequence of a jealous beating, and Beckett submits the experience of disintegration to an implicit inquisition by an unsatisfiable outside agency. The dramatists are not drawn to the accidental.

16. The horror of the scene between Marcus Andronicus and his niece is central to a play that still receives only infrequent production and, in the words of one editor, Sylvan Barnet, "has had few admirers and numerous detractors." The recent production by the Royal Shakespeare Company, directed by Deborah Warner, revealed qualities that textual study had perhaps overlooked. The theme has recently been taken up again, to striking effect, in Timberlake Wertenbaker's *The Love of a Nightingale* (London: Faber, 1989).

17. *Titus Andronicus*, II.iv.16–18.

18. Ibid., 21–25.

19. Ibid., 33–35.

20. The composition of these tensions continues into Act III where Titus and Marcus differently understand Lavinia. Titus, mutilated as he is, plays on

the idea of "hands" and speech. The disintegration is specifically evoked in the references to his possible madness.

> Fie, fie, how frantically I square my talk,
> As if we should forget we had no hands,
> If Marcus did not name the word of hands!
>
> (III.i.31–33)

21. *All's Well That Ends Well*, IV.iii.317–23.
22. It is not my purpose here to inquire whether contemporary drama may in any way respond to a problem sensed in actors and the medium. Nevertheless, in observing the fashion in which plays are written, and which de facto they challenge a pseudostability that is often the refuge of the hard-pressed performer, one may suspect that dramatists are testing a frontier of experimentation. Particularly in an age of screen media, the appeal of the stage resides in a fundamental aspect of performance with which, conversely, actors, increasingly exercised in the film or television studio, are ill at ease or unfamiliar. This is an observation sometimes made by those concerned with staging of classics and the use of large houses and, worse still, both.
23. For information regarding the composition and translation of this work, see Enoch Brater, *The Drama in the Text: Beckett's Late Fiction* (New York: Oxford University Press, 1994), 165, 204.

"Aroun the Worl": The Signifyin(g) Theater of Suzan-Lori Parks

Linda Ben-Zvi

Before Columbus thuh worl usta be *roun* they put uh /d/ on
thuh end of roun makin round. Thusly they set in motion
thuh end. Without that /d/ we coulda gone on spinnin for
ever. Thuh /d/ thing ended things ended.
—Suzan-Lori Parks, *The Death of the Last Black Man in the Whole Entire World*

Make words from world but set them on the page—setting
them loose on the world.
—Interview with Suzan-Lori Parks

In 1971, Ruby Cohn published *Dialogue in American Theater,* a book in
which she discussed the work of four major American playwrights—
O'Neill, Miller, Williams, and Albee—all of whom had created a dis-
tinctive language with which to fashion their dramatic world. Such a
study hardly sounds daring; however, given the theatrical and critical
climate of that moment, the very fact of focusing on language might
be seen as a radical act. American theater was then basking in the heat
of the newly discovered Artaud, and echoing his motto, "No More

Masterpieces." In her opening chapter, "Artaud Versus Aristotle in America," Cohn described this "New Theater" so dedicated to performance over dramaturgy, where "scripted dialogue was being replaced by incantation, improvisation, laboratory, participation—life style." In the years since that book was written, the shift away from an Aristotelian-based theater has continued in America, fed by influences including, but not limited to, Artaud. Experimental works continue to be nonlinear, fragmentary, often incantatory, without delineated characters or recognizable plot. However, language, which in the first flush of this New Theater was seen as the enemy, an archaic reminder of a text-driven drama, has survived, often undergirding a new poetics of theater and even a new critical interest in semiotics, of verbal as well as nonverbal theatrical signs.

Representative of the new generation of American playwrights whose dialogic abilities reinforce a nonrepresentational form is Suzan-Lori Parks, a writer who calls her work "epic theater." In only four years, and with only three major productions to date, Suzan-Lori Parks has made a place for herself on the American stage. The four-part *Imperceptible Mutabilities in the Third Kingdom*, the first two sections of which were produced by BACA (the Brooklyn Academy of the Arts) Downtown Theater in 1988, and restaged there in its entirety in September 1989, won an Obie for best off-Broadway play in 1990. *The Death of the Last Black Man in the Whole Entire World*, her second play, was presented at BACA in 1990, and was given a larger production at the Yale Repertory Theater during its Winterfest program in 1992. Her third major work, *The America Play*, premiered at the Yale Rep in early 1994 and moved to the New York Public Theater in March.

Easy categorization is anathema to any serious playwright; to Parks it is particularly distasteful. As an African-American and a woman she has seen the results of prescriptive generalizations: "I don't want to be categorized in any way."[1] Although her plays are highly political and focus on race, she bristles when people assume that they are only about that subject.

It's insulting to say my plays are only about what it's about to be Black—as
if that is all we think about, as if our life is about that. My life is not about
race. It's about being alive.

She cites as models for her theater Samuel Beckett, Gertrude Stein,
and James Joyce, as well as African-American women playwrights,
particularly Adrienne Kennedy, whom she calls with great affection
and respect "Madame Adrienne": "She inspired me to take weird riffs
and shifts of character."[2] Like Kennedy, Parks fills her plays with
striking visual images that mutate wildly. Yet, while Kennedy materializes specters of a composite self constructed of movie stars, historical
figures, fictional characters, and family members—those "people
who led to my plays," the title of her singular, autobiographical
collection—Parks offers figures who seem to exist solely through the
words they speak.

In her foregrounding of language as image rather than image as
language—poetry in the theater rather than poetry of theater—Parks
seems closer to Ntozake Shange. Both are language-based; both use
dialect, omitting conventional punctuation and capitalization. However, there are essential differences. In her foreword to *Three Pieces*,
Shange explains that what have been called her "acrobatic distortions" of English are her version of Frantz Fanon's "combat breath,"
her own attempts to break free of an imposed "white man's version of
blk speech that waz entirely made up & based on no linguistic system
besides the language of racism."[3] Parks, on the other hand, stages the
process of linguistic deformation itself, the imposition of language
and culture and those strategies of survival encoded in the Black
vernacular. She offers less a face beneath a mask—a language beneath
a language—than the play between discourses: the intertextuality of
dominant and muted forms, foregrounding the very process of linguistic containment, commensurate culture, and political effacement,
indicating both the sickness and the means of healing: the development of a counterlanguage.

With a Kabbalistic belief in the power of even one letter to embody
the whole of a life or a people, Parks concretizes language in her

plays; the way a phrase is said, its rhetorical order, rhythm—even its shifts of spelling—inscribe and circumscribe the speakers in a social as well as historical matrix. As in life, the mispronunciation of phonemes such as /sk/ in *ask* can cost a job or place an individual in a social hierarchy; the shift of a letter—from uhm to humm—can change a life. " 'Thuh,' she says, slumping, 'makes th body /do something very different'—and here she straightens up—then 'The.' "[4] "It is words that push the ideas in my plays. . . . Language is a physical act, not merely some mental thing." So completely does she subscribe to the notion that words can indicate stage action that her plays are devoid of any stage directions or traditional markers for staging. "If you're writing the play—why not put the directions in the writing. Shakespeare did," she says. A director of a Parks play must translate words into stage images and movement. Such possibilities, obviously, allow more freedom of interpretation than do traditional texts. However, Liz Diamond, who has directed all of Parks's plays to date, says that the plays do provide a basis for staging arising from the rhythms, repetitions, and revisions of words, much as they do in Brecht's theater. For instance, near the end of *Last Black Man* the central figure, Black Woman with Drumstick, has the following speech.

> Somethins turnin. Huh. Whatizit.—Mercy. Mercy. Huh. Chew on this. Ssuh feather. Sswhatchashud be eatin ya no. Ssuhfeather: stuffin. Chew on it. Huh.[5]

For Diamond the actions of the speaker grow from the language; something is happening, which Black Woman with Drumstick senses.

> She gives up trying to articulate what she senses for the moment with a "huh." And then she moves on to the task at hand, which is, quite simply, to feed her beloved Black Man feathers which have mysteriously appeared. She must stuff him.[6]

Parks puts the matter more simply: "If you want to know what my world looks like just read the words out loud. They will make you 'see.' "

On the title page of the revised text 6 of *Imperceptible Mutabilities in the Third Kingdom*, Parks carefully defines each word. *Imperceptible* is "that which by its nature cannot be perceived or discerned by the mind or the senses." *Mutabilities* is "things disposed to change." And *in the Third Kingdom*: ". . . that of fungi. Small, overlooked, out of sight, of lesser consequences. All of that. And also: the space between."[7] Parks's "imperceptible mutabilities" become a verbal palimpsest bearing the traces of the forms from which they emerge and against which they react, "the space between" becoming the gestic marks of enforced social systems and their possible de-construction.

Like music, and especially jazz, the play is built on echoing sets: four short plays, *Snails, Third Kingdom, Open House,* and *Greeks.* Each is capable of being performed independently but designed to signify on the others, creating thereby those intratextual as well as intertextual "Talking Books" that Henry Louis Gates, Jr., notes as a primary feature of Black writing.[8] Together the plays create a composite picture of African-American experience, starting in the present, moving back to retell the forced journey from Africa over the Middle Passage, and concluding with two "family plays," which trace, chronologically— from Reconstruction to post–World War II—the devastating effects of slavery on individuals and society. Within each play, there are further subdivisions marked by letters: six sections in *Snails,* and seven each in *Open House* and *Greeks. Third Kingdom,* which functions as a choral ode bridging spatial and temporal divisions, is not subdivided, allowing for the sense of the unbroken—albeit disjunctive—voyage that the piece depicts. While the action in each play is nonsequential, built on linguistic repetitions and revisions, there are nonetheless formal markers, much as in a play by Beckett. For example, each play has five characters, the names usually rhyming or the same. In *Snails,* three roommates call themselves Mona, Chona, and Verona, although they are called Molly, Charlene, and Veronica, "names what whuduhnt ours." In *Third Kingdom* the voices that trace the Middle Passage are homonymic parodies: Kin-seer, Us-seer, Shark-seer, and Soul-seer, signifyin(g) on the last of the line: Over-seer. In *Open House,* the family members are all named Saxon: Anglor, Blanca, and father Charles; the mother surrogate, Aretha Saxon, an ex-slave, being extracted from the

the figure Black Woman with Drumstick in *Last Black Man*, soothes and provides food—a positive act in Parks's plays not a sign of female servitude. She marks the counterlanguage, a shorthand developed and understood by the three women in the apartment. It is also Chona who signifies on the offending phrase.

> Once there was uh little lamb who followed Mary good n put uh hex on Mary. When Mary dropped dead, thuh lamb was in thuh lead. You can study at home. I'll help.

Mona, however, is unable to take solace in the offer; she is so traumatized by language that she cannot even act. "I am going to lie down. I am going to lay down. Lie down? Lay down. Lay down?" Grammar may encapsulate a gest; it can also immobilize those unable to function within its terms.

Scene two switches from the apartment to the lectern, at which a Naturalist, using a parody of Social Science talk—another example of signifyin(g)—addresses the audience, describing his latest disguise: a giant cockroach, the urban variation of "the fly on the wall," which he plans to don in order to enter the apartment, the better to "insure the capturence of his subjects in a state of nature." The exterminator—"Wipe-um-out-Lutsky with uh Ph.D."—called to rid the women of the invading bug is played by the same actor; thus the solution is conflated with the problem, both imposed on the women from without. Instead of "hosing" the bug, Lutsky hoses the women. Against this composite figure, however, stands another male presence in the apartment: a robber. Rather than the surreptitious robbery of identity performed by the Naturalist/Lutsky, this figure "uses the door." He is also silent: "He didn't have no answers cause he didn't have no speech." Verona, who says he has "that deep jungle air uhbout im," names him Mokus, "But Mokus whuduhnt his name." Mokus becomes a visual mark of resistance, a trace of that now lost African language the absence of which is marked by signifyin(g) practices, which are grounded outside of western tradition.[9]

The image is repeated in the following sections of the play. In *Third Kingdom*, Shark-seer speaks of a figure who "diduhnt have no answers cause he diduhnt have no speech. Instead, he spoke in uh language of codes: secret signs and symbols." In *Greeks*, Mrs. Sergeant Smith explains to her children that her husband's letters are written in a special language, necessary to avoid "the Censors."

> Certain things said and certain ways of saying certain things may clue-in the enemy. Certain things said may allow them to catch Sergeant Smith unawares. Sergeant Smith . . . deals in a language of codes—secret signs and signals.

That is why Sergeant Smith is "figuring his speech," she explains. Figuring, or signifyin(g), becomes a way of dealing with incursion and surveillance from without. The traumatized Mona, unable to speak "correctly" in the presence of the Naturalist, is only able to utter "MonaMokusRobbery" ever faster, the words a kind of incantation against the inscribing language with "Everythin in its place."

In apposition to Mokus, and in collusion with the Naturalist/Lutsky, is the mass media, figured in this play by the person of Marlin Perkins of "Wild Kingdom" fame, who taught an entire generation, Black and White, the television version of Africa. Verona, in the last monologue of *Snails*, moves to the lectern and, against a slide show with images of the three women overhead, relates, in uninflected language, her own upbringing: how she watched the adored Perkins who "loved and respected all the wild things," who "tagged the animals and put them into zoos for their own protection," and on whose program she first learned about "black folks with no clothes." Internalizing the lessons of the television, Verona tells of her own attempts to play Perkins and domesticate a black dog, which she names Namib, and her later revenge at his incalcitrance when, working in a veterinary hospital where she is "a euthanasia specialist," she performs euthanasia on a black dog.

> I stayed late that night so that I could cut her open because I had to see I just had to see the heart of such a disagreeable domesticated thing. But no. Nothing different. Everything in its place. Do you know what that means? Everything in its place. That's all.

The play ends with this chilling image.[10]

A summary of *Snails* may make it seem a defeatist work, the three women powerless against the forces of an imposed language and cultural stereotypes. However, Parks's language militates against such a reading: the Naturalist/Lutsky, who comes bearing hoses to squirt the offending women, is himself exterminated by parody; and the women speak, despite all, a rich, communal language growing out of shared experiences, while Mokus is exactly the visual mark of what Gates calls an irretrievable African heritage, becoming in its stead a signifier "that is silent, a 'sound image' as Saussure defines the signifier, but a 'sound image' sans the sound."[11] By starting her play in the present and moving chronologically back and then forward, Parks suggests less the cultural inevitability of the African-American experience than the societal need to address modes of thinking and speaking that have been encoded in academic, social, and cultural languages. Her anti-Aristotelian, epic form creates Brechtian alienation; it also illustrates the centrality of language in any remembering of society or individuals.

"Everything in its place" and how it got that way are the themes of the next three plays. After the claustrophobic linguistic and spatial world of *Snails*, *Third Kingdom* provides a choral interlude, creating a correlative to what the words describe: the retelling of the voyage from Africa to slavery. Even less wedded to realistic representation than the first play, this section creates, through words, a world suddenly cleaved in two: between a "there," which is rapidly receding from view during the voyage, and a "here" not yet on the horizon. "Last night I dreamed of where I comed from. But where I comed from diduhnt look like nowhere like I been," Kin-seer says at the beginning of the play. The speakers try to hold on as long as they can to their "other self," but in vain.

> My uther me then waved back at me and then I was happy. But my uther me whuduhnt wavin at me. My uther me was wavin at my Self. My uther me ws waving at uh black black speck in thuh middle of thuh sea where years uhgoh from uh boat I had been—UUH!

The "UUH" marks the point of cultural and linguistic expunging—from home, from self, from language, and from history—that is replicated in each play and figured by a different word: in *Third King-dom* by the repeated "jettisoned," in *Snails* by "exterminated," in *Open House* by "extracted," and in *Greeks* by "censored."

As the old self is no longer visible, the speakers in the play create a third self: "My new self was uh 3rd Self made by thuh space in be-tween." Parks again foregrounds a constructed presence to mark an absence. This 3rd self begins by using "you," but switches to "I" to ask, "am I Happy? Is my new Self happy in my new Self shoes." "Must be," the speaker concludes, because—moving to "we"—"Thuh looks we look look so." As Marlin Perkins taught, "Black folks with no clothes" smile. "Then all thuh black folks clothed in smilin." The source of the smile is immediately explained: "They like smiles and we will like what they will like." Before the boat arrives at shore the strategy is set: a strategy of forced smiles and of signifyin(g): "He diduhnt have no answers cause he diduhnt have no speech. Instead, he spoke in uh language of codes, secret signs and symbols," the effaced, silent lan-guage of Mokus. The double voice, again at work here, provides the dialectic of the play: "But we are not in uh boat," Shark-seer says four times in the play, to which Us-seer responds, "But we iz." The voice that speaks in the play is the voice of displacement, the voice in the boat.

The third play, *Open House*, becomes a verbal and visual signifyin(g) on the imposed smile of *Third Kingdom*. Aretha, ex-slave and surrogate mother for a white family, attempts to smile, despite the sadistic extrac-tion of her teeth. Her very mouth and smile metonymically mark the slave experience. As each of her teeth is yanked from her mouth, a process recorded by Miss Faith in a book, Aretha supplies a fact of African-American history similarly "extracted" from white history texts.

While the play begins with Aretha's imprecation to her young white charges, "Smile, honey, smile," and her envy of their "nice white teeth," the language, in counterdistinction to that of *Snails*, traces a growing assertion of self through time. The freed slave who is "let go" because she has "gone slack," extracted from history with only her required "smiling" photograph to mark her presence, be-comes by the end of the play the sought-after domestic, no better appreciated or treated but now the wielder of the camera not its subject. At the end of the play, Aretha, toothless, snaps the photographs of the white family, capturing their helplessness when deprived of her services. When she tells the boy and girl she has raised that they will now have to turn to their mother, they ask in unison, "Who!??!" If she has been extracted, the Saxons have been made impotent by their wielding of white privilege. The section ends with father Charles turning to the camera and Aretha. "Smile!" she says; but they are crying.

Re-membering marks the final play, *Greeks*—the most powerful of the four—signifyin(g) on the Greek myth of Odysseus, played out by a 1950s African-American family that waits patiently to receive what the white society has promised: "distinction." Again employing the photographic image, Parks begins by having Sergeant Smith pose for a series of photographs he will send home, showing himself in various poses of authority: "No mop n broom bucket today!" In his periodic letters, he explains his goal: "The distinctions when one's set upart. Uh distinction's when they give ya bars" for "doing somethin noble." While he waits, his family grows, a child added after each of Mrs. Seargeant Smith's trips "to the coast." Her own marks of distinction parallel his. Instead of seeking rewards for nobility, his wife, a patient, modern Penelope circa 1950, dusts and irons, faithfully waiting, taking her own mark of pride in the appearance of her house, family, and person. As she tells her daughters, when she emerged from the bus that takes her to her husband—at first a bus in which she was made to sit in the back and later allowed to ride in front, both of which she does with equanimity— she "wanted tuh look like I hadn't traveled uh mile or sweated uh drop." Buffy finishes the story, "You were just as proud," and Mrs. Smith echoes, "I was just as proud." All other facts of their lives— segregation, the systematic stripping of possessions in reverse order to the growth of the family—fade against this image, set against a sky that is "Just as blue," echoing the blue sky and coast of *Third Kingdom*.

This modern-day Odysseus comes home in old age, broken, crippied, to a wife who is blind and children who hardly recognize him.

He has finally received his distinction but not as he expected. Instead of being honored for faithful service, he is rewarded for breaking a fall. "Caught uh man as he was fallin out thuh sky," he explains,

> They say he was flyin too close to thuh sun. They say I caught him but he fell. On me. They give me uh distinction. They set me apart. They say I caught him but he fell. He fell on me. I broked his fall. I saved his life. I ain't seen him since.

The lesson Smith has for his family—and the audience—is summed up in his answer to his son's repeated question, which closes the play. Afraid that his father will not recognize him when he returns, just as turtles do not seem to recognize their young, the boy asks, "Are we turtles?" To which Smith replies, "No, we ain't even turtles. Huh. We'se slugs. Slugs. Slugs." Returning to the image that opened *Imperceptible Mutabilities*, Parks substitutes slugs for snails, a linguistic shift that marks the slow unfolding of her theme: even the "shelly cave" created by the women in *Snails* is no protection against racism and reality. As the play indicates, distinctions will not be awarded for good conduct.

The ledger the Smiths faithfully keep, and in which Aretha marks the facts of the slave trade and pastes her smiling photos, is a book of myths, in which, to borrow a phrase from Adrienne Rich, "our names do not appear." In her next play, *The Death of the Last Black Man in the Whole Entire World*, Parks writes her own re-membered mythic tale, not a borrowed tale that doesn't fit, as in the case of the Smiths, but one tailored to fit the voice and the spirit of her composite African-American couple: Black Man with Watermelon and Black Woman with Fried Drumstick.

As the names indicate, the figures in this play are even less characters in the traditional sense than were those in *Imperceptible Mutabilities*. Here they stand as a line of signifiers, demarcating the time line of black experience, a chronicle of death and commensurate erasure from history. The man and woman of this ur-couple have as their signs watermelon and chicken; they have been stripped of meaning by a white society and re-figured as racial stereotypes. In the course of the play, Parks restores them to their place within the lives of the figures. The couple is surrounded by others whose history or functions have been similarly usurped and are re-membered in the play. There are those with names evoking Black history: the ancient Queen-then-Pharaoh Hatshepsut,[12] precolonial Before Columbus, and slave narrator Old Man River Jordan. There are figures depicted as the food that sustains the couple: Lots of Grease and Lots of Pork, and Yes and Greens Black-Eyed Peas Cornbread. There is Prunes and Prisms, a name borrowed from Joyce's *Ulysses*, here used by the speaker as a way of altering her appearance: "Say 'prunes and prisms' forty times each day and you'll cure your big lips." Parks also includes a literary figure, whom Gates describes as taking on an iconic function in many African-American texts: Bigger Thomas, from Richard Wright's *Native Son*, here named And Bigger and Bigger and Bigger, in part to mark his metafunction beyond the text that gave him life. Finally, as in *Imperceptible Mutabilities*, Parks introduces a series of signifyin(g) voices, now figured as individual speakers. Ham becomes a conflation of the Black rhyme, capitalized and repeated throughout the play, "HAM BONE HAM BONE WHERE YOU BEEN ROUN THUH WORL N BACK A-GAIN," and as the biblical Ham who, in the key section of the play, offers his own signifyin(g) on the "begatting" of *Genesis*, peopling his version with the progeny of slavery.

A final voice heard in the play is Voice on thuh Tee V. It is he who reports the latest version of the reported death of the Black man, the central action of the play. Black Man with Watermelon keeps being killed—electrocuted, lynched, hanged—and keeps returning, bearing the traces of his trials and testimony of his suffering, both of which have been written out of history. Once he enters wearing the severed rope of a lynching, once carrying the leather straps and chair of electrocution: "Closer tuh thuh power I never been." What seems important is not simply the suffering that he has endured but the silencing and usurping of his story of suffering. As Queen-then-Pharaoh Hatshepsut explains:

We are too young to see. Let them see it for you. We are too young to rule. Let them rule it for you. We are too young to have. Let them have it for you. You are too young to write. Let them—let them. Do it. Before you.

The shift of pronouns marks in Parks's writing, as it does in the work of other African-Americans such as Zora Neale Hurston, the use often made of free, indirect discourse: here the speaker shifts from her own words to a "theirs" internalized, spoken through her as her voice. To reinforce this sense of experience and its signification on stage, Liz Diamond, the director of the Yale Rep production, doubled each figure of death: one experiencing it and one telling it. While Black Man speaks to his wife about electrocution and hanging, about being chased by dogs and jumping into rivers to avoid detection, a shadow figure enacts images of death, at one point sitting in an electric chair with metal helmet clamped to his head, at another time swinging from a rope over the stage.

Each time, waiting to hear his story and minister to him—as Chona did in *Snails*—Black Woman stands strong, the only figure, Parks has said, who is actually alive. "Everyone else is dead, some more than others, but dead."[13] This mother/wife figure, the sustainer of life and of memory, is not a meek provider of food; she is the active doer— "Struttered down on up thuh road with my axe. By-myself-with-my-axe. Tooked tuh stranglin." At Black Man's last return, it is she who bathes and feeds him, cradling him in her arms. She also speaks the last individual words of the play.

Not separated into short plays, *Last Black Man* is divided, instead, into seven discrete sections: Overture; Panel I: Thuh Holy Ghost; Panel II: First Chorus; Panel III: Thuh Lonesome 3some; Panel IV: Second Chorus; Panel V: In thuh Garden of HooDoo it; and Final Chorus. The result is a play that approximates, even more closely than her earlier work, a jazz composition, with repetition and revision in both language and action providing the forward thrust of the piece. However, instead of employing the traditional musical technique of having the Chorus repeat a refrain while the alternating sections carry the new motif, Parks reverses the pattern. Her central couple appears alone in the Panels, during which time "we see them at various points of confusion—which are the same points of confusion over and over again refigured with different variables," as Parks says. For her the idea of such re-figured Panels came "partly from the Stations of the

Cross—the tableau of Christ which hangs in churches." She describes the function of the Choruses as

> the spaces between those tableaux . . . nothing. A blank space. So the Choruses are figuring the blank space between. That's why the Choruses are so weird. They're coming out of that blank, unspoken, unfigured space.

Yet, unlike the traditional Greek chorus, or even choruses in music, Parks's choruses are not repetitions but the place

> where the really new information is presented, where the action really happens. With *Last Black Man* I'm using elements of traditional song and structure and inverting, subverting, converting those elements.[14]

From fixity to movement becomes the thrust or "forward progression" of the play. Beginning with the line "The Black Man moves his hands," Parks takes her people on a linguistic voyage back through African-American experience, historic and literary, animating her characters as she plays with a set of phrases and transformations that alter the former line to read "Thuh black man he move. He move. He hans." In this play the mark of "everything in its place" is a letter, the /d/, which she effaces from han(d), allowing the Black Man movement. The /d/ got fixed in place, Before Columbus explains, once "they" realized the world was round, not flat.

> Them thinking the world was flat kept it roun. Them thinking the sun revolved around the earth kept them satellite-like. They figured out the truth and scurried out. Figuring out the truth put them in their place and they scurried out to put us in ours.

Parks has her speakers re-figure the world, moving toward an erasure of /d/ in order to move their han(d)s and to regain their worl(d) as an active, not fixed form, created by themselves, not imposed upon them. Like the effaced /g/ in signifyin(g), the effaced /d/ unfixes the dominant version of history and allows for the story of Black Man with Watermelon to be told. The last three repetitions of the title read, "This is the death of the last black man in the whole entire worl."

But to *tell* the tale of Black history is not enough, Parks indicates; it must be written down. One of the dominant refrains in the work is this need to "write it down," not have it written for "you" by "them." In the first Chorus, all the actors recite: "You should write that down and you should hide it under a rock." The refrain is repeated with variation through the sections of the play. Having animated the various deaths of Black Man with Watermelon, the speakers have created their own images in that space where there was, to use Parks's description, "nothing." In the final Chorus, Yes and Greens Black-Eyed Peas Cornbread is able to offer this variant on the phrase.

> You will write it down because if you dont write it down then we will come along and tell the future that we did not exist. You will write it down and you will carve it out of a rock.

No longer conditional, the telling becomes active, a call for action. No longer hidden under the rock, it is by the end of the play carved into it.

In *The America Play*, Parks uses the trope of chiasmus as the central image and controlling structure of her third play.[15] When she was a child, Parks wanted to be a geologist; for her the act of writing is a form of digging: cracking open words to discover the secrets that lie hidden, reading in them the stories of times past and of times to come. *The America Play* is excavatory, as were her earlier works. But unlike *Last Black Man*, into which she admits "putting everything I knew," here the landscape is verbally spartan, the repetitions and revisions creating chiasmi that stem more from actions than words; the effect is close to the choreographed repetitions and variations of Robert Wilson's replayed image rather than to a word carrying the kernel of the whole.

"Everyone who has ever walked the earth has a shape around which their entire lives and posterity shapes itself," Parks's leading figure explains. Act I of the two-act play is entitled "Lincoln Act," in which the figure named The Foundling Father, as Abraham Lincoln, a digger by profession, shapes his life in accordance with a "historicized" version of "The Great One," gleaned from "The Great Hole of History," that "Theme Park" where the past is paraded and distorted before an eager public. Bearing a striking resemblance to the "real" Lincoln, the Black Lincoln lookalike, calling himself "the Lesser Known," spends his life imitating not the life but the death of "The Great One," a historicized version made up of re-membered facts, fictions, and myths that have accumulated around the evening at Ford's Theatre and that pass as history. Standing between a bust and a cutout of Lincoln, nodding first to one, then winking at the other, he enacts the death of Lincoln, played as a kind of carnival sideshow in which people pay their money and take their shots while speaking a variety of phrases loosely attributed to the people connected with the event. The first act thus stages the primary term of the chiasmus: the Foundling Father, as Abraham Lincoln, provides a visual diagonal transference of the terms of the Great Man, himself effaced by the distortions surrounding his person and his life. While the goal in *Last Black Man* was to "write it down," here Parks indicates how difficult it is to reconstruct history.

Act II becomes the shadowed variation. Entitled "The Hall of Wonders," it focuses on the attempts of the Lesser One's Wife, Lucy, and his son, Brazil—"named in a fit of meanspirit after the bad joke about fancy nuts and old mens toes"—to dig for the remains of their disappeared husband and father. The act of digging constitutes the major part of the play; the second act is three times longer than the first and is subdivided into ten sections. Four of these relate to elements in the earlier act, providing bits of information about how Lucy and Brazil got to where they are. Two, called "Echo" and "Archeology," also echo the earlier act. Three sections provide brief scenes from *The American Cousin*, signifyin(g) on the present experiences of Lucy and Brazil. And there is a concluding scene, entitled "The Great Beyond," against which the first act is replayed, now seen on a television screen.

Again it is the female figure who seeks some sort of understanding and who is not, like her husband, content to "fake it." As she explains to her son while they dig,

Itssalways been important in my line to distinguish. Tuh know thuh difference. Not like your Fathuh. Your Fathuh became confused. His lonely
death and lack of proper burial is our embarrassment. Go on: dig. Now me
I need tuh know thuh real thing from thuh echo. Thuh truth from the
hearsay.

How the past shapes the present is a central theme in each of
Parks's plays. In the first two the emphasis has been directly on the
experience of slavery; in this play, she illustrates how difficult, if not
impossible, it is to have even a sense of "the boat." History in *The
America Play* is merely a set of variations on a variation: the Foundling
Father as Abraham Lincoln, with his disguises, "playing" the Great
Man, is himself figured as a set of constructed images (the log cabin,
the stovepipe hat, even the scene of death). For all the digging of Lucy
and Brazil, the only vision of the past that remains is a silent re-
running of the first act, a made-for-TV version of history, complete
with canned laughter. If a chiasmus re-figures the first term of a
sentence, Parks seems to be saying that to signify unendingly upon
the terms of the dominant culture can only lead to "nothing," since
that which is being signified on is only a series of distorted "his-
toricities," a "Great Hole" and never the (W)hole. To pattern one's
own life or story—or language—on such distortions is to be trapped
in a structure the terms of which finally imprison, like chiasmus itself.
One is left at the end of *The America Play* with two possibilities: the
total failure of language to do anything more than create disguises
that pass as truth, or the need to stop signifyin(g) on the dominant
discourse and occupy, at last, the initial clause.

NOTES

1. Unless otherwise noted, all the statements by Suzan-Lori Parks are
   quoted from my conversations with the author.
2. Although Parks had long admired Kennedy, she only met her in the
   summer of 1993 when the two, and Ntozake Shange, participated in Los
   Angeles on a panel on African-American women playwrights. They took
   an instant liking to each other, and after the conference Parks convinced

Kennedy to visit Disneyland with her. Parks described her discomfort on the panel when Shange began to speak for "The black woman playwright," using a collective "we," asserting that at times white audiences were not needed, a position that Parks does not share: "I don't want to be so narrowly defined; I want as many people to see my works as possible." See also Alisa Solomon, "To Be Young, Gifted, and African American," *Village Voice*, 19 September 1989, 99.

3. Ntozake Shange, *Three Pieces: 'spell #7'; A Photograph: Lovers in Motion; Boogie Woogie Landscapes* (London: Penguin, 1981), xii.

4. See Alisa Solomon, "Language in *Last Black Man*," in *Bedford Introduction to Drama*, ed. Lee A. Jacobus (Boston: St. Martin's, 1993), 1375.

5. See *The Death of the Last Black Man in the Whole Entire World*, in *Bedford*, 1367. All subsequent citations from this play are to this edition.

6. See Solomon, "Language in *Last Black Man*," 1373.

7. All quotations from *Imperceptible Mutabilities in the Third Kingdom* come from the revised version of the text, corrections made in September 1991, which will be published in *Vital Voices: An Anthology of Woman Playwrights*, ed. Linda Ben-Zvi (Ann Arbor: University of Michigan Press, forthcoming). The major changes from the original play include the lengthening of the Naturalist's two speeches, the omission of the double names for the three women in *Snails* and the slide show in *Open House*, and inclusion of several of the footnoted items now spoken by Aretha within the text. See also the text of the play as printed in *Theater* 24, 3 (1993): 88–115.

8. On this point, see Henry Louis Gates, Jr., *The Signifying Monkey: A Theory of Afro-American Literary Criticism* (New York: Oxford University Press, 1988). On the influence of jazz, see Houston A. Baker, Jr., "Belief, Theory, and Blues: Notes for a Post-Structuralist Criticism of Afro-American Literature," in *Studies in Black American Literature*, vol. 7, ed. Joe Weixlmann and Chester Fontenot (Greenwood, Fla.: Penkevill, 1986). *Greeks* was performed separately, and effectively, at the Manhattan Theater Club's Downtown/Uptown program.

9. Gates, xxii–xxiii.

10. Joan Schenkar, in *Signs of Life*, and Maria Irene Fornes, in *The Conduct of Life*, have similar images of people desiring to dissect the dead. In both cases the dissector is a man, and his desire is power over a woman or a politically oppressed person of either sex.

11. Gates, 46.

12. In *People Who Led to My Plays* (New York: Knopf, 1987), 96, Adrienne Kennedy says that she kept a photograph of Queen Hatshepsut on her wall and would look at it and Beethoven's statue in turn. "I did not then understand that I felt torn between these forces of my ancestry . . . European and African . . . a fact that would one day explode in my work."

Is the English Epic Over?

JANELLE REINELT

My title question poises on the convergence of world-historical events, British domestic politics, theatrical and artistic innovation, and the relatively recent representation of diverse subjects within British culture, including theater. The thesis of this essay is that, while epic strategies have saturated political drama and become absorbed within theatrical practice almost beyond the point of recognition, they are still a constitutive part of political performances. The recent striking conflation of history and theater has effected a critical and rhetorical shift in theatrical language; but the degree to which *epic* will disappear from critical discourse is still open. As for the English part of English Epic, it is indeed over because in the 1990s the voices, perspectives, and cultures—both of writers and their representations—are and will be demonstrably more diverse than the hegemonic writers' profile of past decades.

It may seem strange to speak of left-wing writers who have battled censors, critics, and funding agencies all of their professional lives as hegemonic. Yet in important ways Edward Bond, Howard Brenton, David Hare, Trevor Griffiths, Caryl Churchill, Howard Barker, David

Edgar et al. have become institutionalized as *the* political theater writers. For thirty years, political theater in Britain has been largely English and Epic; English insofar as the major writers have written as English writers with a critique of Englishness. Imperialism, class privilege, ethical bankruptcy, sexism, racism—the list is long, but the perspective is in-house. They have worked as friends and colleagues in institutionalized and nationally funded theater venues (as well as many other places), and their work has dominated critical writing about the British theater as well.

These white, English, middle-aged writers have developed a theatrical style loosely identified by themselves, the press, and academic critics as epic.[1] Often, *epic* is used as a deliberate reference to Bertolt Brecht's Epic Theater traditions, which have provided a substantial legacy to postwar political playwrights.[2] At other times, *epic* refers to a wider tradition, encompassing Shakespeare as well as Brecht, usually invoked as a contrast to realism. Sometimes, as in Kimball King's formulation, *epic* simply seems to mean large in size and scope;[3] at other times specific structural features constitute the epic aspect of a play. Many tight, semi-independent scenes, for example, echo Brecht's insistence that "the episodes have to be knotted together in such a way that the knots are easily noticed."[4] Other epic features include character externally rendered as social and class positioning (in contrast to inner psychological subjectivity), and the dialectical movements of history and context within the narrative. In addition to the dramaturgy of certain writers, the English Epic is associated with theaters such as the Royal Court and the National, with companies such as Joint Stock and Foco Novo, and with directors such as William Gaskill and Max Stafford-Clark.

The English Epic, then, is a broad umbrella term that has become widely recognized as signifying British political theater. However, as an adequate description it does not always work well. Consider Sarah Daniels and Mustapha Matura, both successful and established writers with important productions of new plays. Yet neither of them fits comfortably within the English Epic canon, and neither has received extended critical attention. The tendency of critical nomenclature to exclude, or at least diminish, the visibility of variations and alternatives constitutes the sense of the hegemonic that I have employed here. This hegemony has never been absolute—particular writers, theaters, and companies have resisted or simply diverged from its pull, but until recently these alternatives have not seriously challenged the ongoing dominance of the English Epic.

The conjuncture of three recent developments has opened a space for a reconfiguration of the political theatrical canon, especially necessitating a reappraisal of left-wing ideology and dramaturgy. These three are the end of the Cold War, the legacy of Margaret Thatcher's domestic policies, and the emergence of diverse new theatrical perspectives in the wake of postcolonial and multicultural critiques.[5] Each of these has destablized the English Epic and contributed to the present possibility of a new cultural formation for British political theater.

The revolutions of 1989 and the collapse of socialism in the Eastern bloc have thrown the identity and the program of the Left in Britain (as elsewhere) into extreme crisis. The end of the Cold War has also had several direct consequences for political theater, to the extent that most of the established Left playwrights were associated with an ideology, indeed a "side," that lost. As Fred Halliday writes,

> The End of the Cold War . . . [is] being achieved not on the basis of a covergence of the two systems, or of a negotiated truce between them, but on the basis of the collapse of one in the face of the other. This means nothing less than the defeat of the Communist project as it has been known in the twentieth century and the triumph of the capitalist.[6]

While Brenton, Bond, and the others were never uncritical advocates of communism, they were committed socialists who knew their Marx and believed in the possibility of radical change toward a classless society—not naively, not reductively, but nonetheless concretely and in the language and categories of a recognized Marxist discourse. Thus, the perceived rout of the Left political binary also seems to defeat them by association, or at least to make their previous work seem obsolete.

Theater, as a form of performative discourse, had embodied the Cold War struggle in a highly codified and stable system of signifiers. When the Cold War vanished as an organizing principle of debate, it also vanished as a credible axis of dramatic conflict in the representation of political life. Or, rather, since drama is structured in terms of action and conflict, its ability to represent economically a bipolar conflict like the Cold War is in part the function of genre. In the combination of political material and theatrical form, British theater had come to signify a Left cultural practice within state institutions (and thus an obvious target for Thatcherism). In addition, the particular association of epic plays with Bertolt Brecht also linked the tradition of contemporary political theater to an East German communist who, even before the fall of the Wall, had become increasingly discredited artistically as well as politically.[7]

This sense of the falling off of the relevance and efficacy of the English Epic came into focus after many years of Thatcherism slowly but surely underfunded alternative theater that not only created and produced political plays but provided a substructure of venue and opportunity for new leftist writing. The stories of the demise of such companies as Foco Novo, 7:84, and Joint Stock are typical of the deliberate destruction of leftist companies under Thatcherite arts policies. At the same time, and perhaps even more importantly, Thatcherism participated in the dismantling of the Left opposition through ideological means.[8]

In fact, in much the same way that the changes of 1989 made the bipolar opposition between East and West obsolete, the Thatcher revolution has succeeded in making the traditional British distinctions between Left and Right, Labour and Tory, similiarly imprecise. It was a victory for the Right, and yet Thatcherism has redefined the Right. In his analysis of this formidable feat, Stuart Hall emphasizes the coming apart of the postwar consensus, which he sees as a "bargain between conflicting social interests."[9] Under its terms, the Right agreed to live with the welfare state, comprehensive education, Keynesian economic policies, and the goal of full employment, while the Left accepted modified capitalism and identification with the strategic interests of the Western bloc. This agreement allowed government to go forward and it also structured a stable and partisan set of disagreements—in short, an oppositional Right/Left identity. As the 1960s and 1970s saw the gradual disintegration of this "deal" under the pressures of weak economic growth and low levels of technological advance, insufficient financing and spiraling public-sector costs, each side reiterated its opposition to the constellation of values endorsed by the other. The rhetoric, the categories, and the conceptualization no longer represented reality. This Margaret Thatcher realized and exploited; she set out to "disorganize common sense."

Many of the major changes of her era were even disorienting to her own party—such as the abolition of municipal government or the central administration of "quality control" in the National Health Service. The most significant realignment, of course, has been the unprecedented number of skilled and semiskilled industrial workers, trade unionists, and even urban unemployed who have been persuaded by Thatcherism's rhetoric of "value for money" and "free choice." While there are many aspects of this change of allegiance, one that was shared by the governments of the Eastern bloc socialist states is the misunderstood role of material goods and services in the cultural consciousness of working people.[10] Similarly, in Britain, the Left had underestimated the relationship between popular culture and real needs. Thatcher did understand, and was able to align the positive aspirations of people for material benefits to the market and capitalist ethics, thereby conflating disparate notions of freedom, creating the kind of political vaccum that produced a "lack of any radical hostility to capitalism itself."[11]

This turning over of the general categories of explanation that structure everything from mass media and advertising to scholarly analysis and parliamentary debate interacted with the historical crisis of 1989 to inflect further the post–Cold War situation. I believe this climate, this structure of feeling, as Raymond Williams would have it, provides the context of theatrical reception as well as posing a formidable challenge to playwrights indentified with the Left Old Guard.

One of the positive keys to understanding the shift in tone and emphasis that has occurred over the past decade is the emergence of writers who stand apart from the established political writers, either because of their theatrical route of travel or because of their cultural backgrounds and experiences. I have in mind the important contribution of feminist writers and companies, gay and lesbian writers and companies, and various diverse ethnic writers and companies. The theatrical Left, like the wider political Left, fragmented along identity-politics lines throughout the 1980s. While this fragmentation has had severe consequences for coalition politics, it has also spawned a vital and prodigious cultural renaissance, including theatrical production and especially playwriting. Thus, the Left weakened, but some important individual constituencies coalesced, ironically growing stronger while under financial and ideological seige. Not that these theater writers are completely distinguishable from the established ones—many of the writers I have in mind have had plays produced at the Royal Court, for instance, or have worked there in various capacities, for example, as script readers. The Court, that perfect representative of the politically hegemonic, has also encouraged and produced part of its own opposition.

Hanif Kureishi, for instance, worked for several years at the Court, and had his first play produced Upstairs at a Sunday Night without Decor, and yet he describes the distance between the inside and outside to which I allude.

> The obsession of the many professional gossips at the Court, their focus, as it were, was not only sex but class, the origins of those working there and what these meant precisely. . . . This dissection had originally been a Marxist tool, a way of clarifying what was fatuous and cruel about England, but it had become self-hatred, a form of categorization, exclusion and contempt. I've never known any group of people more gripped by the aristocracy and the business of the royal family.[12]

Apart from the obvious critique of the management from one of a younger generation, this way of lumping the established Royal Court personages together, and defining his point of view as different, establishes Kureishi's "different" context. In describing his work with Joint Stock on *Borderline*, a play about Sikh immigrants in Southall, he identifies the experience as "a setting-out of the themes that would absorb [him] for a long time" in his discovery of the "diversity and drama of the Asian community."[13] At the same time, the Joint Stock theatrical-production experience, while interesting and acceptable, did not really work for him; divergence rather than affiliation with Joint Stock is memorable in his account of the project. And, significantly, the word *epic* does not appear anywhere in his comments about this play.

Similarly, the plays of Mustapha Matura, Tundi Akoli, and Jacqueline Rudet have been presented at the Court, the National (Cottesloe, of course), or the Hampstead Theatre. Yet these playwrights diverge from the hegemonic voices of, say, Brenton, Bond, Hare, Churchill, and Edgar even when they are contemporaries (like Matura) or close political allies-cum-collaborators (like Akoli with Brenton). Kureishi remarks that the "structured and better-written radical drama of the 1970s," citing Barker, Brenton, and Bond, "resembled a debate between friends."[14] It is this common ground and informal identification that marks the group I call "hegemonic" in my attempt to stress that social and cultural factors rather than aesthetics mark a separation which is by no means as absolute in emergent writers.

Of course, this formulation seems to fall into the old trap of separating politics from aesthetics. But, while Epic aesthetics entail some political assumptions, affinity groups may collaborate on shared political agendas without forming a deeper sense of inclusivity or community. Thus, the notion that new work by writers whose primary affiliations and commitments are different from those of the "old" writers does not necessarily mean that there is no structural or even thematic continuity among the work of both groups.

Feminist writers and gay and lesbian writers have especially benefited from techniques we would call "epic." Cross-dressing, concerns with women's history, music in juxtaposition to narrative, camp and drag "alienation" devices—these have been well documented in performance criticism.[15] Yet feminist, gay, and lesbian writers and companies have also made specific theatrical interventions based on other sources—punk music, surreal imagery, and dance, and the reemergence of psychological realism as a powerful emotional tool.

The lesbian company Siren, for example, has worked eclectically in many styles, but their music, an important component of Siren productions, owes more to punk's anarchy and displacement than to an epic sense of juxtaposition and clarifying dialectics.[16] A feminist socialist writer like Michelene Wandor has written plays in a variety of styles over the years, including the surreal or imagist (*Whores D'Oeurves*), the situation comedy (*AID Thy Neighbor*), or the romantic epic (*The Wandering Jew*).[17] Monstrous Regiment experiments in similarly diverse styles, although, significantly, they are perhaps still best known for Caryl Churchill's English Epic *Vinegar Tom*. One of the three founding members who has stayed with Monstrous Regiment through its twenty years has always created work based on images and nonliterary effects: Chris Bowler's *Enslaved by Dreams* and *Point of Convergence*, two of her shows from the 1980s, rely for their structure much more on painterly images and bodily movement than on any recognizably epic strategies.[18]

Psychological realism, often considered in opposition to epic technique, has been reconfigured in the work of feminist and multicultural writers and now reasserts a utility in relation to changing cultural and political goals. While bourgeois individualism is usually ideologically coded in psychological realism, that is not always the salient feature of feminist or ethnic representations.[19] Egyptian-born Karim Alrawi, for example, writes emotionally charged material that comes out of process-oriented workshops and privileges character over plot, often stressing characters' personal resolutions. In place of the cool detachment of epic structure, which frames perceptions of characters' feelings in order to analyze and critique them in political terms, Alrawi emphasizes the relationship between expression and power.

> I think it is much more interesting to look at a situation from the point of view of the person with less power. . . . If you have a lot of power, a lot of your problems are solved. If you have little power, then your problems are magnified.[20]

Giving a speaking voice and focus to those with little power can mean a privileging of character and a desire to move people emotionally.

While aspects of Alrawi's plays can be considered epic (featuring many scenes and a culturally wide and diverse landscape, e.g., *Fire in the Lake* and *A Child in the Heart*, both written for Joint Stock), issues of identity, family, and a personal past make for an intense, almost psychoanalytic experience in his plays. As with some feminist work, the personal becomes the political.

Of course, many feminist writers have been criticized for the bourgeois ideology mapped in their work.[21] However, some women with socialist commitments have deliberately worked with nonepic form— Pam Gems, for example, tried to rework the melodrama of *Camille* to foreground class issues. The attempt to capture and explore female subjectivity has meant that dreams, images, and inner states have mobilized feminist work for which epic is too confining a label. Sharman Macdonald is an example of a writer who draws heavily on realism within scenes to capture individual experience while establishing a context—somewhat epic by placement and construction—that situates female personal lives within Scottish life and culture. *The Brave* (1988), set in Morocco, raises cross-cultural issues of race, gender, and class within a plausibly realistic frame. As in the case of Alrawi, she achieves political effects through empowering and juxtaposing diverse voices rather than through epic's analytic distance.

I am aware that this argument pulls in two directions. On the one hand, it seems to indicate that the presence of this diverse work renders "epic" plays passé; on the other hand, much of this new work contains some epic elements, whether in the structural features of many tight scenes that employ contradiction or juxtaposition, or in the historicization of the incidents through cultural or chronological contrasts. In fact, while the presence of diverse perspectives renders "English" an obsolete epitaph, it also modulates the importance of "epic" as a strategy for viable Left political theater. The plays of writers like Kureishi, Alrawi, Macdonald, and Matura illustrate a hybrid combination of priorities and techniques that renders "epic" inadequate as a description but not irrelevant to an understanding of theatrical elements and strategies forming British political drama in the 1990s.

To return to the socialist writers here called "hegemonic," it seems significant that Howard Brenton, Caryl Churchill, and David Edgar almost immediately wrote plays in response to the revolutions of 1989. *Moscow Gold* (1990), *Mad Forest* (1990), and *The Shape of the Table* (1991) show that the "old guard" are alive and well, rethinking the meaning of socialism in the post–Cold War era, and in the case of Brenton and Churchill still writing epic plays. Perhaps what is telling is the shift of perspective: Russia, Romania, and Czechoslovakia locate investigation in these plays. One might even say that the English focus drops out of their work—in construction if not in reception.

In order to clear a space for the explorations at hand, each playwright has represented the excesses and abuses of the old communist regimes. Brenton graphically recounts Meyerhold's torture and death, Edgar depicts the corruption and ruthlessness of Czechoslovakian leaders, and Churchill spends the first third of *Mad Forest* representing the personal and political "silencing" of the Ceausescu regime. This attention to naming the grave injustices of "really existing" socialism can be seen as a formal and necessary sign that the plays will not merely offer a defense of socialism or a denial of historical fact. However, the playwrights also build into each play the warning that the popular revolutions of 1989 will not guarantee democracy and personal freedom, capitalist luxury, or social justice. In this sense, they offer a critique of the interpretation of the end of the Cold War that sees a clear victory for consumer culture in a global free-market economy. New World Order, indeed.

As for dramaturgy, however, there is no strong evidence of a repudiation of epic theater, and little reason to think that this is at issue for the established playwrights. With *Mad Forest*, Caryl Churchill actually wrote her strongest epic play since *Cloud 9* and perhaps her biggest critical success as well. She employs a Brechtian structure of scene titles, various gestic alienation devices,[22] and epic narrative techniques in order to show the way ideology is inscribed in daily life and how it shifts and changes under various social pressures. She shows people who are caught up in the days of the Romanian December revolution but do not have an alternative vision nor even an understanding of what is taking place. This confusion is clarified in the concise, orderly skeleton of Churchill's epic dramaturgy.

Brenton, together with coauthor Tariq Ali, while invoking Meyerhold over Brecht,[23] created a broad comic epic, which structurally resembles Brecht's *The Good Person of Setzuan*, but with two possible endings, each problematic—quite fortuitously as it turned out a short time later when the Gorbachev/Yeltsin change of power shifted history (at least for a time). Although it is devised with Meyerholdian pageantry in mind, *Moscow Gold* is also a formal, coherent playtext with clean structural lines. In each of two symmetrical acts, six scenes juxtapose reflections on making difficult political decisions with "close-ups" of Soviet life, dramatized through the experiences of a Moscow family, and scenes depicting the social, political, and economic contradictions that threatened the success of reforms, dramatized through the Gorbachev/Yeltsin conflict.

Edgar's *Shape of the Table* more nearly resembles a well-made play: a causal string of events brings a central conflict to gradual resolution through a series of disclosures. Obviously patterned after the historic revolutionary events in Czechoslovakia in 1989 (although Edgar does not specifically name the country), the play gives a close-up of the official workings of radical change through mostly peaceful means. Even in this play, however, certain recognizable epic effects obtain. Most striking is the deliberate foregrounding of political rhetoric as ideologically constructed—this cuts both ways, critiquing the past and the present, the Left then and now.

A case can also be made for the gradual development of the established playwrights beyond the English Epic. Brenton has experimented with media and performance art/dance in collaboration with the Amsterdam Mickery Theatre (*H.I.D.* [*Hess is Dead*], 1989). Caryl Churchill and David Lan's *A Mouthful of Birds* (1986) deliberately seeks to represent the irrational and psychic experiences of its characters. Its style developed out of workshops that relied on images and dance. Edward Bond has in recent years both consolidated his epic work (*The War Trilogy*) and moved beyond it to develop his own (contra Brecht) notions of TEs (Theatre Events). His most recent play, *In the Company of Men*, uses epic scene structure and strong scenic and character gests, yet it takes its major stylistic note from Beckettian minimalism; in fact, the play is like Beckett with politics.[24] Its major premiere took place in France in the fall of 1992 and won the prize for the best play of the season awarded by the Syndicate Theatrale et Musicale.

The English Epic, then, is alive and well but dispersed and partially eclipsed. Cultural diversity has broken the hegemony of any "English" canon, while a realignment of the relationship between Left politics and dramaturgical strategies makes *epic* problematic as a term of dominance but not as a component part in the panoply of possibilities and practices that mark British theater in the 1990s.

NOTES

1. See, for example, Howard Brenton's characterization of epic in Malcolm Hay and Philip Roberts, "Interview: Howard Brenton," *Performing Arts Journal* 3 (Winter 1979): 131–41.
2. See my study, *After Brecht: British Epic Theatre* (Ann Arbor: University of Michigan Press, 1994).
3. "Many critics and theatre professionals have warned that both Brenton's *Greenland* and his collaboration with Hare, *Pravda*, would, for financial reasons, possibly be the last neo-Brechtian epic dramas on the London stage. The expense of using so many actors, props, and scene changes has emptied the coffers of the Royal Court, Barbican and the National Theatre," writes Kimball King in "Howard Brenton's Utopia Plays," in *Howard Brenton: A Casebook*, ed. Ann Wilson (New York: Garland, 1992), 118.
4. Bertolt Brecht, *Brecht on Theatre*, ed. John Willett (New York: Hill and Wang, 1964), 201.
5. While it would be an overstatement to pronounce a new pluralism as a fait accompli in British theater, the late 1980s saw a diversity of work produced and even some consolidation of feminist and gay and lesbian theatrical constituencies, despite the ongoing Thatcherite attack. In 1986, Joint Stock, for example, adopted a policy calling for 50 percent of their project participants to be Black and 50 percent of their Policy Committee to be female. See Susan Carlson, "Collaboration, Identity, and Cultural Difference: Karim Alrawi's Theatre of Engagement," *Theatre Journal* 45 (May 1993): 158; and Joyce Devlin's "Joint Stock: From Colorless Company to Company of Color," *Theatre Topics* 2 (March 1992): 63–76.
6. See "The Ends of Cold War," in *After the Fall*, ed. Robin Blackburn (London: Verso, 1991), 86.
7. In Germany, East and West Germans rejected or canonized Brecht or

considered him exhausted. See John Rouse, *Brecht and the West German Theatre* (Ann Arbor: UMI Research Press, 1989); and Klaus Volker, "Brecht Today: Classic or Challenge," *Theatre Journal* 39 (December 1987): 425–33. For an assessment after the fall of the Berlin Wall, see Marc Silberman, "A Postmodernized Brecht?" *Theatre Journal* 45 (March 1993): 1–19.

8. For accounts of the Thatcher squeeze-play, see Loren Kruger, "The Dis-Play's the Thing: Gender and Public Sphere in Contemporary British Theater," *Theatre Journal* 42 (1990): 27–47; and Tom Maguire, "Under New Management: The Changing Direction of 7:84 (Scotland)," *Theatre Research International* 17 (Summer 1992): 132–37.

9. Stuart Hall, "The Toad in the Garden: Thatcherism Among the Theorists," in *Marxism and the Interpretation of Culture*, ed. Cary Nelson and Lawrence Grossberg (Urbana: University of Illinois Press, 1988), 40.

10. "We must not confuse the practical inability to afford the fruits of modern industry with the correct popular aspiration of modern people to learn how to use and master and bend to their needs and pleasures modern things. Not to recognize the dialectic in this is to fail to see where real people are in their heads. . . . The left has never understood the capacity of the market to become identified in the minds of the mass of ordinary people, not as fair and decent and socially responsible (that it never was), but as an expansive popular system," writes Stuart Hall in "The Culture Gap," in *The Hard Road to Renewal* (London: Verso, 1988), 216.

11. This is a gloss on Fred Halliday's characterization of contemporary communist parties of Western Europe. See Blackburn, ed., *After the Fall*, 96.

12. Hanif Kureishi, *Outskirts and Other Plays* (London: Faber and Faber, 1991), viii.

13. Ibid., xix.

14. Ibid., xv.

15. See, for example, Elin Diamond, "Brechtian Theory/Feminist Theory: Toward a Gestic Feminist Criticism," *The Drama Review* 32 (Spring 1988): 82–94; Jill Dolan, *The Feminist Spectator as Critic* (Ann Arbor: UMI Research Press, 1988), 106ff; Susan Carlson, *Women and Comedy* (Ann Arbor: University of Michigan Press, 1991); and Janelle Reinelt, "Beyond Brecht: Britain's New Feminist Drama," in *Performing Feminisms: Feminist Critical Theory and Theatre*, ed. Sue-Ellen Case (Baltimore: Johns Hopkins University Press, 1990), 150–59.

16. For a discussion of the Siren Theatre Company, see Joyce Devlin, "Siren Theatre Company: Politics in Performance," in *Acting Out: Feminist Performances*, ed. Lynda Hart and Peggy Phelan (Ann Arbor: University of Michigan Press, 1993), 181–200.

17. For a discussion of these plays and their stylistics, see my essay,

"Michelene Wandor: Artist and Ideologue," in *Making a Spectacle*, ed. Lynda Hart (Ann Arbor: University of Michigan Press, 1989), 239–55.

18. See my essay, "Resisting Thatcherism: The Monstrous Regiment and the School of Hard Knox," in Hart and Phelan, ed., *Acting Out*, 161–79.

19. See Dolan's contrast between Brecht's epic and realism in *The Female Spectator as Critic*.

20. Quoted in Carlson, "Collaboration," 164.

21. For an early instance, see Michelene Wandor's critique of *Trafford Tanzi* and *Steaming* in "The Fifth Column: Feminism and Theatre," *Drama* (Summer 1984): 7ff.

22. *Gestus* was Brecht's term for physicalization, which clearly showed the social implications of individual behavior. A gestus may be performed by an actor or incorporated in a scene, and it may include scenic and other semiotic systems (see Brecht, *Brecht on Theatre*).

23. "If you look at the subject, what to do about how to put Gorbachev's career on the stage, and how to represent how he came there, what the stakes in the Soviet Union are, and what the problems have been—now, how do you do that? It's unbelievably difficult and if you say 'I am a Brechtian,' you're not going to get very far. Brecht represents a parable theater, which means very clean lines. So you turn elsewhere, need to think of other things" (Howard Brenton, interview with the author, 16 January 1991).

24. See Bond's "Commentary on the War Plays" for a discussion of Theatre Events (TEs) in *The War Plays*, rev. ed. (London: Methuen, 1991), 298ff.

Acting Out the State Agenda: Berlin, 1993

SUE-ELLEN CASE

Berlin as stage is a role assigned to the city from the time of Frederick the Great, who perceived the broad avenues as military parade grounds and its basic domestic architecture as backstage *Kasernen* (barracks) for housing mercenaries. While Frederick's personal sense of cultural production withdrew to the French-aping *Sans-souci*, he left the city with an impressive opera house to signify the central urban site for performance within his matrix of state space.[1] Heiner Müller's play *Gundling's Life Frederick of Prussia Lessing's Sleep Dream Scream* sets German drama and intellectual production at this Prussian, military site, revealing the intersection of state military spectacle and theatrical tradition as the central semiotic vortex for the twentieth-century German stage. While in the eighteenth century the business of war set Berlin's map, in the nineteenth the city was once more redesigned—this time to accommodate industry. The barracklike domestic architecture burgeoned to accommodate workers, providing whole zones of one-room apartments for the proletariat.

Meanwhile, in the city center the great department stores were built with an acute development of the show window and the case display of wares.[2] The design of Berlin, then, conjoined military and mercantile space to create a sense of city as stage for the display of arms and wares.

In this century, Berlin continues to stage the spectacle of military zones, wares, and urban redesign: from its canal waters consecrated by the slain body of Rosa Luxemburg and Hitler's firey finale in his bunker underground, to its proscenium wall delineating East and West, framing West Berlin as the showcase (literally *Schaufenster* 'store window') of capitalism. Department store and political spectacle worked as one in West Berlin's showcase status. Moreover, Berlin set the stage for the agonic dialogue between communism and capitalism. In fact, it was such the definitive site that John F. Kennedy made a personal appearance there to deliver the line "Ich bin ein Berliner—" as if that identity were a role one might assume in any of the NATO-pact countries.

The apotheosis of this compound occurred through the politico-media representation of the "fall of the Wall." West Berlin's showcase status opened out into the former East, spilling the signs of economic victory through the Brandenburg Gate. Berlin's streets became *the* processional ground from East to West, for immigrants, and from West to East for consumer goods. Without the Wall, Berlin served as both the major department store for the spread of capitalism and the semiotic center of a new kind of unity where state and market unite as spectacle. Berlin as the set for this production appeared on TV and in magazines distributed throughout the world. Now, with the Wall gone, the center of Berlin will, once again, be completely reconfigured—the only major city in the late twentieth century to redesign its central area. Redesign itself has become an earmark of Berlin and perhaps the key to the future urban sensibility, as Arthur Eloesser described it in 1912:

> everything is provisional, and whoever was born in Berlin finds himself less at home there than a newly arrived inhabitant, who does not have to cast off any inhibiting memories or troublesome sentiments in order to

jump into the flowing present and swim toward the shoreless future. (qtd. in Jelavich, p. 23)

While Berlin itself has been slated to be a state stage, it has also been sited as the center of the German stage. The major monumental theaters were erected there. The proletarian movement at the turn of the century was housed in the Volksbühne, the Deutsches Theater produced Brahm and Reinhardt, Brecht rehearsed the new German state at the Berliner Ensemble,[3] and the Schaubühne on the Hallesches Ufer[4] architecturally centered the social drama of the 1970s. In other words, Berlin images the theatrical movements of the century in its architecture. As Berlin divides and reunites, the location of these theaters within the city is likewise suggestive of the state's political agenda and the project of commercial enterprise.

The representation of Berlin as stage of market and state, as well as state stage, was consolidated into the founding of a theater festival designed to define the state of the art: the Theater Treffen. Begun in 1964, the Treffen followed on the heels of the construction of the Wall. The project: an independent jury of theater specialists convened to select the representative German-speaking productions of the year and bring them to Berlin. While (West) Berlin remained an island in the midst of the GDR, this project meant transporting West German productions over to the closed city of Berlin, constituting it as a cultural center in the time of its geographic isolation. Surely the political point could not be missed, if only in accounting for the immense outlay of money necessary for such an impractical importation of sets and ensembles. The aim of the festival was to foreground Berlin as the cultural capital of the capitalist Germany. As a result, the productions became representative of the Federal Republic's political and economic agendas.

Staging the reunification of Germany in Berlin intensified the denotative power of the festival title as a *Treffen* (meeting). As the two Germanies, even more, the two Europes (East and West) "meet" in Berlin, the meeting of representative theatrical productions in the major houses is made to mirror the reunification process. Thus, the productions serve as a laundry list of state agendas and issues. The

introduction to the 1993 festival program illustrates just how deliberate this conflation of theater festival and state project has become.

> The theater of the German language needs a Treffen; because in a federally
> constructed cultural landscape, it is necessary to produce a sense of correla-
> tions (*Zusammenhänge*) for the development of standards and project ar-
> eas. . . . The Treffen of German-speaking theater needs Berlin; for it is the
> soundboard of a critically experienced audience, suitable theater spaces, a
> rich theater landscape, set in the capital of a changing, yet charted land,
> whose dismissals and perspectives the theater should mirror, both in its
> content and its aesthetics. . . . Today, the Treffen in its appropriate region is
> the proper instrument to further the development of cultural contours and
> changing political circumstances. (Festival Program, p. 3, my translation)

With the Treffen so constituted, its audience acquires the role of "criti-
cally experienced" citizens—literally, the representative public (the
word for audience in German is *Publikum*). The theater, then, embodies the state, as one jury member of the Treffen began his article:

> "Deutschla-a-and!" The scream rang out across the stage of Theatertreffen
> 1991 and 1992. An anonymous "caller" . . . shrilled his keynote for a yet
> unfathomable condition in the arena. (Festival Program, p. 5)

One might say that "Deutschla-a-and" registered as a keynote call
specifically in the arena of the Treffen. The festival, then, is embedded
in the new Berlin, the new captial of the new Germany, in such a way
that this Treffen produces a kind of semiotic archaeology of the German state/store/theater of the present. From the productions, to the
houses, to the road traveled among them, the Treffen organizes a set
of correlations for new cultural standards and projects. As a semiotic
archaeologist, attendance at the Treffen operates like an excavation of
it as a dig.

DIGGING THE TREFFEN

What, then, were the productions selected for the 1993 Treffen and
what do they represent? The program consisted of three Shakespeare

productions: *King Lear, Romeo and Juliet,* and *A Midsummer Night's Dream;* two other kinds of classics: *Oedipus* and *Woyzeck;* three plays from the Eastern bloc: Gombrowicz's *Yvonne, the Burgundian Princess,* Alexander Wampilow's *Last Summer at Chulimsk,* and Mark Galesnik's *The Possessed;* a period piece: Hofmannsthal's *The Tower;* and three plays about contemporary German nationhood: Christoph Martaler's *Kill The European! Kill Him! Kill Him! Kill Him! Kill Him!,* Hochhuth's *Westies in Weimar,* and Johann Kresnik's dance theater piece, *Wendewut,* or *Rage at the Turning Point* (the reunification). The general profile suggests a return to the canon, from Sophocles, through Shakespeare, to Büchner; a recognition of the Eastern bloc as part of the new Berlin; a nod to period reconstruction; and three pieces that stage the anxiety, frustration, and violence embedded in the present historical moment in Berlin. Digging a little deeper, the semiotic archaeology of the state agenda becomes evident in the selection of texts, the houses to which they were assigned, and the overall presence of the Treffen in Berlin. Certain productions collect to serve as poles or axes of the state process at this historical juncture, while others simply shore them up. Particularly unimportant were *A Midsummer Night's Dream, Yvonne, the Burgundian Princess,* and *Last Summer at Chulimsk.* *Midsummer* was a bit of formalist fluff to shore up what will be described as the pietist pole, while *Yvonne* and *Last Summer* represented familiar, assimilated versions of Eastern bloc theater: *Yvonne* the Polish comedy, and *Last Summer* a derivative of Chekhov's *The Cherry Orchard.* The following plays, however, ground the new state ideology, both in their production values and in the location of their theaters.

Oedipus[5] was assigned to a small rehearsal stage in Kreuzberg, the erstwhile Turkish, punk, alternative quarter. The theater is located near the end station of the notorious subway Line 1, which runs from the central train station out into the quarter. Line 1 played the title role in a leftist musical about Berlin produced by the Grips Theater. The plot concerned innocent "westerners" (a term that used to mean, in West Berlin, those who came to visit Berlin from West Germany) who take Line 1 only to descend into the social and cultural badlands of Berlin. The train runs directly past the church where, during each

May 1 celebration, a revolt was staged, which often culminated in a violent clash with the police, involving the torching of cars or buildings. The participants were generally punk activists; and the issues were often centered around squatting and the threat of intense gentrification. This year, the papers reported, the revolt was an orderly parade: a formal monument of its earlier engagement—a puzzling state of affairs, since Kreuzberg is now an area sited for gentrification because of its more central location between the "two Berlins." *Oedipus* appeared (like the Sphinx) at the last station into what will become the new center of the city. What was once an end station, in the time of socially critical theater, would now become a historical monument in the time of reunification.

Dieter Hacker's version of *Oedipus* was cast as a one-man show. This choice could have represented the sorting out of state contamination within the individual. Absorbing the chorus into the self could have served as an apt metaphor for the assimilation of former GDR politics of state collectivity into capitalist individualism. Instead, *Oedipus* played as a classical text read aloud as a source of inspiration for a painter in his atelier. The set, costumes, and props were basically white. This monochrome effect intensified the monologue style of the production. The painter read Sophocles's text aloud in a meditative tone, as if thinking through its formal structure. He had prerecorded his reading of the choral sections, accompanying the tape as he listened. Other characters became focal points for his delivery, such as helmets hung on the wall. Tiresias was a white stick in a white paint can. The painter brought on huge, empty canvases, which he proceeded to cover with images only indirectly related to the text (dogs in the moonlight, for example)—moody, lyric paintings, perhaps related in the director's mind to the translation—for the translation is Hölderlin's glorious Romantic verse.

However, Hacker's choice of Hölderlin's verse did not foreground its reception history as earlier treatments of Hölderlin texts had done.[6] For example, in 1977, the Schaubühne produced *Winterreise*, a performance that historically situated Hölderlin's literary project. Culled from *Hyperion* (his novel of the Romantic return to Greece), the performance took place during freezing December nights within the fascist

Armin Rohde in Dieter Hacker's production of Sophocles's *Oedipus* at the Schau-spielhaus Bochum.

architecture of Hitler's Olympic Stadium. The Schaubühne production illustrated the inheritance from the German Romantic imagination of the classics to the architecture and intent of the fascist arena. At a time when Berlin is pushing to house the Olympics 2000, perhaps to celebrate its new, powerful, pan-European status by holding the games in that same stadium, it would seem that such a theatrical deconstruction of Hölderlin's aesthetics would be on the historical mark. In contrast, Dieter Hacker's production of Hölderlin's *Oedipus* emulated Hölderlin's Romantic nostalgia for the removed, classical aesthetic. The production suggested that a private, meditative use of the classics might provide a palliative for state pollution. Moreover, that cultural production of a formalist sort buttresses the construction of a state.

The critics offered various interpretations of this production: one version asserted that it explored the relation between painting and theater; a more sophisticated one, in the leftist paper *Taz*, insisted that it concerned semiotics and cultural production. The oracle, after all, was the first state institution set up to interpret signs—and Oedipus is a man in search of a sign, so to speak. While this production of *Oedipus* was arguably about cultural production, any sense of the determining role that institutions or the state play in the process was precisely what the staging abjured. Rather than semiotics, *mummified* came to this critic's mind. The mise en scène of white on white reproduced not only an old cliché of opulent interior decorating but also the tattered color of mummy costumes in movies about archaeologists who appropriate classical remains. In the movies, the mummies take their revenge on the grave robbers. Berlin's own Pergamon Museum stands as a rich testimony to such practices and might be seen as an appropriate target for avenging mummies.

Rather than deconstruct either the protofascist ideology embedded in the return to Greece or the colonial politics of unearthing its riches, Hacker's *Oedipus* imaged the assimilation of the classical text as a building block in the production of an isolated, internal, individual self. The emergence of this self, even if mummified, suggested that what is actually unearthed in this production is not so much classical Greece as German pietism. This Oedipus turned inward to read the classic as scripture—a meditative text that suggests modes of production. Given the emphasis in the play on state pollution, his meditations implicitly served as inspiration for the production of the internal profile of the good citizen in a time of danger and degeneracy. There is a specifically Berlin tradition of linking pietism with nationalism in this way.

Friedrich Schleiermacher, preaching from the early nineteenth-century Berlin pulpit, was the first to place pietism in the service of nationalism. The state "as a work of art," the individual, internal model of national unity, and the firm basis of the concept of nation in cultural production are all the leading elements in Schleiermacher's brand of nationalistic pietism.[7] Hölderlin, also trained in theology, scripted a translation of Sophocles that configures a nostalgic, Romantic return to Greece as a model of how to ground a nation in a utopic cultural past, distant from the troubling issues of the time.[8] The conflation of cultural production with scripture and the morally good citizen as a foundation of the state is basically the lesson Oedipus learned, ridding the state of pollution in his blinded, exiled state. The citizen is thus brought to a condition of repose, encouraged to imagine his distance from the disturbing elements in the state as a kind of moral perfection, and that perfection as constituting the cleansing element of state pollution.

Today's Berlin is torn by an internal strife that challenges such repose. More importantly here, it has also lost its ideological center. Marxism is officially dead, both as a critique and as a constitution of an Other system, taking with it the once-powerful polemic of "western" capitalism, which set out to prove that consumer goods were a testimony to success. The exit of the East and the consequent conclusion of the West's argument have left an ideological vacuum upon which some notion of national unity must be configured. Several historical forces have resurrected pietism as the practice that will fill the vacuum—particularly the leading role the church played in unseating GDR power. Since the church led the final successful charge against the GDR government, it has renewed its organizational strength, and pietism along with it, as its traditional ideology. In the future center of Berlin, Kreuzberg, Hacker's *Oedipus* stands as a beacon for the good citizen who, in repose, is distant from polluted, warring elements.

From this perspective, Thomas Langhoff's period production of *The Tower* may be considered as also serving the same state agenda of reinstalling nationalistic pietism as its base ideology. Even the nature of the production, a period reconstruction of Hofmannsthal's attempt to grapple with the demise of the old order in Austria, seems to match the curent historical moment in Berlin. Like *Oedipus*, the production marks its treatment of an earlier time as a historical review upon which the future might be based. In both, a certain nostalgia for the past emanates from the production, marking the sense of that golden past so familiar to Romanticism. Hofmannsthal's revision of Calderón's *Life Is a Dream* pits the isolated man, who was raised in a tower, against court intrigues and plays of power. When we first see him in his tower, he resembles the mummified look of *Oedipus*, dressed in white, caked makeup, and wrapped in shredded rags. The narrative actually elevates the barbaric man, suggesting that his isolation has produced a purity of sorts, in contrast to the fallen practitioners of state politics. This essentialism constitutes the barbaric as pure, if not purifier. An offshoot of nationalistic pietism, the barbaric purifier today haunts the streets of Berlin in the image of skinheads. They pose as individualist, barbarian purifiers of a culture ridden with foreign (read outside) polluters. Langhoff's production finesses this concurrence by, in fact, staging the end of the play as a fascist takeover but inserting a fake double of the true barbarian as the cause of it. In other words, he both admits the structural connection between the espousal of this myth of barbarian purity and contemporary, right-extreme icons of it, and he eschews it, by establishing the persona of the fake Sigismund embraced by fascists. Yet *fake* in Langhoff's production works like *foreign* in the dominant ideology. The true removed citizen still remains as a testament to the pure and the constitutive element of the "good" state.

Pietistic nationalism's erection of the state rests on myths of common origin and an elevation of the German language as civilizing, unifying speech. Constructing the new Germany upon the notion of common origins and a shared language provides a breeding ground

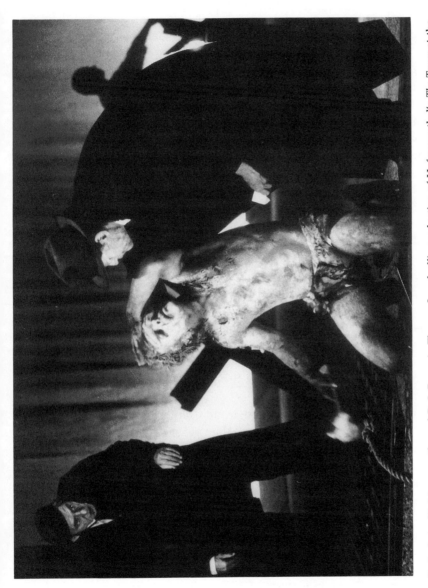

R. Ludwig, D. Morgenruth, and R. J. Bauer in Thomas Langhoff's production of Hofmannsthal's *The Tower* at the Deutsches Theater.

for racist attacks on outsiders. What both *Oedipus* and *The Tower* fix as one pole of the current state agenda is the pietistic notion that there is some correspondence between a specifically German, internal morality and the successful future of reconstituting the state. Buried beneath this nostalgic meditation on unearthed shards of Romanticism and pietism is the successful eradication of the polluting GDR notions of collective organization (in contrast to the isolated individual) and materialist values (in contrast to an internalized morality). What follows is the call to a further purification of other "foreign" values. Although not narrowly foreign, women also fall under the category of elements in society that may denote pollution.

For these plays are about men. In *Oedipus*, the single female figure of Jocasta completely disappears into the male painter's monologic subjectivity. *The Tower*, with its cast of twenty-eight characters, affords only three women's roles: two servants, who appear briefly in a court scene, and one farmer's wife who likewise is rarely seen. In fact, in *The Tower*, the absence of the mother becomes the site for both the bonding and the murderous conflict between the barbaric son, Sigismund, and his corrupt father, King Basilius. Langhoff staged their first meeting in the room of the mother's deathbed. Father and son first see each other through the dark veils of the empty bed. Sitting on the bed, the king gives his son his ring of power. On and around the bed, the son physically attacks the father/king, biting his neck and almost killing him.

If "woman" is a site for nostalgic mourning of the dead mother and concomitant male, filial violence, then what constitutes the body of the state? Do these productions promote the specifically male body as citizen, with the empty site of dead women as the space of sociality— a social meeting (*Treffen*)? Several plays in this Treffen bore titles of male personae: *Oedipus, King Lear,* and *Woyzeck*. Methinks the Treffen doth protest too much. This overstatement of the centrality of the male citizen accompanies the insistence on partriarchal power in the reunification process. The loss of abortion rights and state-assisted child care, along with the new status of unemployment for a majority of former GDR women, confirmed that the new state would abandon any gains women had made in the former GDR and continue the resistance against any change in their second-class status in the former BRD. Thus, the ideal citizen in retreat is specifically a male who sets himself up as moral judge within the state, guaranteeing the success of legal changes such as the antiabortion restriction. If the repose or the isolation of this citizen is disturbed, he might be forced to become the agent of violent purification.

Woyzeck is just such a good man; though not in retreat, he is certainly an outsider whose moral purity leads him to violence against women—the murder of Marie. It now appears that three of the productions in the Treffen actually shore up one axis of the future state project: from two plays that proffer the male citizen in retreat to one that enacts the scenario of purification. Further, Valentin Jeker's[9] staging of Woyzeck illustrated how racism works with misogyny, establishing a category of foreign pollution. Taking a liberty with the text, Jeker created a character he named the Jew. In his first scene, the Jew appears as a dissolute drunk in the village tavern. The ominous moment came when the Jew appeared as a stereotypical salesman—the one who sells to Woyzeck the knife with which he will stab Marie. After the sale, the Jew danced about the stage with his money in some sort of simulated ethnic step. There was no perceptible audience shock or anger at seeing this character in this role on the Berlin stage at a time when the rise of anti-Semitism has become a burning national problem. When Jeker was asked about this portrayal at the press conference following the opening, he replied that the Jew is simply an outsider like Woyzeck. Jeker claimed that his representation somehow dealt with contemporary social problems. But, in fact, he had duplicated them. Since the figure was not received as a puzzling, or even disturbing, invention, he must be seen as playing some commonly understood role in the society. "Naturally," the Jew, polluted by his love of money, would sell weapons to a lone vigilante on a quest.

From the perspective of pietistic nationalism, it would seem that Woyzeck is merely the aesthetic, pietistic character in retreat who now turns his Janus face of violence against women. Woyzeck is the soldier whose militancy is private and moral: the nineteenth-century Mambo. The constructivist set for this production located the violence within a kind of serene abstraction, suggesting that such action is neither local nor eccentric but somehow structurally reproducible and legitimate. Ironically, this production of *Woyzeck* was imported from Bonn.

The production was assigned to the Free Volksbühne, formerly the center of the Treffen. The theater was built in 1962 to replace the loss of the original Volksbühne to the GDR—claiming that kind of social, progressive theater movement for the West even though the original building had disappeared behind the Wall. This theater is now slated to lose government funding. Its future may lie in privatization. The Free Volksbühne is situated in one of the newly chic quarters of Berlin. A few blocks away is Uhland Strasse, once a kind of trendy but underground scene, now undergoing major structural alterations to include an expensive mall with fountains and designer stores. If *Oedipus* played at the end station of artist-as-citizen, set in the old punk Turkish quarter, which is retooling to become a simulation of itself—a kind of Berlin Greenwich Village—the violent, racist *Woyzeck* is set near the Ku'damn, where cellular phones proliferate to make quick deals for "reclaimed" Eastern territories, and where the newly arrived businessmen and diplomats seek to establish themselves in what will become the signature cafes.

MUMMY, DEAREST

In spite of these dramatic witnesses to a growing reactionary position, there is still something like the return of the repressed to be played out on other stages—primarily those located in the erstwhile East Berlin. If not yet "mummies," the former citizens of the GDR, and those in support of them, seem to rise in revenge against the looting of their territories. On Rosa Luxemburg Platz (a resonant woman activist's name), the Volksbühne's ensemble played Frank Castorf's version of *King Lear*. *Lear* is a play about the division of lands, civil war, and treachery. The performance opens with a woman playing Slavic melodies on an accordion. In an almost punk delivery, she wildly and darkly delivers Gloucester's text about the broken, violent world in which "our best times are behind us." This is not the rhetoric of reunification.

Nor is this the spectacle of the male Lear in retreat from treacherous women. In fact, women dominate the stage. The three sisters enter with pails and rags to begin scrubbing the floor. These are big, strong, hard-working women who greet Lear over their shoulders while continuing to scrub. The scene of the measure of love and the division of lands culminates in an erotic pietà, with Lear and Cordelia, upon whom the sisters throw their dirty washwater. They all exit except Cordelia, who remains on stage to piss long and painfully in her bucket. When the King of France enters in a white suit, she throws her urine on him with the line, "drink, France!" For her dying scene, Cordelia is pulled from the water standing on a blood-drenched, floral-print sofa, reading aloud from *The Gulag Archipelago*. Although nearly dead, she still signals the return of the repressed; she is still on her feet and secure in her critique.

The strength of the female characters is due, in part, to the construction of the role by the actresses in the ensemble, particularly Heide Kipp, who played Regan, and Walfriede Schmitt as Goneril. Kipp and Schmitt have been active in the GDR women's movement and in the women's theater scene. In her interview with Renate Ullrich in *I Am My Own Capital* (*Mein Kapital Bin Ich Selber*), Walfriede Schmitt discusses her participation in the women's movement in the GDR and her sense of being a woman onstage. Her major tactic onstage, she notes, is to play in contradiction to the classical women's roles.[10] Schmitt's project is aided by the Brechtian acting tradition in the GDR, which focuses on physical acting—the *gestus* as the material circumstances of the production, which take over the text. While some feminist critics might argue that this kind of counterproduction is still mired in the original, patriarchal position for women onstage, in the GDR's physical-acting tradition such counterplaying is capable of wresting the character away from the narrative movement of the play. It yields the portrait of a powerful rather than a cruel woman.

In this *Lear*, the gender issue remained tied to the context of the national history of the GDR. Although a gender critique did reside within the production, the agon was basically fought on the grounds of nationhood. Lear's divided kingdom situated the semiosis within the terms of national politics. As signs of the GDR, Edmund runs to

A. Kruschke, W. Ortmann, H. Kipp, and W. Schmitt in Frank Castorf's production of *King Lear* at the Volksbühne Theater.

and fro about the stage, exchanging consumer items in the frantic manner of the first days after the destruction of the Wall; and Edgar's letters appear as articles in the (*Bildzeitungen*) cheap dailies from the West, which were imported soon after the Wall opened. Castorf also introduced a chorus called the Seven Samurai. These are Lear's whacking, wacky soldiers, dressed in fragments of medieval armor, sometimes reduced to their long underwear, or worse, half-naked. They often speak English: lines from the Shakespeare text, cigarette ads, sports slogans. Do they signify the American presence in Berlin? NATO? They fight wildly and without strategy or control. They pull Cordelia from the sea then stuff *The Gulag Archipelago* in her mouth and rape her.

Castorf's production proliferates such signs of East/West/gender/ reunification without channeling the meanings. The anger plays, the loss as well, the sense of something torn apart, the working body, the poverty. By the end of the play, the classic text is difficult to cull out of the environment of things and gestures. The play *King Lear* is merely one sign among many. Semiosis intensifies until the "forms crack." Within this dangerous, mad state, the necessary distance for nostalgia is not available. Consumer objects fly out of orbit, work produces nothing, and battle is without goal. Instead of the citizen turned inward, this one wanders a geography of state, which turns out to be a destructive and powerful maze. In the former GDR, the land of the now-dead critique, the motor of the revolutionary impulse runs on to animate even the corpses and sling them back onto the high capitalist stage. They gesture memories of state censorship in a present of "free" looting.

The program for the performance was composed of quotations from works by Canetti, Horkheimer/Adorno, Theweleit, and Virilio on the verso, while the phrase repeated on the recto was "Stop the Pogrom!" The program combined something like leftist political graffiti with the construction of a Euro/post-Marxist critique. In that same vacuum that yielded a rebirth of pietism, this project begins to organize, from heterogeneous sources, the new kernel of a critical theory along with a new style of performance. "Stop the Pogrom!" calls out for change to the contemporary streets of Berlin. Unlike the Bonn

Lear's army, designated as the Seven Samurai, in Frank Castorf's production.

production of the Jew in *Woyzeck*, this program strikes out against the rise of anti-Semitism. From this perspective, what begins to emerge from the housing and production of the Treffen is a simulation of the two former Germanies. In the "Free" Volksbühne near the Ku'damm, the outraged citizen commits acts of violence against pollutive elements in the state. In the original Volksbühne on Rosa Luxemburg Place, the call for change rings out across the stage of GDR history. Must "nation" still organize the complex social relations of the new Europe? Will the same two axes continue the division of East and West?

On the subway to the Volksbühne, a man announced to the passengers: "I am thirty-eight years old. HIV positive. If you don't give something to me, then please give to the AIDS Action Center." These kinds of social problems, related to sexual practice and gender bias, still remain beneath the heap of national contestations. As long as the political axes organize along the old state lines, arguing national histories first, then these problems will remain underrepresented on the stage. The 1993 Treffen took place at the same time as the sixtieth anniversary of the Nazi burning of the books. The papers printed a photo of the conflagration, which has newly emerged from some lost archive. The photo, along with some eyewitness accounts, testified that the head of a stone bust had been waved on a stick above the crowd and then thrown onto the heap of books. It was the bust of Magnus Hirschfeld, the founder of the sexual institute, who fought the law against homosexuality. His charred bust rested on the pile of books.

This kind of image and historical fact, which indicates the institutional role the state plays vis-à-vis sexual practices, still remains lost to the stage. Is it because the discourse of public state politics cannot address "private" issues as political? Or is it that both the reactionary and the critical axes of the state agenda, in spite of their struggles over certain issues, retain a common sense of national issues as proper politics and relegate other kinds of issues to the categories of decadent and foreign? In the previous Marxist-Leninist tradition, gender and sexual politics were deemed bourgeois, which smacks of both decadence and distance from the socialist state. In the pietist tradition, both are morally disallowed. Sander L. Gilman, in his article on AIDS entitled "Plague in Germany, 1939/1989," argues that the disease has been constituted as African or American in the German imagination.[11] Thus, the notion of Germany as set apart from the source of decadence parallels the notion of the citizen whose distance determines his moral right to citizenship. Pollution, unlike policy, is, then, imported by foreign elements, which are marked by the struggles for liberatory institutional practices regarding gender roles and sexual preferences. As long as representative theatrical productions continue to exile these forces from socially committed productions, they will emulate the agenda of the pietist state.

Nonetheless, the tortured dying of one nation does convulse Germany at this historical juncture, so questions of nationhood do retain some place on the stage. At the Berliner Ensemble, formerly the official theater of the GDR, a Senecan dying scene was staged in the form of a rationalist oratorio of statehood entitled *Westies in Weimar*. The title is haunting in its resonances. Weimar, the "classical" home of Goethe and Schiller, had been part of the GDR, now reclaimed in the reunification process. Expensive hotels and restaurants opened, transforming it into a showcase of "classical" German culture for rich tourists. The war of cultural ownership, as well as that of private property, was the focus of this production.

First, the private ownership of cultural production was at issue in the relation of the performance of the text. In this scenario, the individual, virtuoso artist from *Oedipus* came to life as the outraged playwright, Rolf Hochhuth. Before the curtain, programs were sold with the warning "this book has nothing to do with the production." Tucked inside the program was a copy of an official letter from the co-Intendants of the Berliner Ensemble, Matthias Langhoff, Fritz Marquardt, and Heiner Müller: "We print the reply from Rolf Hochhuth [to this production] and distance ourselves from its form and its content. We consider his play *Westies in Weimar* important and wish him further productions. Also in Berlin." Hochhuth's long, angry statement followed, asserting that "Einar Schleef destroyed and falsified my play." Hochhuth reported that he had attended a rehearsal in which he did not hear a word of his own text. Moreover, he was perturbed to find other texts in the production and concerned that the audience could not discern that he, the playwright, had not selected them: "for example, Brecht's praise of the communist party." In terms of production values, he found the following most disturbing: "The people disappear into choruses . . . it is totally without a stage set." Hochhuth concludes: "Schleef's perspective on people, as he portrays them onstage, is insultingly inhuman."

The performance began in the dark. An actor shined a flashlight around the theater, resting the beam on the ornate decor of Baroque angels and decorative shapes of the Berliner Ensemble building. The theater as real estate, embellished real estate, opened the show. A twenty-minute prelude followed. The text was composed of fragments from Schiller's *Intrigue and Love*. A back-lit line of women and one of men stood on the apron of the stage, dressed in army overcoats and combat boots. At one point, the men took off their coats and stood nude. The "classical" text was delivered in rhythmic choruses, without inflection. The Schiller play had long ago set up the notion of a subject in state politics. If Schiller created a suffering, individual, psychological subject in contradiction to the state, the director created a raging, collective subject as the dying state. Wrenching the text from the individual playwright and having (individual) "people disappear into choruses," as Hochhuth charged, the director returned the Berliner Ensemble stage to the GDR ideology of the collective citizen. Schiller shored up the collective as subject.

An intermission followed the first twenty minutes. The audience was informed that the performance would run for three hours, without further intermission. The audience spilled out into the square before the theater, around the bronze statue of the seated, "friendly" Brecht. In contrast to that monument, this performance would be the direct offspring of the radical Brecht of the learning-play years— particularly of *The Measures Taken:* bare stage; minimal props; one or two set pieces; brick wall upstage; actors nude under army coats and boots; placards pinned to the front of coats with handwritten titles (minister of state, professor, farmer); one chorus of men, one of women; choral recitations that break sentence rhythms into complex, eccentric patterns; absolute precision in unison; choral leaders with simple hand gestures (the *gestus* of the arguments); spare, repetitious blocking patterns.

Scenes: men with half-shaved heads, axes high in hand, run toward audience, shout "Execute!," dig axes into stage floor, return, repeat. A man from Essen wants to buy a hotel in Weimar. Nude, back lit, the chorus interrogates his right to do so. With his outline against the brick wall, with money in hand, the chorus asks repeatedly, "Who is the Party?" Farmer: "The Russians, in their agony, threw us away behind them as they left." Farmer: "A VW buys my land. The 'original' owner reclaims it. Where shall I live? An apartment in the city?" Suicide stories are delivered from the boxes in the house. The chorus sings "Oh sacred head now wounded" while wearing placards that ask "But who is the Party?" A lengthy argument is recited from a court case. The female chorus in a box on one side of the house argues with the men on the other. The argument does not concern gender. The question posed: what constitutes ownership of land? If you live in a house for forty years and take care of it, or if you owned it before the GDR and produce the deed, is it right, although it is legal, to reclaim it with no restitution? A woman in a red evening dress, hand raised like the Statue of Liberty, reads Bonn's proclamations concerning the reclamation of border lands without restitution. Final scene: the singing of an old Schumann/ Heine song with the line "Bring a large casket." This is the state funeral of the collective subject without private property.

The nudity in the production was always male—there was no pornographic exploitation of women. This choice enforced the notion that nudity represented the condition of having been stripped bare by the West, plundered. Nudity imaged the unemployed and landless. The burning pain of lost national values and opportunities overcame any other kind of politics. Gender played only as a structural element that separated the choruses. Sexual practice remained outside the context of the representable. Housed in the Berliner Ensemble, this production continued the role that theater had assumed, a monument to the state. Castorf's *Lear* at the Volksbühne retained the role that theater had played in the GDR (under the tutelage of Benno Besson and Heiner Müller), part of the state, but offering a critique of its objectified subject. Nevertheless, the state remained the actual subject on the stage. The outraged oppressed, in Mohawks and boots, with axes, also became the extreme-right attackers. Contradiction moved the narrative flow.

Today, angling between the two theaters, Oranienburg Street has become the new scene for the political punk underground.[12] Warehouses still half-destroyed from World War II are now the locations for underground films. One of the synagogues attacked on Kristallnacht has opened a bustling kosher restaurant. The punk style combines the militancy look with cross-gender masquerade. The Semite, the queer, and the punk political activist come together on this street to create a culture of resistance that does not quite reach the dominant stages, even when their work is in the critical tradition. Underground film has better responded to the new political sense. The gay and lesbian film festivals in the United States include numerous films from Germany. Women filmmakers, who chronicle the history of women in Germany, and Jewish directors offer a variety of films that reflect the new look as well as the new kind of critique. The stage, which still belongs to the state, lags behind in its old questions of nationhood. Yet the punk and the entrepreneur go hand in hand on Oranienburg Street. Is the privatization of cultural production really the answer? Can one buy politics? Will "style" be effective as resistance?

Perhaps the performance that came closest to imaging the intersection of state politics with those of gender and sexuality was the wordless "choreographic theater" (as he calls it) of Johann Kresnik from Bremen.[13] Kresnik, along with Pina Bausch, is the foremost practitioner of Tanztheater, or "dance theater," in Germany. His production in the festival, *Wendewut*, or *Rage at the Turning Point*, was based on a semidocumentary book on the GDR written by a state official—no remnant of a play could be found on this stage.[14] However, certain "characters" did emerge during the performance—some from the documentary history of the GDR, such as Erich Honecker, and one major player who represented its history, designated as The Woman in the program. While "the people" of the GDR play in various scenes, the overall narrative shape of the politics of reunification is borne by a single woman. Kresnick thus feminizes the object of oppressive forces and the subject of the performance.[15] She plays out the subject position in the collective, personalizes a dependence on the state through dances with Erich Honecker, and suffers its final condemnation and defeat as parts of her body are measured and stamped like meat with DDR (GDR) or SED (the Socialist Unity Party) to the applause of the victorious crowd of onlookers. Her body is inscribed with allegations of cooperation with the state, which followed the fall of the Wall. His repertoire would suggest that this approach is an ongoing critique in his work, for his former pieces were entitled *Ulrike Meinhof* and *Frida Kahlo*. The female body in motion reads resistance and oppression through its wounded strength (in *Kahlo*) and its activism (*Meinhof*), which resulted in state execution. Here the figure of the woman danced with the state, survived its history, and bore its humiliations. In the end, she traveled along the walls of the theater, feeling with her hands the new walls of institutions, which replace the single wall of national difference.

Theater as an institution of the state was implied by the design concept of the production as well as the choreography. The historical situation of the audience was illustrated by a net "wall," which ran through the center of the house—the ghost of the Wall that still operates in the psyche of the German public. The audience was thus constituted as the German people. The viability of the stage, the arena of representation, was literally deconstructed at the end of the piece as real stagehands destroyed the set, sawing holes into the floor of the stage and dumping set pieces down into them. The action was violent and disturbing. The woman's flight along the walls was accompanied by the destruction of the space of performance. How could that space be reproduced in reunification? The performance left that question with the divided audience.

Music and dance were also interrogated for their roles in state production. During parts of the performance, a large woman dressed as a party functionary sang Schubert lieder. Marion Kant, a leading GDR authority on dance, informed me that there had been a deconstruction of these song cycles in the offical GDR music scholarship. Apparently the critique concerned Shubert's project of the musical setting of the words to both *Die Winterreise* and *Die schöne Müllerin*. Written by Wilhelm Müller, a political activist at the time who had

A. Colemann (left) as the Woman in Johann Kresnik's production of *Rage at the Turning Point*.

fought in the War of Liberation, the lyrics could be interpreted as alluding to political action. However, Schubert's invention created an emotional, personal, musical tradition. GDR musicology insisted that the words suggest, instead, a concrete critique of social forces. In Kresnik's production, stage pictures of political violence accompanied these song cycles, reclaiming them from the dominant German celebration of Schubert while situating them within a historical moment that itself has already been surpassed. Kresnik's signature treatment is to create a contradictory tension running through his choreography of images.

The basic contradiction of the performance resided in the simultaneous creation of both a sympathetic and a critical portrait of the GDR. For example, a depiction of Honecker ran through the piece that challenged both his role in the GDR and the post-Wall reception of it. His most violent and memorable pas de deux was with an SS officer. The officer, with lipsticked clown mouth, kissed Honecker against his will then stripped him down to his shorts, performing violent anal penetration. He then dropped eggs down into his shorts and smashed them with his hands ("eggs" in German is a slang word for "balls"). One could interpret this action as either a sympathetic reference to Honecker's early days in a Nazi prison camp and their lasting effect on his decision-making process or a suggestion that he "went to bed" with fascist practices. At the end of the performance, Honecker ran furtively around the stage with his briefcase, which was finally opened to reveal a fire burning within. This scenario no doubt signified the opening of the Stasi files, Honecker's flight to Moscow, and the specious trial that was slated to follow. Kresnik's ensemble created a choreography of images that provided a critical, historical shorthand for these occurrences, suggesting two contradictory readings at once.

"The people"[16] of the GDR also played a dual role in the piece. They were dressed in gray suits, wearing the thick-rimmed glasses that have become a stereotype of Eastwear (the slang term in the United States is Buddy Holly glasses). Potatoes were their identifying prop: they planted them, harvested them, ate them, took pratfalls on them, choked the peels down their throats, and puked them up. In

O. Ventriglia and H. Bailey in *Rage at the Turning Point.*

several scenes, the GDR people struggled with wolf-headed creatures. The wolf was a standard symbol for capitalism in the former
East, but here it also seemed to connote the official, restrictive nature
of GDR policy. These were violent scenes, with the wolf-headed dancers climbing over the others, chewing on them, in daring versions of
"lifts." The fall of the Wall was enacted by Westies wearing oversized,
gold-lamé versions of Bavarian wear, reclining in chairs and eating
fast food. The East people, dressed in their customary gray suits,
worked at their simple stations—both sincere and industrious and
drab and ineffectual. The partying West people finally pushed the
wall east, in their sloppy, loose delights, crowding the East people
toward the edge of the stage until the wall collapsed.

The improvisatory nature of Kresnik's ensemble scenes plays a role
in the flow of his images. On the German stage, so controlled by the
director, this modicum of agency on the part of the performers seems
refreshing. It is reminiscent of the feel of early performances by the
Living Theater in the United States, for example, where the relationship between improvisation and the political aim of the performers
played a major role in focusing the audience on the movement of
bodies as signifiers of social conditions or of a resistance to them.
Perceptible cues denoting the end of a section, resulting in a lack of
perfect ensemble timing, create a sense of heterogeneity to the corps's
numbers.[17] Susan Manning has published several works concerning
fascism and the history of avant-garde dance in Germany. The stark
contrast between Kresnik's loose ensemble pieces and Schleef's perfectly tuned choruses in *Westies in Weimar* signals the relative distances between performance and state. Kresnik portrays the state—
but loosely and imperfectly, pointing to it without emulating its bureaucratic organization. Schleef, on the other hand, creates a smooth-
running performance, which, while it critiques the state, emulates its
goal of bureaucratic efficiency. Could it be that Kresnik's base in
dance, rather than theater, offered him the necessary distance from
the institution to find, in improvisation and without text, a subject
and a form that does not replicate entirely the state agenda? In his
press conference, he made it clear that there was no "place" for work
such as his. As choreographic or dance theater, his only venues were

the opera houses, which were unsuitable for his project, or his isolated performance spaces in Bremen, though his invitation to the Treffen signalled some kind of assimilation, however imperfect.

The above productions constituted the foreground of the Treffen. In the background, a "play market" (Stückemarkt) filled some afternoons, with readings of plays as yet without productions. Selling plays seemed a sanctioned aim of the new sense of Treffen. Official discussions between the production teams and interested viewers were slated after certain performances and in the afternoons. Questions often revolved around finances, since many theaters had been closed and others were being required to produce more of their own funding than in previous years. Discussions of traveling productions that had earned revenue in Switzerland, for example, accompanied questions about the semiotics of staging. An official press conference was held to announce the reestablishment of the journal *Theater der Zeit;* it had served as the GDR theater journal, had collapsed with the Wall, and now was to be published by a small press in Essen. Questions of economic survival came from the floor—how this journal might compete with *Theater Heute,* for instance. A new undercurrent of economic panic stirred beneath the Treffen. Market competition was no longer masked by aesthetics. Somehow the central role of state-funded theater did not seem as financially or dramaturgically secure. Even the Treffen had lost some of its luster. Tickets were still available for many productions—a totally new phenomenon. Some houses were only half-full. Perhaps the fall of the Wall collapsed the centrality of state in both former Germanies. Without the national division, international markets of entertainment, as well as local, more subcultural ones, could infringe upon state enterprises.

Since the 1993 Treffen, the world news has carried the report of the sudden, unannounced closing of the historic Schiller Theater, along with continued neo-Nazi violence and the German Army's first foray since the World War I outside state borders to fight in the new United Nations' (international) peacekeeping army. The competition to see which architectural firm would plan the new center of Berlin has been decided, and there is an urgency to begin building. The fever is to construct nationhood, even as it dissolves into competing markets, and to construct an architectural, geographic center as it dissolves into cellular-telephone virtual space. Will the stage itself as a concept hold, or will "The Woman" from Kresnik's production continue, with less and less success, to find something beneath her hands as she feels along the concrete institutional walls?

NOTES

I would like to thank Marc Silberman for a helpful reading of this manuscript.

1. For a discussion of this function of performance spaces in city planning, from the time of Frederick onward, see Marvin Carlson, "The Urban Hub," in *Places of Performance: The Semiotics of Theatre Architecture* (Ithaca: Cornell University Press, 1989), 61–97.
2. For a brief, concise history of Berlin, see Peter Jelavich, "Berlin's Path to Modernity," in *Art in Berlin 1815–1989* (Seattle: University of Washington Press, 1990), 13–40. Subsequent references to Jelavich are indicated by page number in the text.
3. For a personalized history of these theaters, see Carl Weber, "Crossing the Footbridge Again," *Theatre Journal* 45, 1 (March 1993): 75–89.
4. Although the Schaubühne is technically on Lehniner Platz, not the Ku'-damm, it is effectively situated on the main street of the erstwhile West Berlin.
5. Sophocles, *Oedipus*, trans. Friedrich Hölderlin; director, designer, and costumer, Dieter Hacker; actor, Armin Rohde; Schauspielhaus Bochum.
6. For a study of the radical reception of Hölderlin, see Helen Fehervary, *Hölderlin and the Left* (Heidelberg: Carl Winter Universitätsverlag, 1977).
7. For a discussion of German pietism and nationalism, see Koppel S. Pinson, *Pietism as a Factor in the Rise of German Nationalism* (New York: Octagon, 1968). Chapter 7 includes a discussion of Schleiermacher.
8. Perhaps it is worth reminding the reader that Hölderlin wrestled with the relationship between the "spiritual" aesthetic realm and the state in his works, particularly in his various versions of *Empedocles*.
9. Georg Büchner's *Woyzeck*, directed by Valentin Jecker, from Schauspiel Bonn; Rudolf Kowalski as Woyzeck, Susanne Seidler as Marie, stage and costumes by Thomas Dreißigacker.
10. Walfriede Schmitt, "Die Dimension des Vorgangs," in *Mein Kapital Bin Ich Selber*, ed. Renate Ullrich (Berlin: Zentrum für Theaterdokumentation, 1991), 59–75.

11. See Sander L. Gilman, "Plague in Germany, 1939/1989: Cultural Images of Race, Space, and Disease," in *Nationalisms and Sexualities*, ed. Andrew Parker, Mary Russo, Doris Sommer, and Patricia Yaeger (New York and London: Routledge, 1992), 175–200.

12. Since the original writing of this article, Oranienburgerstr. has changed. The punk scene has moved to Mainzerstr. in Prenzlauer Berg, and Oranienburgerstr. has become a tourist spot.

13. One of the only articles in English on Kresnik's work is Gautam Dasgupta, "Kresnik's *Ulrike Meinhof*," *Performing Arts Journal* (May 1991): 64–66.

14. *Wendewut*, by Johann Kresnik, Bremen; original book by Günter Gaus, first Federal German permanent representative in the GDR (1974–81); music by Serge Weber and Franz Schubert; stage concept by Penelope Wehrli; Woman played by Amy Colemann.

15. For a full development of the idea of the feminization of the GDR in the media, see Katrin Sieg, "The Revolution Has Been Televised: Reconfiguring History and Identity in Post-Wall Berlin," *Theatre Journal* 45,1 (March 1993): 35–47.

16. "The people" refers to the use of *das Volk* and *ein Volk* in the state-inspired media representation of the reunification process. Kresnik's stage pictures recalled that sentimentalized sense of the public.

17. A discussion of the relation between Tanztheater and cultural difference, or relation to the state, was published in *The Drama Review* 30,2 (Summer 1986): 57–97, with Susan Manning and Johannes Birringer.

Sitelines: A Ground for Theater

Jim Eigo

[As I use the word *theater* it embraces plays, performance, dance, opera—any live act in which actor is seen to assume (to any degree) a persona; it has a history & is one, it is both the place we go & what takes place there. I don't with a single voice put forth a case. But theater is I argue at base polylogic. Even as the object of my deep regard remains divided, I do. Much of what follows is incomplete & incompletely compatible metaphor (analog, model). The theoretic writing most useful to me has been artistic hypothesis. While I don't believe in truth, I do hope for a truer, which is what these successive, unsuccessful hypotheses aim at.]

(oversite: a foreword)
THE END OF CAPITAL IS ULTIMATE LIQUIDITY,
WITH EVERYTHING & EVERYONE WORN SMOOTH OF ALL FEATURE
TO FACILITATE THE CIRCULATION.
TERMINAL TO TERMINAL,
THE QUIET SHUTTLE OF CIPHERS MIGHT BE ALMOST SOOTHING—
& LOTS LESS EFFORT THAN PUSHING DATED PRODUCT.

"I DON'T EVEN HAVE TO MOVE & I GO, & SO I DON'T ANYMORE."
AND YET. . . .

/ #1 A GROUND /

1.1 /Theater is not a visual art.
It is not its simple procession, a kinetic concatenation of emblems, the sum of successive tableaus (production numbers). Though a show that doesn't in some sense "show" of course isn't.

1.2 /Theater is not a verbal art, though often in its split consciousness, watched & watcher (& vice versa), it speaks a dialog.

1.3 /Theater is not broadcast, which is properly neither here nor there while theater is both. It's more nearly fully sensual than the merely telegenic is. It, even when it relives experience, is itself primary experience as the electronic vomitorium (with the viewer as toilet/terminal) can never be. And it's public.[1]

1.4 /Theater more than to see is to be with, is animated diagram, is more a matter of getting from here to there, in place.
Put pure & simply, theater is dynamics framed to palpable shape in (actual) time & space.
So plainly it's geometry. Theater, in the subjunctive mode, as well is (ad hoc) a deficit history, an event that sits aside from events and, history preeminently fabrication, is an anthropology, & so, unnatural history. Yet, like calculus, theater (value onto value, Hamlet onto Sam however imperfectly) maps.

1.5 /Sensual & mental, things & thinking, any art is means & what it means (the latter never entirely the former, nor ever fully not). The very idea of art is in this sense stereoscopic.
Theater in addition is where art & art cross. The confluence that is performing space is irrecoverably creole (& better be so proudly).

1.6 /What's seen there varies night to night, man to man, woman to man, woman to woman, here & everywhere else.

So how is this seeing believing? Such sight were more efficiently used in the service of disbelief.

Containing as well its doubt, which is there in its innate self-consciousness, ceremony is the ritual of the faithless (being all who are incompletely faithful, faith being all or not). Closer to ceremony (for which ritual today is irretrievable ur-text), theater today would be an act of nonbelief.

1.7 /Task abstracted from function is play (what drama & sport might share), an almost pure intent.

Ideally play is transcendent ludicracy. Where it has content it's blasphemy, transgressive, fugitive. It matters less what it flees than that it has to.

The thing we call a play assays to plot play—too often the patient's died on the dissecting table. Play a peculiarly human acumen, drama is its (humans being the unnatural creatures they are) formal elevation. What perverse itch in human nature would pitch a play (artificial thing, that makes of even the breathing body an object) on the site of the self? Perhaps because it's the sole ground on which to experience death & desire, sole topics worth our breath. The body is there in a play as in no other art; any art not alive is finally graphic art: it can be salutary, utilitarian, but theater alone is experiential; the body is there in the theater as nowhere else.

Imagine a play a sequence of incompletely compatible placements. In imbalance (asymmetry, contradiction) it finds (as does every temporal art) its dynamic. Pods at maturity part; plays (a one-way organic mechanics) open, but plays as well unfold, roll forth. Play is a willfully perverse projection of a player's unreasonable idea onto an intractible preexistent landscape.

Its irrevocable content I repeat is flesh. So that play at sufficient pitch might, in a broadcast age, be seen as the erotic in all its public dimension (broadcast being corporate, private).

1.8 /In the temporarily unabandoned shells that mark the artists' quarter in an after-urban era, there still from time to time flares among the undead something like theater. Under a video drizzle and in the face of a digital wind. Imagine the will it soon will require to—like a fist of the spirit—appear out of the nothing we're slated by millenium's end to have become. With its simple being so exhausting, can it ever again mean more? Is it anymore even that?

In a broadcast age an act can happen only where we've retrieved from the encroaching spectral an actual place, only where?

/ #2 ITS SPATIAL & TEMPORAL CONFIGURATION /

2.1 /There's state we say & then there's the state we're in. In this place every surface is at this time negotiable: it's in the nature of stages not to be all walled in.

Is stage then the field of play? How then place the playhouse (how many ways)? Conventionally planes in recess, theater is (at base) plane in formation.

2.2 /As building extends the plan into the real so performance story. The scenography of theater is one therefore that, rather than picture or sculpture, is more an architecture,[2] but specifically: that *negative* architecture that archaeology is. Archaeology being where history's become geography. Which space is a space of theater.

2.3 /So yes theater is visual but is of some idea in the visual.

Which is neither to say a pure & simple conceptual art.

There is pattern that is the track of process & pattern the track of idea so that, like geometry implied when a circle's run, theater is able to delineate invisible.

2.4 /Structure is a framework & lines of force: what infects the event is more than its physical shell. Even as the theatric accident & the structure it inhabits clash, unbalance, mutually elucidate.

In art is no pure structure: to articulate structure brings (de rigueur) pictures to (human) mind.

Every thing we experience, being by way of perceptual apparatus, is a picture; every picture is a representation. Adding a level of (conceptual) mediation, art is, in addition, reflection.

Though usually less obviously than photo is to negative, all art is a trace, a diagram of a structure left on a plate in the perceiver's mind, a picture. The art object or event, means & mediation, occasions a flash that screens & captures perception. In the move of mind any art makes, picture to description (& paradigmatically from photo to caption), we've three levels at least: thing, picture, name—the shortcut specimen-to-label (as in unexamined life) is of a more reductive order than art.

Art is & art pictures a structure of nature-slash-culture, mirrors or distorts it. Art is not opaque or transparent, wall or glass. While not strictly utilitarian, art functions: it is an object, it has an object. And in theater, unless image is at some time a thing as well, it isn't at all. Image in time implies pretext, foresight, direction, directive. Just as any structure pictures, pictures (implying succession) structure. The shape of the picture in theater is station, discrete gesture, action's cross section, a real-time snapshot, & is for all that insufficient to theater. In lapses between the "stills" as well, and in their enveloping aureole, is theater. Pieces that structure moments & sequences, not wholly unlike slides or clips, remain nonetheless pieces, unlike a finished film. Because theater unlike other art is framed & at once continuous with the world.

2.5 /Here in the frame time is space's traversal in a more palpable way than it is outside: to move or fail to measures all. Being point plus direction, theater time (whether body or not) is trajectory, vector; it is place. Theater is of all the arts most territorial. Who controls the space drives the drama. At its starkest the mise en scène (direction), deployment in time over space, has as its task charting the campaign. Theater is a moving target until it's not.

Every point in isolation is transition, if in motion is (potential) pivot. Hinge at once bridges & signals breach. There is in the interim, as ever, the future to think of. A stage is in essence one among more: it can't be set like a table, which for one thing is level while even the stodgiest stage is raked. Saying what a scene missing means is ever the theater's wild surmise (& unspoken motive).

Narration in film is succession of shots. In theater it's literally plot, where, so much an art of prompt & response, even the non sequitur, given the pressure that motion in a closed time & space makes for, tends to be perceived as an element in a (shadow) causal train.

So story is prospect. For us it's the all but apprehensible shape of similitude at history's end; thus it as well foreshadows. Its delineation is drama's configuration. Fiction is history's supplement; if we can term it as well an absent landscape,[3] theater is that landscape telescoped, landscape collapsed. Theater seems to me truer to its nature when, a succession of specific terrains, it, rather than representing indelibly a single specific place, in a sense is never quite sufficiently even one to let us forget we're in fact here. Where now might that be?

2.6 /Site determines the object, scale the art (said the site artist Robert Smithson). In theater, how far is scope then a question of location? Space we can safely say isn't what takes place.

But how much (how little) is situation in theater the landscape? Landscape is space in time &, more than mere set, in theater today does some of what mise en scène did formerly (the unfolding from a strong initial spatial configuration standing in as it can for the ineluctable suction of classic drama's fate).

Where spatialization of time stops, we've time pure & simple, or space—but not in our theater: all we can do with time is bear it witness or alter our sense of it. Here place can replay as time as now time with place. Suspension of time is the place (we're asked to believe) that classical theater was, just as suspension of the general state enabled stance, at a time when place & stance were unremarkable. But even site in a broadcast age erodes in a halo of zone, commodity's locus, all things already their currency. Today placement will likely require a stronger focal than visual.

2.7 /What in a video world is not irrevocable? What is irrecoverable? The reproducible is replaceable, & if temporal, reversible; theater is strictly speaking neither. Events simply speaking represent nothing. Being complex the theater event *can*. But, never just a record, it must as its first concern take place.

Is being & taking place here one & the same? Nothing in theater simply takes place (& never less so than now): a place is taken. The player's intent is requisite. (To imagine untenable space is to place it if only in absentia, increasingly the domain of today's theater practitioner.) In performance, place (for now) is the ground delimited by the line thru the points the players pace.

2.8 /In acquisition of reading skill, apprehension of a project develops; the move of the mind of the child is from that which simply is (letters / phones) to what it (phoneme /morpheme /word /phrase) in context must be. Ideally reading puts to the test the stretch of cognition. (In adults reading is often simply pattern recognition: one sees a sentence & says ah that's it.)
Configuration (conceptually) is that which, discovered, will let us in the audience (if just for an instant, so in a sense falsely) read as unit what we till now have seen as more (& may well again); it occurs where readers wright.

/ #3 THE TIE WITH THE AUDIENCE   THE OTHER THAT IS US /

3.1 /The player is never alone.
Theater charts a psychic correspondence, a system of the other in serial.[4] The site of performance is terminally the auditor's eye. (I identify, I identify with or I don't, I ingest.) Art but for the audience might be a falling tree; its presence can make of any observed passivity action.

3.2 /At the heart of theater is the implicit pact between spectator & performer. Audience assents to (temporary) general suspension: for this time in this space we agree to rewrite rules, to hold alternative views of now, to entertain an other. This in a way is theater in essence: at the juncture of here & a there, now & a then, reaching with ease into either (both).

3.3 /The suspension that is theater is literally ecstatic—beside itself, though never fully unhinged: we would a here & now beyond this time & space, yet we remain. Though it may be tenuous or sporadic (as in postmodern performance) or abstract (as in some dance) in the very act of framing a live event, a suspension that is an invocation, requisite to all nonutilitarian performance, we conjure an other-than-here-&-now—which of course is never really. Even when there's a particular "otherwise" here represented, nothing can annul the presence players present: a flat can fall, a line fall flat, an actor faint or worse. And players age no slower (or faster) than off. And while this palpable otherwise never cancels the here now, unlike the otherwise of other arts, in theater the otherwise underway is physically indivisible from the here that is.

3.4 /Theater telescopes to its moment, each one a potential pivot, peripeteia, weathercock spins & counters. It is its threshold, its juncture, the crossroads where space turns place & back again, a charming spot.[5]
In theater a point as well implies a past & future. When's echo denser than original? When repetition's repetition. Any question here is really two.
As every hybrid has split lineage, theater, at root a forked art, is dialogic. Any person, even in monolog, implies an other. To whom else does the showman motion? (& just who's that?) What onstage the watcher is to sleeper, offstage onlooker is to both. How far is a spectator sanctioned voyeur? To be put on the spot is after all what a player's for.

3.5 /It's not so much that the artist (in that she creates) is godlike as it is that humans (in that they articulate) are. That insight that art is more accurately articulation than it is fabrication is superseded by the one that says that that articulation (a pact an art & its public have, identifiably if tacitly, indirectly made)—is significantly fabrication too, only the site of the manufacture is the beholder.

3.6 /Everything is like a lot and nothing is anything other. Yet anything here (if let to) will conjure its opposite. Which is only natural: our truest perceptions even of self, of need, admit of an other, for to look at the self, the self (outwitting nature to capture its sole innate blind spot) has at least doubled.

So when the I looks outward? Contradiction sustaining imagination's scrutiny is paradox; content tells when difference constitutes otherness. Is the calculus of pathos a simple displacement (I you we you they)? Was there ever a more significant other than I in other words? Well just about.

Thru the long saga of consciousness the other has functioned often as just another that one is conscious of; simple animal compassion can be somnambulistic or cannibal. Yet even at those moments when most relatively fully felt, we are in empathy with the other as we catch sight of something like self. If the double (prime target of this century's theatric probe) is self in objectification, where's that leave the subject? Can the other that one projects be so full blown the double becomes the globe? Or a host within which a second I lodges & sets up shop? Worm or weevil, real heart eaten, will evil heart beat out a brain? Not likely (though even the thought haunts): empathy is only & always as discontinuous as consciousness itself; the self at its most empathetic shuttles between other (as self) & self (as not).

3.7 /Even as horror scenario, such full consummation of self would seem dated. Till recently there was information about oneself only another body could relay one. Modern play had at base this knowledge (& was as a consequence infused almost with a low-grade desperation). As postindustrial culture's self-monitoring methods improve we grow more truly independent of the other &, to the degree we do, less needful of theater proper. And the end of the meaning of origin that the circuit of replication bodes is the end of the meaning of other as well is it not? Still there's the pleasure I guess.

3.8 /Theater being a live art, a being art, better the audience be up close, smell the players as well (& vice versa) for as long as it lasts. How else will you know you've been there? What else has it to offer anymore? A scent survives a sighting. Or feel at least the breeze in the wake of their passing, brush of electric fields, the heat then the chill.

/ #4 THEATER & ITS ABSENT THINGS, THE THINGS OF LIFE
(ABSENCE THE PRESENCE BETOKENS, PRESENCE THE ABSENCE) /

4.1 /Does nobody appear? Would anybody do? If it's theater there
usually somewhat suddenly is (as ever), out of conceptual nowhere,
some body.

Theater being here & now, its base allure is that of life. Its stuff,
uniquely for art, is living: its progression, haltings, alterings, its re-
versals, its alternates. This dispensation that is theater is a pocket,
bracketed, parenthesis within which to (literally) quote make believe
unquote.

Theater is too much presentation ever to be fully representation, "minimal" art in the commonest sense of the term: there being the least
distance between the materials & the product, there's been the least
(art) done. What is now before us was largely so from the start, flesh
rendered flesh, body body. Where no special makeup or attire, the
transformation in player is purely intentional, the body the flag you
need to read the wind, a dress the breath wears (disguise being but a
subset of guise)—this while it might seem street clothes is costume, a
functional emblem as well as a parallel apparel elementally other.

4.2 /As a freeze frames, so a frame freezes—what is it framelessness
frees? It's only thru frames of mind we perceive. The frame, material
or intentional, is every art's minimal precondition. Every room is a
frame (& vice versa). A mirror binds all in its frame in a scene: to
frame a space is to stage. Stage space itself is framed from the start, so
onstage freeze is a frame within a frame. The fear or desire that flick-
ers no nearer than the margins, the obscene is by definition out of
frame (& anything framed, dismembered). As in high notes in opera
when song is an only slightly lesser bloodletting, the most outrageous
poses, when the frame is in freeze, only increase our awareness of the
realness of the beating heart there.

In life the glance is our picture; in art the picture is never just our
glance. With the former the frames coincide, or better, the framing
itself is the frame; in the latter they can't. So that, while one cannot

say art is wider than the world, one can say art, wider than our experience, shows us, if not at our best, then at least at our most. Art then colonializes nature? Other art conducts taxonomies; theater, anatomies. Art, when event, is as well a natural process; when object, it's the end of one.

Production values aren't art's even where they coincide. Its province being perceptual, art generates beyond all necessity, a surplus value not precisely that of capital exchange. More than merely a more exotic eat, art in addition to inquiry ought to essay to draw from it all the better to draw it all (only sometimes depiction). More than make statements it states. Art as suspension of life has its limits, as art as extension of love has. A different desire entirely, art is (at times) articulating not art. Utility is to action as function to perception. Not a blunt but blunted object, art (is it not a victimless crime?) is failed utensil, & far from useless.

4.3 /Theater is the many arts at once. Into gap between word & gesture, or any of two of theater's many interlocking codes, comes no holy ghost.[6] Theater is its nonmystical self-invocation. Where things cross & eyes stop, tell me what it conjures. We see all history's precipitates, or rather culture being the nature people have intervened in, its fossils, its every monument being a carcass (here they're animate).

Isn't art the other science? Mock document is fiction. Would only art that truly failed be real? Fiction is fact in the nimbus of gaze (art is life in a glance). So clearly fiction's an other: there's a slant inheres to glance—might drama be glance reciprocated, reciprocal fiction? With all art being transfer of a sort, the idea of correlative is close to the heart of theater, mapping (like the algebraic, a to b) a set of values onto foreign (neutral) material, by first the artist & then the audience, an establishment of correspondence (the performer the correspondent). This mapping is the movement of mind central to the fiction drama is, the projection required of any audience, a value displacement with empathy the (provisional) mapping of self on other. It isn't our fictions defang us but how they function for us.

4.4 /Is any behavioral sequence dramatic? Disaster is faster than fate: drama projects the urgency of the former onto the latter's base. How then was the Socratic dramatic? Theatrics today can be as little dramatic as drama is sometimes theatric. If conflict (widely) is drama's essence, theater is the quintessential art of (place for) the play of difference. With durable thought the product of collision, drama is that art most naturally thoughtful. Life fundamentally unresolved (& drama irredeemably knit to life), theater, embracing the widest dynamic range of irresolution, seems the art (while the least closed) the least incomplete.

4.5 /In theater the here before us is also the here that is not.[7] Nothing here is itself. Theater presents the absent.
Can agent be absent action, absent object? Actor object of absent action? (Palpable lack gives pleasure & instructs.) What would live performance do with full possession anyway? Theater locates (& concentrates) here before us the energies of absent action: something that happened, or ideally happens, prior or elsewhere, is palpably happening; it's a trace & at once its tracer.
Is simple displacement in series action? Is fictional action distinct here from actuality? Action is intentional, directed activity; activity is action of reduced intent. Real action is no longer theater or has yet to become it (reel action never was or will be). Flattening action makes it spectacular. Attention as action is sensing with intent. Like workers of Marxist lore, doers of action invest neutral matter with what significance it has (& can a moment later with another). As futile as running in place, doing here is even more useless.

4.6 /So much the art of the thing in the flesh, theater (being framed) is always at the same time more: presence more tangibly (sensibly) absent for being more imminent, presented & denied at once, possibilities more certainly closed to us for being so impossibly close. (Is that why classically death was obscene?)
So that here the thing itself, at once what is & what appears to be, is, in its very untenability, theater.[8]

4.7 /Theater in that it's framed is of course art: that art that even as it presents represents. In time & space, in a time & a place & maybe two, theater is the immediate as it's reflected, mediated, life & likelife, a confoundingly distant proximate, original with recollected in a single spot. Actions in the theater are at once representations because detached from origins & complete context, & are presentations because imperfectly impossibly reattached to their new ones. As that presence that re-presents, all action in theater is in addition narrative, metaphoric no matter how bald its mechanics. Being at once here & there, it is of all the arts the art of longing, re-presentation being presence & a presence again, no sooner an "I" than a "you" (no sooner an eye than it u-turns).

And that which pretends presence? Presents a pretense I guess it's safe to say. How establish constantly a (consistent if not a constant) presence when it's always instantaneous dissolve?

Nothing's rent essence like sentience (unless it was presence).

And nothing out of context is fully verifiable or not. Is every thing in theater here equally? Nothing not tautology is perfectly true. If truth's to be the whole truth, errors are a part. Though not a truth, there seems a more or less false (gradations of which inventory theater), therefore a truer toward which.

4.8 /Theater (for all that) is perhaps the art least capably completely abstract. Theater is never real; theater is always actual. Theater is that actual that is not real, where something may be actually but never be really done; to hammer a nail in play space can be actually to hammer a nail but never really to hammer. As a fly that strays into stage space now is "fly" in quotes. You finally don't need agency for theater, just the actual.

Even ideas in theater must have sensory consequence. In the metamorphosis of dream, the perceived form is corrected in accord with (subliminal?) shift in (linguistic) intent. Where the sentence's subject had been *boot* (for example) it now is *tree*. The sensual surface of dream realigns itself. What (subliminally) of image does mind retain thru the changes; is messge attached? Whose to whom, has *it* changed? Does fresh encounter later retrieve, reinforce, reinvigorate?

Alter or wipe it out? By great risk one means not the risk to mean nothing but the risk not to mean, but scant chance. In the giggle at fissure (incongruity) itself is meaning. Inavoidably, things in theater have extrasensory consequence. Every image has a mental sensuality & here as well has a corporeality—from which it can as quickly un-hinge to a personal delectation that, diminished or enhanced, sur-vives its inital instant—can any thing limit pleasures of appearance? The experience of any art (& intensified in theater) is actively reflec-tive (though the shimmer shatter) because we've forever a sense of surface of water there as well as depth. Is comprehension apprehen-sion with depth? Depth a function of duration, is comprehension apprehension over time? Absolute transparency might baffle most (but I wouldn't sweat it).

/ #5 PERFORMER PLAYER ACTOR PERSONA CHARACTER /

5.1 /And as the player is never alone, the player is never herself alone, simple channel, vessel for a message. Nor ever not herself. The thing is never alone the thing we think it is. In the West, theater begins when there's a second one, too; contention is a precondition to signifi-cance. This root duplicity we at times call dialog; nor does its choral core melt in solo performance, being the course the self & a role (internal verse & chorus) go.

5.2 /Dialog is at times soliloquy by other means. Is it action's simple soundtrack? How captions function varies. They can labor to pack it all in, or can modify, supplement, cancel, compound, even work at cross-purpose to the captioned. (A caption might saccharine the sick picture it can't detoxify, only to intensify viewers' nausea.) What the most efficient caption says, the captioned has not or it wouldn't have to be captioned. The very notion of action & its words rehearses the dialogic split at character's heart.

5.3 /Character is (for one thing) so the other can read one: when maximal contrast is not sufficient detectible dissimilarity, confusion can occur. How far is character the sum of tics? Just what is character acting? Shtick? (Is a tic typical? Is archetype? Or is archetype paradoxically atypical?) So what might characteristic be?

5.4 /Theater irreducibly carnal, how far does terming it body art go toward explaining it? Though agency in any broad sense is in today's market problematic (where amid reels of feedback locate heart's desire?), here every player is a framed agent; every framed agent is in addition persona.

We can eliminate character from performance but never persona, that by which performance is perceived to be one, a veil to read the breath of intent by, never transparency, not near opaque: see thru to the backdrop that backs it up (but what?).

Put simply, performing is human being at its most. Player is actor plus desire & is character only when player is in conflict with persona, the latter being the frame that (like a language) enables & delimits them all. So player is her own carnal construct (& so on agent); the actor is sculptor, a self the sculpture. The soul of the actor is nomad. Kleist locates the soul in the axis of motion. In the spotlight just being is doing & is more than how I move—as motive seems more than mechanism for motion but is at least that. Performance space is energy field within which matter (body) is energy clot; every scenario (countercreation) accelerates clod to dissolution of a sort.

5.5 /Where is gesture language? When do gesture & (literally) word at war cancel? When reinforce? how far is gestural lexicon a repertoire (how project, reflect or render actors' gender now I ask you)? *Gestus* (as Brecht used the term) would seem that gesture that explicitly is at once its gist (you get the drift): it's action's cross section as exchange, that is, a packaged, dispatched, utilitarian activity that as interaction has (as well) its value added.

Perched between character & actor, Shakespeare's fool is character at minimal characterization, whose character is function, his function his action, his action activity, & that activity largely diction. Jester is more than mime with words; mummery is less than mimetic. Not every framed endeavor is mimic: what is the minimal simulation qualifies? The mimic mirrors, the mimic distorts. One strain of new performance seems semimimetic art, mimetic gesture only discernible for all it's been short-circuited.

Here event is our (hardly sole) agenda. How accurately might actors explain the shape of event as postures maintained thru succession of gesture? For audience, shape is what thru trail of sensory data we grasp (& whom). Its shape in fact matters.

5.6 /Spectacle is succession of effects; how's a performance more? The thought/word/deed of the scholastic dragged the Platonist's picture/ name/thing toward performance; Hamlet's grave digger's act-do-perform was practical (mal)application of its Elizabethan extension (reflection-resolution-execution). So theatric performance as much as process is presence (much as infusion of self into song is measure of vocal performance). What has performing to do with seeking truth? Some cycling doesn't make a circle: thru time & space the performer, product & process, progresses thru repeats. Progression to death is (potential) endpoint: live performance's mortality is its central fact.

5.7 /But don't because of that privilege too much the individual. Not that there's no self but, genetic & social, inheritance & confluence (& never the same stream twice), where locate it? There of course is a body. But self is a point you can isolate only in the way any locus of trajectories is. How might a point of intersection be said to be? Did unaided mirror-state in psychology's self-regarding subject differ from that induced in today's closed circuit? Theater's death potential is as well circuit breaker.

5.8 /Here everything fronts for something (people included): we who are incarnate can't, & so we impersonate. Less indeterminate than undetermined, is any one adequate stand in? Who but as oneself does one do the things one does as (to whom else would you listen in silence for long)? Persons are (epistemologically) less a succession of opinions than their chronic preoccupations, stable as their consistently changing viewpoints can never be. Theater saw what a second demanded, at which point either a third. (The whom here is ever who's measure, & so on.) A troupe is a society; every actor knots a particular packet of interrelations performance focuses. Space is a field of force, powerlines are drawn & redrawn, within which performer is point, pole, node—or points there. Any line & point outside that line defines a 3-d space (theater).

/ #6 THEATER'S SOCIAL FUNCTION (CURRENT EVENTS & TO COME) /

6.1 /As it was in the beginning, might end be word too? Information is the invisible (non)industry. Contemporary move more & more from material to quasiverbal (bits), if completed, only wants an effective silencer to snuff all. (Talk is only comparatively cheap; is any art as seamlessly duplicitous as sentences? Art's most socially mutable medium, language now metamorphoses beyond.) Such entropy, not a dead weight but an evaporation, undifferentiated rest, were a death of exhaustion, loss of breath.

The ultimate victory of private enterprise will paradoxically be the utter destruction of the private, which even now is largely the construct of images frozen & framed, mass produced for ease of broadcast. Might a theater push that day into forever-receding near future, eternally asymptotic to now? Has even a system as nearly perfectly total as state capitalism leaks? In the face of collapse of public spaces, has theater in the ethos of our epoch any public place deeper or broader than your diversion/my expression?

With broadcast (retrieval & replay) & biogenetics, the industrial age's (& replication's) crisis of the authentic is swamped in a crisis of origin, a crisis of location. When significance evacuates its former haunts, the body (not just the self but the seat of material experience) is less than ever a stable entity. For a carnal art like theater, what does our progressive (broadcast) dematerialization bode? Having ever been the embodied apparition (things seen & in between & in between the scenes its province), theater would seem (too easily?) a fit antithesis to the specter's specter haunting the postindustrial.

6.2 /Perhaps today tv sport most nearly embodies people's aspirations as (classic) theater did. If so, those aspirations have certainly been abstracted (& alienated). Who believes in true give & take still? There is not a woman or man today of vapidity compact enough to stand as cipher adequate to the howling hole at the heart of the country today—it wants company. But most performance has all the political charge of a tv game show—which is not to say not any, but that participants have yielded meaning to unexamined format shaped outside. At least our dead theater collectivizes audience isolation.

When's specimen before us exemplum? Adequate performance metaphor is minimal (not sufficient) precondition to a theater in any sense activist. Politics is art of the possible; theater decidedly not. Yet while other arts can be political, theater, being irrevocably social, embodies (more than mere metaphor) irrevocably a politics.

Introducing the truly unexpected into any severely regulated system extends beyond aesthetic rupture into the political—so art in real socialism is more than social realism—the argument goes. But is a turning from tradition founding another or reinforcing?

6.3 /Is every theatric (trans)action of itself (without special emphasis) emblem? The hallmark of the postmodern in theater (all the world's a preset) might be said the "pretense," the pictorial as the emblematic &, over time, allegorical. Allegory is parable without the key. So what do you do with (obligatory) happy end to begin with? There & back (& we've been there) is epic basically; our picaresque is of epic inconsequence (epic of inconsequence), all blastedly pastoral.

Actual replication is (meta)physically impossible; yet incessant virtual replication is a (the) condition of contemporary existence, how square the two? Where better try than in theater, where thing is thing & image, where image, image & thing, the logical place to focus on the difference at the heart of replication (new time, new place, perhaps new face: its material conditions dictate)?

Where thing is as well irredeemably here, in theater we'd also seem best positioned to probe (mass) mediation: in the way it's irreducible to image (or any one other regime) its value to us (acutely today) resides. It's the place unashamedly false enough to permit wide inquiry into questions of truth. The medium of most messages at once, theater could be social theory's synesthesia.

6.4 /No remaining public space is so shot thru with social potential—not that there's much competition (shopping malls, theme parks, conference calls). Could theater be effectively the last stand of the social & the real presence?

But how occur without center? Should nothing in the future in particular take the stage, what takes place? At circumference center seems several, an art of disparities all strand & transition. Incessantly decentered centering, gyro is accurate (mental) figure for a woozily self-aware (end of the) century's time-space continuum.

Theater doesn't just render the sensible, it renders sensible, wrests from the blank a reading.[9] Theater rediscovering what to do would at this time uncover surviving structures of interchange, transpersonal art, involving of necessity persons expressing, outstripping expression, its function in the info network to dysfunction, indigestably carnal, an art at heart systematically anarchic.[10]

6.5 /What might art at optimum change? Theater doesn't change the world. Hasn't it at times changed thinking? Can it? Theater entertains the possibilities.

Thucydides said, to fit change of events, words too had to change their usual meanings. Don't in fact once syntax changes acts change? Drama is epidermal. All being not a becoming here risks being not. Were skin again theater's primary eye (was it that in "pure" play? in ritual?) we'd have intriguingly fluctuant focus. Action may be theater's core but transformation's its essence (soul); the readiest door to theatric transformations is exchange. Essence of drama is in fact interchange, transformation its body: to uncover exchange disinters integers' interplay. This human circuit (projection perception) ideally creates a dynamics of equals.[11]

6.6 /Predicated on presence & absence, the exchange that theater is is at once a product & not. Mightn't it, then, one foot in the market, one out, be a particular tool for commodity critique? The modern market is both the square & its potentially boundless extension. Theater, a place of exchange, is a place where thing is something more (value added) than it might naturally be. The other that is theater's concern can be particularized twice: the promise the thing cannot itself be & the one at the other end of the line.

6.7 /Systematic deployment of cultural detritus in a framed time & space would be theater. (And, more than info synthesizer, would be at least that.) Art's channel has inherently two terminals, but then there's all that external as well—just activate tactility & somehow deanimate the static). As a defined entropic system, its lines would be its winding down, (re)cycle a spiral must sometime sputter to. Earlier in our century, in art, decontextualizing elements to combine into a new art often drained those elements of content; content, when any, became a function of a new form, of the elements' relationships within the new object. But in theater a utility shadows every object (or, if unaddressed, haunts it). A theater piece an amalgam of objects doesn't, despite decontextualizing them, drain them of meaning: they are rather hypostatized, intensified in being framed. There in addition can be (as it earlier was in art) the meaning that accrues to the novel form.

6.8 /For an art to trans-form: what's performer to do? To retrieve the tension postmodern theater lost when it demoted plot & the (externally) dialogic, make theater that's turns of event: at the point where invisibility appears, silence sounds, theater here & there for which performer as site of transaction is articulator. Let theater as well be inquiry, let theater essay. Philosophy as well as manufacture, eclectic & collective.

In hearings, tribunals, courts & deliberative bodies in general, the action, as in Greek theater, takes place elsewhere. The tension this makes for is inherently dramatic. Increasing the draw of the literally obscene (necessarily offstage action), how might contemporary theater re-implicate the audience in stage happenings? Enveloping us, not only would what is before us engage us, what is behind us as well would. Theater can be the spatial representation of (social) state. More than define or conduct taxonomy, such pieces would chart relation. The task is to draw powerlines, expose how coercion works (where so much of the clutter of theater now just covers up).

/ #7 EPILOG A (META)PHYSICS OF (DIS)APPEARANCE
(& A REHEARSAL) /

7.1 /Theater touches as life does but affords the viewer a regard the speed of life cannot. Fiction, forensic inquiry, in the theater is autopsy.

7.2 /Being here is what it's about—or so it appears. Theater is the art at once carnal enough to embody desire & ephemeral enough to outrun it.

7.3 /Like figurative sculpture (suspended animation) in reverse, theater (at once action & reflection) animates suspension. What's happening has (in a sense) already, so is at the same time a record of it. All theater is a type of hell: one does it over & over, & though it's over will do it. (It's only prospects of paradise paralyze).

7.4 /Theater is impossibly art: while art aims to rescue from time, theater (even in the ecstasy of a player beside herself) is of its time irredeemably—not the most tightly focused spot can reclaim from the moment its object. Ecstasy in theater can't be remotely besottedness but in fact demands that I the performer, standing beside myself, be at once what sees me[12]—god & her creature? No eye is neutral or it's divine & I for one don't for a moment believe it: nothing here is neutral (& that's about all that is). The ecstasy of intellect we might term insight has here a nagging fact.
The human is by flashes capable of insight & ecstasy, making one human, almost redeeming life of its accumulating deadening; but one had better position oneself for these flashes, for where they occur is very far from the safe, the clean, the convenient.[13]

7.5 /The transforming power of such an art would be, by one measure, the movement of mind required. (But better get your body there as well.)

7.6 /As with every sequential art, theater (covering its tracks, eliminating its others) even as it unrolls irredeemably conceals.

Is theater player's refuge? Player's trap? Player's escapes? Theater was ideally its trapdoor. (Is trapdoor a fourth wall maybe trap deeper?)

7.7 /This is the art that, brief as life, moves as life does. That theater is not life (even though it is) tells us what?
Theater is the art more fragile than we because it's we "concentrate," a compound corruptible.
Let's speak concretely of ephemera: has even evanesence essence we can apprehend? How is it this art form that least exists most is? Fact is a body an act can leave behind; but never here where sole precipitate is change. And yet, though performance evaporate after: theater that is theater (history tells us) we can track like an isotope can infection.

7.8 /We here are always working thru the dark. Theater is what has left when the house lights come back up (what is left is what we call life). Is this then clear? In every potential clearing is arguably theater.

NOTES

1. The earliest instances of the word *theater* in surviving English texts occur about 1380 A.D. in translations of antique works. Theater is the place of ancient theatrics & not applied to the native drama until it too had a home of its own (& it would take nearly two more centuries for that). In 1382 the Wycliffe Bible glosses *theater* as: a common beholding place. The phrase is amazingly succinct & full for so early a characterization. *Theater* here is inherently social, & in making "beholding" the central act of the audience, it invokes mind as well as eye: more than mere viewing, beholding is a seizing at a disclosure, an attempt to apprehend (comprehend).
2. Into the silence the hulls of a culture will speak: unoccupied architectural space appears the theatric negative; and for me it conjures its figment productions the more insistently the more impressive it is as a space.
3. The revolutionary aesthetician Viktor Shklovsky said plots are homeless.
4. Didi who watches a sleeping Gogo wonders who watches him. A theater within a theater (within a theater . . .) figures to some extent in every Beckett play. The double is as central to modern theater's first practitioner, Alfred Jarry, as it is to its patron saint, Antonin Artaud (who named his theater for Jarry). Each substantially theorized the privileged role modern theater accords the act of perception: Jarry's " 'pataphysics"

would project "virtuality onto limits"; a theology of surfaces, its calculated savagery might seem a comparatively cool blue progenitor to Artaud's incomparably white-hot "metaphysics of the skin." In a neat sequence, the actor-director Roger Blin, whose first professional acting and directing jobs were under his friend Artaud, directed (and acted alongside) the first Didi.

5. On twelfth night, the medieval theater's feast of fools, the idiot's word is sage: is inversion essential to epiphany, the world this once seen upside down? The ass on the backs of the sons of the son of man was for certain dramatic reversal.

6. Theater, so many systems, doesn't lend itself neatly to semiotic taxonomy, which may be why constituent analysis in theater theory seems comparatively impoverished (impossibly cluttered). The codes of theater have more to tell semiotics than semiotics theater. What's a dramatic grammar (what's a grammatic drama)? It should be said: recognizing its systems has been important to some contemporary makers of theater: in postmodern performance practice there has often been willful mismatching of the multiple codes of performance that in the West, since the Renaissance at least (except in marginal forms), have been fit together (inevitably imperfectly) as close as can be.

7. The sacrifice of the Mass, where real presence is staged sacramentally as absence, is nothing if not theatric.

8. Beckett says the object in Proust is a symbol of itself; for things in the theater this is the natural order.

9. Klee (in my translation) has said art doesn't render the visible, it renders visible.

10. Expressionism a spider web, formalism is grid. In mannerism form survives belief—how far were form decorum (decorum form) anyway? The new form is the one of as yet imperceptible rhetoric (& so lies).

11. To relate Brecht & Artaud to each other & to us today, consider how each thought (& sought to bring) about change. It's why they were important to the activist theater of the sixties & early seventies, & potentially salutary to us today but, as things stand, how impossibly far away they seem. Both believed change (1) possible (2) desirable (3) the province of art. To effect the change each saw as theater's province, Artaud (like Rimbaud, an early model for Brecht as well) would derange, Brecht reorder. Hugo Ball, thinking theater alone could create the new society, extended Dada into cabaret; I think a similar impulse later in the century diverted art into happening. The former director Herb Blau was fond of telling actors: art changes nothing but at least it changes that (unspoken corollary: theater, concerted public action, is the likeliest place such change would mean). Now that Blau has advanced to writing theory (& we to reading), could

his aphorism stand without crippling qualification? The avant-garde is dead not because experimentation has ceased (it's slowed) but because no one experimenting (who is neither fool nor trickster) believes she is leading anyone anywhere. But to those of us for whom even the ghost of a chance for a change in things someday remains important, Brecht & Artaud remain.

12. It's because theatric ecstasy end-distances quite literally that Brecht & the ancients in the theater meet.

13. Thus are contemporary megainstitutions ultimately antihuman: promoting an ethic that will sacrifice anything to achieve the safe, the clean, the convenient, they promote a narrowing of the human, even unto liquidation.

Afterthought from the Vanishing Point: Theater at the End of the Real

HERBERT BLAU

For some months in 1993 I was, unexpectedly, equivocally, and rather amused at my reluctance, commuting from Paris to the United States to direct a sort of opera, which opened in Philadelphia and was later seen in New York. This was a remarkable piece, actually, with remarkable collaborators, but putting that aside (a one-shot deal, I say), I had not been active in the theater for more than a decade, a terminal condition, it seemed, for which my friend Ruby Cohn has never quite forgiven me. At the time I stopped my theater work, after more than thirty-five years of it, I wrote a book on the activating pretense (or enabling fantasy) that what, in the last phase of that work especially, had been happening on the stage was continuing on the page: a certain elliptical and circuitous density of performance whose energy came from an obsession with disappearance, or the forms of disappearance, now you see it now you don't, the ghostliness of the referent, it all, it all, as Beckett might say, encapsulating thus the unspeakable whole truth of its fatal attraction—whatever *it* might be. So far as

I understand that obsession it arose from the grounds of impossibility out of unabating desire, in theater, now theory, to get as close to the thought of theater as theater would be if it were thinking about itself, crossing the critical gamut and teasing us out of thought. Ruby never quite approved of this either, especially when it seemed, as it did to her, that I was personifying the theater and presuming to speak for it. Perhaps so. It may not in any way appease her, but it should be apparent in what I have written that if I were somehow speaking for the theater I didn't always like what is said. Meanwhile, obsession being what it is, to some degree arising here again, I shall try to keep presumption in the subjunctive, to allay if possible the still quite agile astringency of her doubt.

Thus: *if* the theater were thinking about itself it might be concerned, as a preface to any reflection on its cultural politics or the current state of the art, whatever it has come to be, with how it materializes to begin with from whatever it is it is *not*. That there is something other than theater, prior to it, by whatever name—life, reality, manifestations of social process, or relations of production—is not in itself a foregone conclusion (no more than the staple of theater history that theater is derived from ritual instead of, possibly, the other way around). Not, at least, it would seem, if we took seriously what troubles the theater, so far as that can be deduced from the canonical drama, with its long rehearsed suggestion that the theater, *which always needs to be watched*, has never trusted itself. That's a suggestion taken up in the work I did at the end (with the experimental group KRAKEN) and the book derived from it (dedicated to Ruby), which initiated, in a period suspicious of ontology, a sort of ontology of performance—or just this side of "essentialism," a subatomic physics. That book was entitled *Take Up the Bodies: Theater at the Vanishing Point*, which is the originary text of all I've been thinking since, even when, presumably, I'm not thinking about the theater.

The subtitle of the book also accounts for the title of this essay, whose subtitle—"Theater at the End of the Real"—will have more or less reality depending on your perspective or, for that matter, your critical view of perspective with its notorious vanishing point. For there we encounter the liability, even the vice, of representation, implicating the theater in the recessive economy of mystification that, according to much recent theory, supports the imperious logic of advancing capitalism, as if it came with the bourgeois enlightenment out of the blinded sockets of Oedipus's eyes as formed in Plato's Cave. Things have advanced so far, however, so fast, that in the vertiginous excess of the postmodern scene, its obscenity of image, we seem to be living a redundancy of theater, so much so that even the system of representation appears to be obsolete. Or it's possible to think, as it is now being thought, that where the real has ended the spectacle begins, or that the commodification of the spectacle *is* the end of the real. Whatever the case may be, as distinguished from the real, the case is defined by the interaction of theater and the phenomena of photography, which from its foundational moment, by a man of the theater, was also obsessed with disappearance.

That accounts in some measure for the theoretical work I am doing now, on photography and fashion. I mean by fashion not only the commodification of style, what's in, what's out (not at all inconsequential), but the movement of contingency through value that, with the seeming precision of aleatoric perception, makes a seductive puzzle of "life," raveled as it is in appearance. The old metaphor of the Theater of the World was fascinated with the play of appearance, but if it now seems overloaded with the play within the play that's because the dominion of appearance is facilitated and augmented by the random exactitude of the camera: not that *this*, not this *that*—the metaphor suffused with metonymy. Yet, for all the instamatic adjustments in the high-speed film, it's as if there is still a kind of friction in the shifting signifiers. What appears to be life may be theater, but for all the dazzle of appearances even fashion carries with it, as in the erotics of makeup, its "natural look," that thought of something more authentic, dative, other than mere appearance. That there is an artifice to this dubious look does not necessarily diminish the thought; nor does the theoretical animus against anything like the authentic, with its suggestions of an irreducible core or the truth-claiming authority of an original, make the whole issue any the less fascinating. It is, of course, the fascination effect that links fashion and theater, and both have gone through phases in which they have also tried to resist it.

The puzzle has been made all the more seductive through the twentieth century, as fashion became a virtual creature of photography, in turn responsible for the anthropology of fashion, even while escalating its theatricality. In the incursion of fashion upon art there has been, with an accelerated blurring of genres, a radical testing of the parameters of performance and performance theory, along with the whole spectrum of supportable ways of looking at what, through the entire history of modernism, resists being reliably imaged because it's always subject to change. In this regard, the early history of photography, with its desperate measures *to fix the image,* seems the emblematic double of emergent modernism with its objectification of subjectivity in strategies, techniques, configurations as diverse as the verbal icon, or the ideogram, or the Brechtian *gestus* or—as with Benjamin's "chips of Messianic time,"[1] arrested into a monad, pregnant with tensions—the radiant Image itself. When photography managed at last (*hypo*-thetically) to fix it, it had already become the referential problem lamented in Beckett—"It? (*Pause.*) It all"[2]—so that the grammar of being seemed to have broken down, the object itself dispersed into the activity of perception.

What we were left with, bereft, is the residue of an appearance with the look of being looked at. And by the time of Beckett's *Play,* so far as the human presence was concerned, not entirely sure of that: "Am I as much as . . . being seen?" (*Shorter Plays,* p. 157). The terror of *not* being seen, pandemic to the landscape of Beckett, had its inverse (or perverse) objective correlative in "the anguish of perceivedness" of *Film* (p. 163), along with the paranoid symptoms of the syntactical variants, no *being* seen (no presence, that is), no being except *as seen.* There was also, long before Beckett, the anguish of perceivedness doubled or compounded if it ended up on film, as in the horror of photography expressed by Balzac and reported by Nadar. Balzac's paranoia was such that he saw every photographic portrait as a successive deprivation of being, each time the shutter closes a layer peeled away. What we seem to have confirmed, however, in a world now thoroughly photographed, saturated with exposure, is that in the fragility of a specious substance there was no being to begin with.

About this unnerving eventuality there might be, in the postmodern era, paranoia or *jouissance*, but all of it brought us back to the foundational anxiety of photography that is the ongoing problematic of its theory: the "emanation of the referent,"[3] as if photography *were* theater—which is what, in the bereaved (and belated) phenomenology of *Camera Lucida*, Roland Barthes said it was. The semiology of his book *The Fashion System* might have been a somewhat different thing had it been revised after *Camera Lucida*, and the affective experience of photography as a form of primitive theater, or *tableau vivant*, "a figuration of the motionless and made-up face beneath which we see the dead" (p. 32). The sacramental image in Barthes's book of the dead is that of his mother, whose Winter Garden photograph was preserved, as if it were a chip of Messianic time, only to his own view. Whatever the futureless radiance of the Image, he cannot risk its being seen. Whatever he adds to the photograph, engorged as it is with time, the principal anxiety is change. Any way *you* look at it the Image is troubled by sight.

There is much more to be said about the potential abrasion of presence by sight, through photography, in theater, which is brazened out on the catwalk, with the engendered problem of the gaze, in the world of high fashion with its spectacular *défilés*. The theater itself—explicit source of fashion in previous periods, or a function of it in a relation of reciprocity—has always, of course, been subject to change, which *is* its subject. I wrote of the theater long ago as a time-serving form, but with the insubstantial pageant fading, cybernetically, into the feedback systems; it's as if we're dealing now with an overwhelming accession of temporality that, in the proliferous imaging of the mediascape of the postmodern, collapses time (into) itself. If this seems to be the totalization of theater into the apotheosis of fashion, it is also a considerable nuance beyond what Benjamin meant when, distinguishing fashion from history, "whose site is not homogeneous, empty time, but time filled by the presence of the now," he described it, even in its avidity for the topical, as "a tiger's leap into the past" ("Theses," p. 263). What we think of now as retro, with a refurbished subjectivity in the recycling of vintage clothes, is in its pastiched sense of history a tamer version of that leap.

What are we to make, however, in this context of the standard conception of the theater as a paradigm of society, on which I was asked
recently to give a keynote address at a conference in England? Those
attending were leftist theater directors and neo-Marxist scholars, brim-
ming with cultural materialism, but given the British variety, with a
strong disposition to think—just as tenaciously as John Major—of
society, and thus the paradigm, as more than less intact. If, to say the
least, the reflective paradigm needs some drastic revision, that's because in the age of mechanical reproduction or, at the leading edge of
advancing capitalism, "digital image manipulation," the parameters
of the social have also broken down—assuming that the social (contrary to Baudrillard) really did exist.

They were already breaking or broken down, of course, at the time
of the emergence of the Theater of the Absurd, when Ruby Cohn and I
were assigned the same office at San Francisco State College (not yet a
university) because of our common interest in Beckett, considered by
some elitist and by others merely fashionable. Revered as he is now,
Beckett was barely known then in the academic world, and people still
resisted in the theater, when I first staged his plays, the bleak and
discomfiting vision of an entropic universe, atoms whirling around us
with aimless half-life energies and, as if the cosmos were claustrophobic, the most minimal life support. That was bad enough, but it's as
if the cataclysm of value described in the participial present—"All
faiths are tottering"—at the opening of Ruby's early book on the comic
gamut in Beckett, were now inarguably and devastatingly complete; in
the semantics of the unnamable, all substantives emptied of value:
"religion and science, personality and ideology, family and nation,
freedom and imperatives, subject and object. . . . "[4]

Yet, with faith so foundering, will miracles never cease? For in its
exhaustive enumeration of the exhaustion of value, its apparently hapless mimicry of the incapacity to act, *Waiting for Godot* was about to
become something like the ground rhythm of dissidence for the politics
of the sixties. That impotency could be so activist was, for some interested in a political drama, as inexplicable then as it is today in much
cultural critique, particularly in the ideological assault on the paradoxes and tensions of modernist form, which, for all its antidrama,

Godot still masterfully represents, along with the elegiac remnants of a "disempowering" nostalgia. What was also called fashionable then, though it seems reasonably transparent now, was the "obscurity" of the play—which at some performances at our theater sent certain spectators up the wall—though some obscurity would seem to have been inevitable amid the contradictions of late capitalism with no principle of coherence and, in the ceaseless metonymic slippage, everything falling apart.

The litany of tottering faiths consists, to be sure, of truisms about modernity that, if second nature in art and thought, and the cataleptic agenda of Beckett, were never quite admissible, certainly not in their entirety, to a party platform in any democratic society of the post-industiral world. Yet, not long before the levees on the Mississippi were also breaking down (happening as I write this in 1993), swelling the federal deficit and turning western farmlands into a postmodern setting for Noah's Ark, we heard an apocalyptic voice that did not, however, resonate with near derangement as in the annals of emargination. The voice was formed, rather, in the Cartesian tradition, and if there was a note of dispossession (to which we'll turn in a moment) it came from a region of established power that had just been inundated by the same widespreading calamities—economic and demographic, with joblessness breeding rage, and the media surveying it all—that not only complicates the gridlock here but makes it next to impossible for any party to govern in any western(ized) democracy. Among the calamities, on a geopolitical grid where nothing is distant anymore, are the formerly totalitarian states released into the atomic whirl, with fragmentation, tribal rivalries, and ethnic cleansing—the monstrous free marketry of illusory liberation that in still other parts of the world are making a compelling case for neocolonization. That may be very hard to swallow in our cultural studies, with its politics of difference and, with certain reigning pieties, discourse of power. History, it has been said, is the thing that hurts, but if we're really keeping up with that history it may also be time for a slight revision of the protocol from Benjamin that has become a virtual doctrine in our antiaes-thetics: if the monuments of culture are accompanied by a history of barbarism, the history of liberation has been accompanied, more often than not carried away, by the momentum of barbarism, which also has its monuments—some of them obscene or grotesque by any standard, not only that of the older aesthetic, and not as valorized in the carnivalesque of Bakhtin.

What happened in all this to the socialist dream that still shapes the agenda of critical theory, as well as the fantasy text of dissident theater practice? It is as if for the sake of renewal in the detritus of the dream a kind of homeopathic violence were required, and that's exactly what the former prime minister of France, Michel Rocard, discerned when, after the debacle of the legislative elections, he prescribed a "Big Bang" for the Socialist Party in France. Rocard did so in language that might have been sifted from poststructuralist theory, or, with ideology battered all over the world, the repressed or begrudging awareness, if not the worst-case scenario, of British cultural materialism. If not the end of the real, then the end of social class, and with that, too (also hard to swallow), the end of collectivity, with lingering fantasies of it—plaintive legacy of the Left—for the utterly dispossessed. There would seem to be obvious implications for those of us in theater studies, where we've had, in a modified recycling of the participatory ethos of the sixties, much theorizing of a shift of power in which, with repositioned subjects, meanings would be determined, or "constructed," by the members of the audience. But what audience they would be members of, in any public sense (with scale), is as indeterminate as meaning itself in the metaphysical slapstick of Beckett. Speaking of cultural materialism, it was one of its tutelary figures, Raymond Williams, who foresaw against his disposition (and before Baudrillard) the dissolution of the social, in an unguardedly elegiac moment of an essay on the drama of a dramatized society: "Privacy, deprivation," he wrote, "A lost public world; an uncreatable public world."[5]

What was ironic at the time that Ruby Cohn and I were first drawn to the drama of Beckett is that, despite the epistemological caveat of the plays and Beckett's own insistence that he was writing into a void, we couldn't quite believe that the possibility of a public world was entirely lost or, if so, uncreatable. But while disaster may create a provisional sense of community, as on the banks of the Mississippi recently, erosion seems much less ineluctable there than it does with the illusions of collectivity at the end of the real. That end may merely be, if not its foundation myth, the most mordant master narrative of the postmodern; but if the real returns as ubiquitously as ideology—whose end has also been frequently declared—the cost of its return is, with an increase of entropy, further subtraction from the body politic, or in Rabelais's essentialist phrase, its substantific marrow. What we are confronted with all over is the difficulty of a feasible politics in the insatiable suction upon the social, which collapses the ground of a public life. If we should desire to recreate it—whether at the utopian horizon of postmodern thought or out of modernist nostalgia for the world in which it appeared to exist—where would we find, in the absence of supportable value, any credible figure of authority as an armature for possibility? As for socialism's die-hard prospect, the chiliastic notion of class warfare, it is, according to the autocritique of Rocard, like centrist, technocratic management of the economy, a concept ready for the ashbin of history.

The Big Bang may need to be bigger than he dreams, and in the immediate pathos of history Pierre Bérégevoy, Rocard's successor as socialist prime minister, gave us the bang with a human face when he committed suicide, shooting himself after the elections. Nobody, of course, knows exactly why, though subsequent allegorization of the suicide saw it as either his taking of responsibility for the crushing defeat of socialism or a sacrificial act impelling it into the future. As the parable dissipates in the appalling fact, what Rocard says of France seems true of all those industrialized countries "where the sentiment of belonging to a class, or a collective movement, is no longer perceived as a reality, where change is effective only if it touches the individual."

The notion of class may remain, despite all, obdurate in the English theater, its last-ditch referent, without which, perhaps, its dramaturgy would fall apart. And there is in France, as there is not in the United States, the last-ditch insistence of its Communist Party, though in the general state of dispossession some of its waning percentage points are going over to the reactionary/racist politics of the National Front. So much, so far, for residual collectivity. The rest is a national scandal (more or less exteme, depending on the nation), with ecology as a last resort (though it did woefully in the French elections). As

Rocard said—with nobody in the Socialist Party having yet come up with an answer—"When the French can no longer find their identity in a social class, in a religion, a profession, a generation, or the amount of money they make, what is left for them to identify with?"[6] They have, of course, the perennial figures of a national theater, but if the Comédie Française is, when not merely regressive, a mecca for tourists, like the Royal Shakespeare Company or Stratford-upon-Avon in Britain, the theaters at the Maisons de la Culture in the *banlieues*—where the workers live on streets still named Lenin or Aragon—are patronized for the most part, as the Berliner Ensemble once was, by liberal and leftist intelligentsia from elsewhere. It is, I think, a familiar story, this desire for a populist theater in an urban space where the locals remain indifferent. So it was with Joan Little-wood when I saw her work at the end of the fifties in the Jewish quarter of East London. With its ebullience and strategic optimism it was, as we might expect, a success on the West End before Littlewood turned to other populist projects and disappeared from the theater.

Not everybody disappears, but the paradoxes remain, with disheartening complexities in the American theater, on which I have written extensively before. As for the illusions of *théâtre populaire*, they first brought me to Europe in the 1950s because it seemed the correlative of what we were trying to do then in my theater in San Francisco, fulfilling in a city with a strong labor tradition, and the still-vivid memory of a general strike, what still amounts to a socialist dream: to create an audience of workers, students, and intellectuals. (There were several members of our company from the old San Francisco Labor Theater, and our stage manager then seemed an incarnation of the dream: a marvellous man named Kershaw, formerly a steward in the teamster's union, a self-taught Marxist who seemed to move behind the scenes, implacably, like History itself.) Calling for a revolution, *The Impossible Theater: A Manifesto* (published in 1964) was a testament to the dream with, however, an existential turn of mind, conscious that any apparent unity in the theater was, irreparably, in the reality of fracture, an essential rupture, for which the idea of community itself has always been a cover-up, as Euripides knew in his critique of the festival of

Dionysus, the theater's foremost illusion. Why did we pursue it? *Because* it was impossible.

This paradox might be further defined around the concept of the audience, which is not so much, for me, what exists before the play, a congregation of people gathered before the curtain, but the thing about to happen in the subjunctivity of performance. I must add, however, that what happens more often than not is not always for the best. If this is a somewhat Beckettian idea, it is not construction theory. Whatever construction you put upon it, give an audience a chance and it will inevitably be wrong. A statement to that effect, from *The Impossible Theater*, is probably the most inflammatory I ever wrote, though it appears to be the recurrent subject of the play within the play, which appears now to be culture itself, confounded by theatricality or—in the vision running from *The Bacchae* to *The Balcony*, which I staged in the early sixties—constituted by it. Perhaps I should have left it at that, but many years later I published a very long book entitled *The Audience*, which ramified the subject, with no polemic, and by gathering into the concept of the audience, as heuristic principle, just about every issue that besets performance, from questions of power and authority to the vissicitudes of perception to the secretions of theater into the rhetoric and psychopathology of everyday life.

The book has nothing to do with reception theory and very little to do, though it draws on psychoanalysis, with current views of, say, the gendered spectator. It does reflect, however, on "gradients of the gaze," and begins with a woman's voice: " 'No audience. No echo. That's part of one's death,' " wrote Virginia Woolf in her diary at the start of World War II. She was working on *Between the Acts*, in which the audience, "orts, scraps and fragments like ourselves," is brutally and equivocally mirrored in its dispersion. Her dread over " 'this disparition of an echo' . . . is a conspicuous deepening of one of the major anxieties in the history of modernism, extending into the indeterminacies of the postmodern. If the audience is not altogether an absence, it is by no means a reliable presence." In the first chapter, and elsewhere, I examine the various ways in which the appearance of a gathered public has been looked upon with scorn or distrust by seminal practitioners in the theater, like Brecht and Artaud, and by social and critical theorists, like Gramsci, whose dramatic criticism was even more caustic than Brecht about the culinary audience. The harshness of their judgments may be attributed to the urgencies of the period or the necessities of an insolent politics, but the gathering needn't be quite so soporific or anesthetized to seem, as I wrote many years later, in the last decade of the century, "like the merest facsimile of remembered community paying its respects not so much to the still-echoing signals of a common set of values but to the better-forgotten remains of the most exhausted illusions."[7]

As it turns out, *Between the Acts*, with its parodistic history of English drama, written and directed by the lesbian Miss La Trobe, culminates in a sequence that, in mirroring the audience—orts, scraps, and fragments like ourselves—anticipates various modes of performance that, in an incessantly shattered mirror, and more or less brutally, have been seeking alternatives to the exhausted illusions. Were we to look back on the course of such developments since the fifties and the sixties, it might be with a recognition of something at the heart of theater that, despite all demystifications, has persisted in practice and been dispelled by no theory: whatever the alternative modes of performance, either by reducing the scale to local forms of intervention or by widening the parameters of what we think of (as) theater, either as it was or may be—as a paradigm of society or a model of power relations or an access to subjectivity and transsexual possibility or, in a body without organs, the prophetic voice of the wide world dreaming, antioedipally, on things that are yet to come—we are still caught up in the future of illusion. Which remains, and ever will, what all ideological struggle is about.

That is the burden of the last book I've published, *To All Appearances*, which moves from ontology to ideology and (as in Marx's camera obscura) its inseparability from performance, whose powers are often invoked, without much tactile knowledge of it, in the vanities of critique, dreaming on subversion or transgression if not a Big Bang.

To attempt the impossible, I always thought, could be more or less realistic, but there seems to me in much academic discourse—whose political desires I mostly share—a muscle-flexing rhetoric making very tenuous claims. The same may be true of performance. Yet, some alternative modes of performance have, with varying intensities, actually *felt* subversive or transgressive, and brought on the censors or a prison sentence. Some have been more or less theorized. Some, with the best intentions, remain psychosexually callow and politically banal, whether or not the censorship is alarmed. As for the audiences of the alternative theater scene, feminist, ethnic, gay, whatever, it becomes increasingly apparent that they can be, if anything, even more predictable, manipulable, or responsive to banalities and stereotypes than the bourgeois audience that, according to now-standard analysis, was ready to support a theater reproducing its own image, even when that image, as in Ibsen, or Strindberg, or Pirandello, was next to appalling and in no way edifying at all.

The liability of automatic response remains with any mode of performance, but when I speak of alternatives I mean for the most part the wide spectrum of events and practices that have already reformed, or will, our notions of theater by departing from the theater or ignoring it to begin with. This has certainly been troubling to those with uninterrupted allegiance to the institutional forms of theater and, with whatever allowance for diverse experiment, the dramaturgy that goes with it. During the sixties the term *performer* was given an honorific turn in contradistinction to the actor who, according to the theorization then, was subservient to that dramaturgy, the playwright, the director, and the whole repressive apparatus of the theater as we'd known it. There were, within the orbit of this critique, performances within the theater that borrowed from or elided with performance in the other arts, and that continues to this day (Wilson, Foreman), along with the ideological dispensation of apparently dissident forms that have not resolved their relationship—in acting method, dramaturgy, visual design—to the old repressive apparatus, counting on a new content, or parody, to do it in. Of those alternative modes, however, outside the structure of theater—from the emergence of the happening out of the scene of action painting, to the situationist *dérive* and its critique of commodity culture, to various manifestations of autodestruction or the aesthetics of the orgastic in Viennese actionism, as well as the new technological order of performance heading through interactive video toward virtual reality—what has been of most compelling interest to me are the variants of body art, with its conceptualized masochism and, through the sometimes unbearable silence of a perverse endurance, its glossolalia of pain.

Here we may come through the most repellent extremities of an apparent indifference back to the sticking point of any serious thought about the theater. (Body art was an offshoot of the presumably impersonal conceptual art of the seventies, but if its major figures are now doing other things, whether sculpture, or photography, or video art, that work is—like the return of figuration in painting—still inhabited by performance, and there are any number of variants of body art on the international scene today, markedly so, it now appears, on the mutilated landscape of Eastern Europe.) In a chapter of *The Audience* on "Repression, Pain, and the Participation Mystique," I rehearse in a fabric of association with body art the immanence of pain in the texts of classical theater, as something more than a ritual paradigm or pretext for catharsis, as something so unbearably present that, even in hearing about it, it seems to have destroyed the codes. "Slave as I am to such unending pain," says Oedipus at Colonus.[8] I mean pain and not a metaphor of pain, though even as metaphor unnegotiable—Philoctetes' cry, Medea's screams—persisting in the theater, as in history, with more or less displacement or repression, though so intolerable in certain periods that it presses to the surface again, as it does in *King Lear*, "where the subject of pain *is* the subject that disappears *into* the pain" (*The Audience*, p. 180). So it is in Beckett's *Endgame*, that virtual model, or manual, or theory of body art, the consummation of a theater that at its excruciating limit, too painful to be watched, out of sight but not of mind (something dripping in the head), really impossible to perform, is almost embarrassed to be theater. And what about its politics? "Use your head, use your head, can't you, you're on earth, there's no cure for that!"[9] What's peculiar about such theater is that, cutting to the brain, its vision can be empowering.

The same might be said of Artaud's vision of the theater of cruelty, which shares a certain embarrassment at being theater, where the body is the merest spectacle cannibalized by representation. This may account for Artaud's own ravenous interest in radiophonic art, ultimate site of no-body, or of an alchemical theater, with its "meticulous and unremitting pulverization of every insufficiently fine, insufficiently matured form . . . "[10] The laminations or overlays of amplified feedback might be, as he could only dream then, a pulverizing force, working on any last insufficiency in what Barthes called the grain of the voice, which seems in Artaud—as in the performance art of Diamanda Galas—to tear itself out of the throat. And when that occurs it's as if, the language lined with flesh, the body is nothing but *voice*, reversing thus the denial in poststructuralist thought of the unfailing complicity between voice ("whose phenomenality does not have worldly form")[11] and an idealizing metaphysics, with the delusional dignity of transcendence.

Various body artists were, to be sure, influenced by Artaud, and in their work—as in his last harrowing performance at the Vieux Colombier[12]—it is a virtual ethical principle to literalize the pain. So it is in the performance of Stelarc today, still striving to transcend the body, making it obsolete, the pure radiance of the (corporeal) Image suspended with fishhooks through its flesh. For Stelarc, however, swaying with stretched skin over street or ocean, it is not merely a matter of masochism as epiphany in the high modernist sense. It may very well be that the performances are that, too, but they are conceived as a way of forcing technology back to the body in a world assaulted by the information explosion, which Stelarc sees as the dead end of evolutionary process and a compensation for our genetic inadequacies. The fishhooks are, in their testing the limits of the genetic, the primitive technology of another genesis. Without the meditative refuge of a mind-altering state, Stelarc deflects the glut of information gathered through the hooks into the astonishment of knowledge, the pain disappearing as if through Barthes's *punctum* (the rip, the tear, the wound) into "a kind of subtle *beyond*" (*Camera Lucida*, p. 59). Such art may appear to be, like the depilation of Vito Acconci, or the vomitings of Gina Pane, or the mummification of Rudolf Schwarzkogler, merely perverse or solipsistic, and, whatever the inflictions upon the body, an aesthetic mystification. Maybe so. While there are few who can even *look* at photographs of Stelarc's suspensions, much less the actual event, without wincing, it is certainly possible, if you can bear the pain at a distance, to see his performances as exquisite or beautiful in an older romantic sense, like much of the meditative work, however perilous, of Ulay and Abramović. Yet, whatever the aesthetic or antiaesthetic, or, in Foucault's terms, self-assumption of the body as a "subject of knowledge," what we also have is the art of risk in a state of emergency, presenting the body as a form of resistance.

We also know that there are bodies all over the world, as in Bosnia or Bangladesh today, that have no option of resistance, which may make a mere vanity of body art. Still, it has its political correlative, when there happens to be an option, in putting one's body on the line. There have been various body artists with specific political intent, and despite its arising from the rather elitist context of the conceptualism of the seventies it was absorbed very rapidly into the politics of identity, as in the early confessional modes of feminist performance. Yet the conceptual power of the practice seems proportioned to its pure *gratuitousness*, which is, as in modernist poetry, almost like a moral choice. And the most challenging part of its legacy corresponds, I think, to the unavoidable movement in theory, and now in history, back to ethical questions, intersecting our politics, for which the most comprehensive paradigm remains the tragic form. It is surely to be expected that, along with theory's turn back to ethics and aesthetics, tragedy itself—shameful site of Oedipus in the critique of phallogocentrism—will also have to be reassessed, for it remains the paradigm of the body in a state of violation taking responsibility for that state, though not yet, perhaps, in possession of its meanings.

Violating the body is, in the paradox of performance, a testament to the human: not only the sign of its endurance but, in either the implacability or mania of self-determination, an inviolable respect. The resisting body is the subject of performance, and always has been, even in conventional theater, even when the body is absent, as Beckett perceived in "the instant of recorded vagitus" of his synoptic *Breath* (*Shorter Plays*, p. 211), haunted to begin with by disappearance. With all the theoretical emphasis on historically constructed bodies—the woman's body, the Black body, the gay body, the myriad bodies of ethnic identity—it is the body in pain that invariably returns us to the emblooded logic of the vanishing point itself, *the essential body*, which is the thing that hurts if history hurts, crossing the politics of difference at the living end of the real.

If we see the body of the performer today flattened into a photograph, as in the case of Cindy Sherman, it is in a sense both living and dead, and the degree of its living depends not only on who's looking but on the emulsified prospect of a residual presence (something grittier than a trace?), the emanation of the referent as well. Sometimes you look and there seems to be nobody there, not the no-body of radiophonic art but the correlative of a cultural theory whose critique of presence, and fear of the hierarchical, has flattened or leveled the heuristic substance of what it deconstructs. That's what it did, it seems, with the figure of Oedipus, who disappeared into a narrative so rich and inexhaustible that, in the critique of representation, the third play is rarely remembered. The new historicisms remind us that the myth, and the tedious burden of its unending pain, is merely culture bound. But what are we to make of theatrical paradigms that, put off as they may be by the representation of fate, make very little provision for the fate of representation, baseless as it may be, its gratuitous necessity, not merely as a sign but as an agency of the real—as Derrida had to concede, with almost tragically poignant resistance, at the end of his essay on Artaud's theater of cruelty and the closure of representation. What is at stake here is something else again than conforming representation to some newly forced perspective (call it a subject position) or, in camp and masquerade, the illusions of multivalency in the ideology of desire.

The score is not in on whether, in the blade-running prospects of our time, we shall develop a better culture or something other than culture, though it should be clear enough—since the fall of the Berlin Wall and, after the euphoria, the demoralization of Europe—that with all the presumptions of recent discourse about the operations of power, the nature of power still eludes us, and we ought to be chastened by that. Overdosed on Foucault, we are callow about power and how to distinguish it from appearances, particularly from certain appearances we happen to convey ourselves when, in whatever minor genres, we acquire something like power. On this issue, nothing whatever in our culture critique seems to me on a level with our canonical drama, or for that matter the theatrical pathos of history itself. "Kto Kovo? Who Whom?" asked Lenin in a conundrum about the Bolshevik Revolution. Who is the subject or guiding force of history and, with no punctuation between, who is the object? With the toppling of the statues of Lenin it's as if once again history has refused the (Brechtian) punctuation, leaving us, amid the prospects and terrors of exponential difference, with the object disappearing into the subjectivity of perception.

Which is not to make the case for, as they say, "releasing subjectivity." If subjectivity is going to be released, it is into a field of crosspurposed metastasizing claims where, with whatever impaired perception, we're not released from the grievous task of making finer distinctions about difference (we want it and we don't want it, or only want it so much), about the subject (particularly the subject who—with a quite valid claim, and in an electoral process, the vote—happens to disagree with us), and about the uses and abuses and indeterminacies of power, and what we would do with it if we had it, since what it means to have it is (as we can see with Bill Clinton or Boris Yeltsin, or Nelson Mandela) also part of the problem. One might prefer to forget in all this, though history won't, and Büchner didn't, the utter derangements of power, or its surreptitious perversions, in those who come to it through the most admirable idealisms. It is not an easy problem because, speaking of virtual reality, it is virtually insoluble—which appears to be why, if there was anything real to begin with, the tragic myth in all its inadequacy came into being itself, with the devastating prospect of its own critique.

That can be painful, so painful that, as if pain were its very emblem, there is no certainty but doubt, which is the one inheritance of the theater metaphor we can hardly do without. Critical theory came on the scene with disdain for that metaphor and the dispensation of mimesis, as if it were the agency that, instead of alleviating pain, sustained and reinforced it. There is something to be said for that, and Brecht said it, though he could no more do without it than can any appeal or demand made on behalf of the marginal or disadvantaged. Even now, as theory passes into cultural studies with an increasing assumption of power in our graduate schools, it remains somewhat schizophrenic in its view of (the) theater, rejecting the institution with its oedipal history while moving off the datum of play inherited from the sixties into more or less appropriation or displacement of the idea of performance. Under the pressure of theory, approaches to theater history and dramatic literature have changed and diversified, more radically so than at any time during the career of Ruby Cohn, with the adamant boundaries of its impeccable scholarship. Recently there have been various books and theater journals concerned with new attitudes toward history and the consequences for methodology, not only crossing genres but epistemological disciplines, a commendable ambition with a crisis of qualification.

What, meanwhile, is the object of our study? As I see it—with or without the dramatic texts or performance texts, as in the recovered evidence of historical practice—that remains what it always was: the precipitation of theater from whatever it is it is not, which like the mystery of difference itself may be indecipherable. If I speak here for myself, it is with the unpurged assumption that released subjectivity is always prey to oedipal blindness. Appearance, and then again, appearance: for the rest, take up the bodies, what else is there to say? Except that not to say it *then* is to start thinking about power.

NOTES

1. Walter Benjamin, "Theses on the Philosophy of History," in *Illuminations*, ed. Hannah Arendt, trans. Harry Zohn (New York: Harcourt, Brace, 1968), 265.
2. See Samuel Beckett, *Footfalls*, in *Collected Shorter Plays* (London: Faber, 1984), 243.
3. Roland Barthes, *Camera Lucida: Reflections on Photography*, trans. Richard Howard (New York: Hill and Wang, 1981), 80.
4. Ruby Cohn, *Samuel Beckett: The Comic Gamut* (New Brunswick, N.J.: Rutgers University Press, 1962), 4.
5. Raymond Williams, *Writing in Society* (London: Verso, n.d.), 19.
6. Quoted by Jim Hoagland, *International Herald Tribune*, 25 February 1993, 4.

Afterword

JOSEPH CHAIKIN

Dear Ruby,

Early on I met you—here and there, but I didn't know you well.

Years ago, I read a little of your work. Then later, after my stroke, I met you Clearly and read your work better. I found it surprising and full of information about Theatre. Brilliant.

Both of us discovered—in our own way—SAM Beckett. He was and is the single contemporary writer that I feel I most identified with. He certainly changed my thinking and mind.

I saw you in Davis, CA; New York; London; Paris; Brussels. You are extraordinary. I'm so glad I met you.

Love,

Joe

Contributors

H. Porter Abbott is Professor of English Literature at the University of California, Santa Barbara. He is the author of *The Fiction of Samuel Beckett: Form and Effect* and *Diary Fiction: Writing as Action*. He is currently finishing a second book on Samuel Beckett.

Linda Ben-Zvi is Professor of English and Theater and teaches at both Colorado State University and Tel Aviv University. Among her publications are *Samuel Beckett, Women in Beckett, Susan Glaspell: Essays on Her Theater and Fiction*, and two forthcoming books: *Theater in Israel* and *Vital Voices: An Anthology of American Women Playwrights*.

Herbert Blau is Distinguished Professor of English and Comparative Literature at the University of Wisconsin-Milwaukee. His most recent books are *To All Appearances: Ideology and Performance* and *The Audience*.

Enoch Brater is the author of *Beyond Minimalism: Beckett's Late Style in the Theater, Why Beckett*, and, most recently, *The Drama in the Text: Beckett's Late Fiction*. Professor of English and Theater at the University of Michigan, his other published work includes *Feminine Focus: The New Women*

Playwrights, Around the Absurd: Essays on Modern and Postmodern Drama (with Ruby Cohn), and *Beckett at 80/Beckett in Context*.

John Russell Brown is Professor of Theater and English at the University of Michigan. He is the author of *Shakespeare's Plays in Performance, Free Shakespeare*, and *Theater Language*. He is also the editor of *The Oxford Illustrated History of Theatre*.

Sue-Ellen Case, the author of *Feminism and Theatre*, is Professor of English at the University of California, Riverside. She is the editor of *Performing Feminisms: Feminist Critical Theory and Theater* and *The Divided Home/Land: Contemporary German Women's Plays* and is coeditor of *The Performance of Power: Theatrical Discourse and Politics*.

Joseph Chaikin, director, actor, and writer, is the legendary founder of The Open Theater.

Bill Coco is a dramaturge, teacher, and writer currently living in New York. Over the past decade he has been dramaturge for ten productions by Joseph Chaikin, including the Obie-Award winning *Texts for Nothing*, featuring Bill Irwin, at the New York Shakespeare Festival Public Theater. In 1995 his translation, with director Peter Stormare, of a new version of Strindberg's *Dance of Death* played at the Almeida Theatre, London.

Elin Diamond is Associate Professor of English at Rutgers University. Author of *Pinter's Comic Play*, her articles on feminist theory and theater have appeared in *ELH*, *Theatre Journal*, *Modern Drama*, *TDR*, *Kenyon Review*, and *Art and Cinema*. She is currently completing her book *Unmasking Mimesis*.

The distinguished French critic Bernard Dort died in Paris in 1993.

Jim Eigo is a writer and AIDS activist living in New York. He was playwright with Herb Blau's troupe KRAKEN, and his fiction, concrete poetry, and dance criticism have been widely published.

Martin Esslin is Emeritus Professor of Drama at Stanford University and the author, among many other works, of the landmark study *The Theater of the Absurd*.

Carla Locatelli, Professor of English Literature at the University of Trento (Italy), is the author of *La disdetta della parola: L'ermeneutica del silenzio nella prosa inglese di Beckett* and *Unwording the World: Beckett's Prose Works after the Nobel Prize*. She is also Adjunct Professor at the University of Pennsylvania and the author of numerous essays on literature and literary theory.

Gerry McCarthy, whose writing on theater ranges from Molière to Beckett, teaches in the Department of Drama and Theatre Arts at the University of Birmingham in England.

John Orr is Professor of Sociology at the University of Edinburgh. His books include *Tragic Drama and Modern Society*, *Tragicomedy and Contemporary Culture*, and *Cinema and Modernity*.

Janelle Reinelt, Professor of Theater Arts at California State University-Sacramento, is the author of *After Brecht: British Epic Theater* and the coeditor of *Critical Theory and Performance* and *The Performance of Power: Theatrical Discourse and Politics*.

Antonia Rodríguez-Gago, Associate Professor of English at the Universidad Autónoma de Madrid, has written many articles on contemporary drama and has also translated many of Beckett's plays into Spanish, including *Rockaby*, *Ohio Impromptu*, *Catastrophe*, and *Happy Days*.

Yasunari Takahashi is Professor Emeritus at the University of Tokyo and President of the Shakespeare Society of Japan. He has translated into Japanese Samuel Beckett's complete dramatic works, as well as Peter Brook's *The Empty Space* and *The Shifting Point*. His collection of essays (in Japanese) on Yeats, Beckett and *noh* is forthcoming.

Hersh Zeifman, Associate Professor of English and Drama at York University, Toronto, is coeditor of *Modern Drama* and has published widely on Beckett and contemporary British and American drama. His work includes *Contemporary British Drama, 1970–90* and *David Hare: A Casebook.*